BLACK+DECKER™

The Complete Guide to

OUTDOOR CARPENTRY

Updated 3rd Edition

Complete Plans for Beautiful Backyard Building Projects

COOL
SPRINGS
PRESS

Brimming with creative inspiration, how-to projects, and useful information to enrich your everyday life, Quarto Knows is a favorite destination for those pursuing their interests and passions. Visit our site and dig deeper with our books into your area of interest: Quarto Creates, Quarto Cooks, Quarto Homes, Quarto Lives, Quarto Drives, Quarto Explores, Quarto Gifts, or Quarto Kids.

© 2019 Quarto Publishing Group USA Inc.

First published in 2014 by Cool Springs Press, an imprint of The Quarto Group, 100 Cummings Center, Suite 265-D, Beverly, MA 01915, USA. T (978) 282-9590 F (978) 283-2742 QuartoKnows.com

Cool Springs Press titles are also available at discount for retail, wholesale, promotional, and bulk purchase. For details, contact the Special Sales Manager by email at specialsales@quarto.com or by mail at The Quarto Group, Attn: Special Sales Manager, 100 Cummings Center, Suite 265-D, Beverly, MA 01915, USA.

10 9 8 7 6

Originally found under the following Library of Congress Cataloging-in-Publication Data

The complete guide to outdoor carpentry : complete plans for beautiful backyard building projects. -- 2nd edition.
  pages cm
  At head of title: BLACK+DECKER.
  Summary: "Step-by-step instructions and full-color photography for more than 30 projects, including swings, benches, planters, tables, chairs, arbors and bridges"-- Provided by publisher.
  ISBN 978-1-59186-618-3 (paperback)
  1. Garden structures--Amateurs' manuals. 2. Outdoor furniture--Amateurs' manuals. 3. Carpentry--Amateurs' manuals. I. Black & Decker Corporation (Towson, Md.)

TH4961.C6543 2014
684.1'8--dc23

2014012732

The following projects are © SCOUT and are used with permission:
Folding Table (page 92)
Sheltered Swing (page 168)
Garden Bridges (pages 188-203) www.handy.scout.com

Cover photo© SCOUT

Acquisitions Editor: Mark Johanson
Senior Art Director: Brad Springer
Layout: Laurie Young
Contributing Photographer: Rau + Barber
Photo Assistance: Adam Esco

Printed in China

NOTICE TO READERS

For safety, use caution, care, and good judgment when following the procedures described in this book. The publisher and BLACK+DECKER cannot assume responsibility for any damage to property or injury to persons as a result of misuse of the information provided.

The techniques shown in this book are general techniques for various applications. In some instances, additional techniques not shown in this book may be required. Always follow manufacturers' instructions included with products, since deviating from the directions may void warranties. The projects in this book vary widely as to skill levels required: some may not be appropriate for all do-it-yourselfers, and some may require professional help.

Consult your local building department for information on building permits, codes, and other laws as they apply to your project.

Contents

The Complete Guide to
Outdoor Carpentry, 3rd Edition

Introduction 6

SEATING PROJECTS 8

Side-by-Side Patio Chair 10

Classic Adirondack Chair 16

Slatted Garden Bench 22

Knockdown Garden Bench 26

Sling-Back Adirondack Chair 32

Porch Swing 38

Porch Swing Stand 46

Recyclables Bench 52

Luxury Sun Lounger 58

Trellis Seat 66

Contents (Cont.)

DINING & ENTERTAINING PROJECTS 70

Trestle Table and Benches 72

Cedar Patio Table 80

Teahouse Table Set 84

Folding Table 92

Occasional Table 96

Children's Picnic Table 100

Traditional Picnic Table 104

Patio Prep Cart 108

Pitmaster's Locker 114

Timberframe Sandbox 118

YARD & GARDEN PROJECTS 153

Compost Bin 124

Freestanding Arbor 128

High-low Potting Bench 134

Trellis Planter 138

Raised Bed with Removable Trellis 144

Versailles Planter 148

Jumbo Cold Frame 152

Pagoda Lantern 158

Firewood Shelter 164

Shelter with Swing 168

Four-Post Patio Pergola 178

SPECIAL SECTION: GARDEN BRIDGES 188

Conversions 204

Credits/Resources 205

Index 206

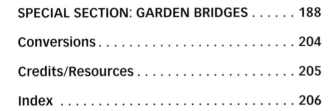

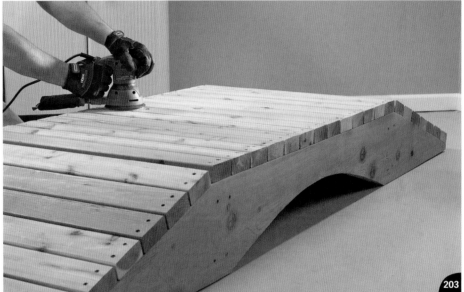

Introduction

Outdoor carpentry is just plain fun. Working away in the elements and fresh air with plenty of space and elbow room. And perhaps best of all, you almost never encounter a fraction like $^{13}/_{64}$ or a cutting angle like "31.2°". The projects tend to be bigger and so do the tolerances. So if you're still pretty new at the carpentry craft, there is no better place to get some experience (and create some cool things for your yard) than working outdoor.

In this new edition of BLACK+DECKER *The Complete Guide to Outdoor Carpentry* you'll find more than two dozen complete projects, from basic benches to large four-post pergolas. Most are made of wood and do not require a lot of fancy tools. Some are highly utilitarian, like Potting Benches (page 134) and Firewood Shelter (page 164), or Cold Frames (page 152) and Compost Bins (page 124) for gardening. Others are meant for visual pleasure, such as the Freestanding Arbor (page 128) and Trellis Seat (page 66).

We've been careful to include projects that represent a wide range of skill levels, but even the hardest among these are doable for the average weekend craftsman. Put together the Traditional Picnic Table on page 104 and you'll practice mitering different angles in the same structural member. The woodworking and crafting lessons go on and on from there.

The ultimate goal, however, is to make additions to your backyard (or front or side yard) that beautify the outdoor space and make it more usable. Whether you're building a place to sit and get a tan, like the Luxury Sun Lounger on page 58, or adding a handsome workhorse like the Patio Prep Cart on page 108, you'll find that all the projects in the pages that follow meet that goal in high style. You bring the tools and elbow grease and we'll supply the photo-driven instructions for projects where function meets one-of-a-kind, beautiful form.

Seating Projects

You'll never fully enjoy your backyard without comfortable seating. Chairs, benches, and swings are mainstays of outdoor living. In this chapter you'll find a dozen seating projects that range from fanciful to simple, classic to retro, and nautical to Eastern-inspired.

Each design in this chapter has been carefully shop-tested for comfort. A couple of degrees of slant in a seatback might not appear to make much difference when you're drawing up a plan, but your body can tell immediately. And if your seating is not comfortable, what use is it? You can be confident that the benches and chairs that follow have been subjected to hands-on (well, not hands exactly) testing from sitters of all sizes.

If you are a relative newcomer to carpentry, consider starting with one of the simpler projects, such as the Knockdown Garden Bench or the Slatted Garden Bench. If your skills are a bit more advanced, think about tackling the Porch Swing and Porch Swing Stand or perhaps the Luxury Sun Lounger that's crafted from mahogany and features stainless steel brightwork.

In this chapter:

- Side-by-Side Patio Chair
- Classic Adirondack Chair
- Slatted Garden Bench
- Knockdown Garden Bench
- Sling-Back Adirondack Chair
- Porch Swing
- Porch Swing Stand
- Recyclables Bench
- Luxury Sun Lounger
- Trellis Seat

Side-by-side Patio Chair

You can share a view, some shade, and a table for snacks and a beverage with a friend when you've got this side-by-side patio chair in your backyard. You might recognize the design, as it was inspired by the side-by-side chairs that were often included in the ubiquitous redwood patio sets popular in the '50s and '60s. Those sets typically included a lounge chair, some small tables, a patio table with an umbrella holder, and a side-by-side table and chair similar to the one shown here.

You'll find that these seats are most comfortable when they're appointed with cushions, but they're still easy to enjoy when left bare. And just about any patio table umbrella can be used with this set—simply size the umbrella post hole to fit. The optional umbrella should also be secured in a weighted base that is placed under the table.

Even a beginner can build this side-by-side chair in a day using less than $100 in materials. It's easiest to build if you have a table saw, miter saw, jigsaw, and router. If you don't have a table saw, then you can use a circular saw to rip the 2 × 4 frame pieces down to 3" widths. The purpose for these parts being 3" wide is to give the set a more refined appearance, but you can simplify the design and avoid rip cuts by using full width 2 × 4s. If you choose to use full-width 2 × 4s, then you must move the front rail notch up ½" and the seats will end up being ½" higher.

Materials ▶

5 1 × 4" × 8 ft. boards	Deck screws (2", 2½")
5 2 × 4" × 8 ft. boards	Exterior-rated glue
1 2 × 6" × 8 ft. board	Finishing materials
1 ¾ × 12 ft. deck board	

This lounge chair built for two offers comfortable seating separated by shared table space. It is a perfect furnishing for intimate conversations or for quiet leisure time spent sharing a bowl of snacks and an occasional sidelong glance.

Side-by-Side Patio Chair

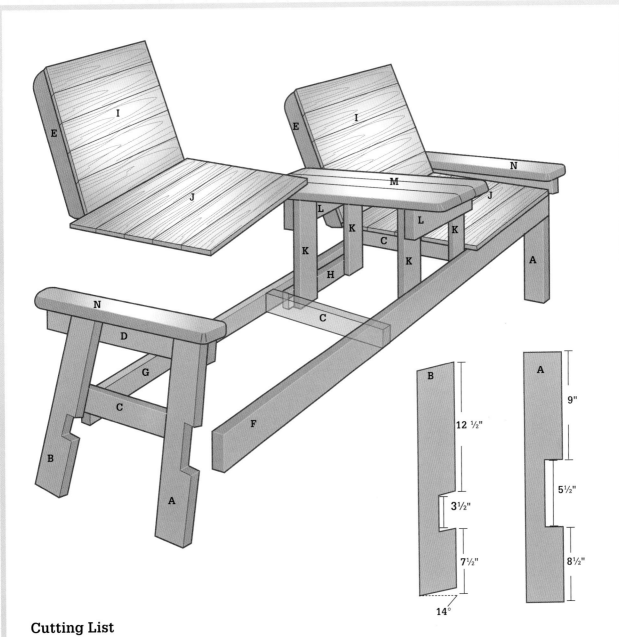

Cutting List

Key	Part	Dimension	Pcs.	Material
A	Front legs	$1\frac{1}{2} \times 3 \times 23"$	2	PT Pine
B	Back legs	$1\frac{1}{2} \times 3 \times 23\frac{1}{2}"$	2	PT Pine
C	Seat supports	$1\frac{1}{2} \times 3 \times 18\frac{5}{8}"$	4	PT Pine
D	Arm supports	$1\frac{1}{2} \times 3 \times 22\frac{1}{2}"$	2	PT Pine
E	Back supports	$1\frac{1}{2} \times 3 \times 21\frac{3}{4}"$	4	PT Pine
F	Front rail	$1\frac{1}{2} \times 5\frac{1}{2} \times 60\frac{3}{4}"$	1	PT Pine
G	Back rail	$1\frac{1}{2} \times 3\frac{1}{2} \times 60\frac{3}{4}"$	1	PT Pine

Key	Part	Dimension	Pcs.	Material
H	Table bottom crosspiece	$1\frac{1}{2} \times 3 \times 19\frac{3}{4}"$	1	PT Pine
I	Back slats	$\frac{3}{4} \times 3\frac{1}{2} \times 19"$	10	PT Pine
J	Seat slats	$\frac{3}{4} \times 3\frac{1}{2} \times 20\frac{1}{2}"$	10	PT Pine
K	Table posts	$\frac{3}{4} \times 3\frac{1}{2} \times 13\frac{1}{2}"$	4	PT Pine
L	Table supports	$1\frac{1}{2} \times 3 \times 16\frac{3}{4}"$	2	PT Pine
M	Tabletop planks	$1\frac{1}{4} \times 5\frac{1}{2} \times 24"$	3	PT Pine
N	Armrests	$1\frac{1}{4} \times 5\frac{1}{2} \times 24"$	2	PT Pine

Side-by-Side Patio Chair

BUILD THE FRAME

Cut 2 × 4 boards to make the legs, back supports, and seat supports. These parts must be rip-cut down to 3" wide to conceal their telltale 2 × 4 look (for best results, rip ¼" off each edge to get rid of the bullnose profile milled into most 2 × 4s). Use a table saw or a circular saw and edge guide to make the rip cuts. It is often easier to cut the parts to length first and then rip them to width because the shorter boards are more manageable.

Use the construction drawings (see page 11) to lay out the notches, miters, and radius-curve profiles on each piece. These details must be correctly noted onto the parts. Lay out the notches that will hold the front rail in between the front legs and the back rail in between the back legs. Drill a ⅜" blade access hole in the inside corners of each notch and then cut the notches out with a jigsaw. Clean up cuts with a chisel or small profile sander.

Miter-cut the ends of the back legs at 14° angles. Be careful to cut the miters in the correct direction so that the notch is on the front edge of the back legs. Miter-cut one end of each seat support to 14° **(photo 1)**. *Note: Parallel angled cuts on the ends of a workpiece are called "plumb cuts."* Miter-cut the bottom

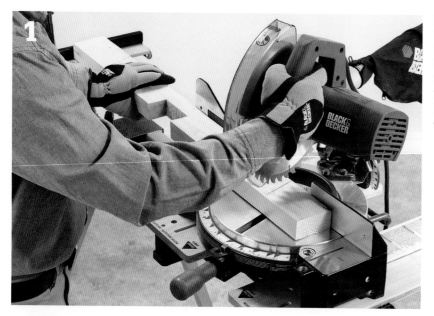

Make plumb cuts on legs. Set the miter saw table to 14° (orient the blade to the right side of the 90° mark). Position each back leg so the notch is facing away from the saw fence and trim off the right end of the back leg. Make a parallel 14° miter cut on the other end.

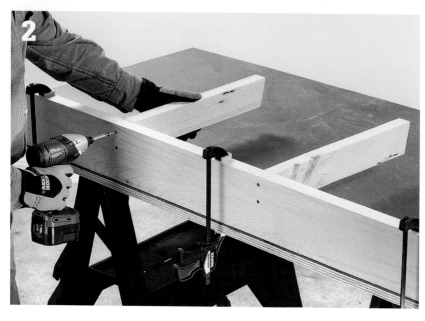

Attach the seat supports. The seat supports should be attached to the front rail using exterior wood glue and 2½" deck screws (use at least two screws per support).

end of the back support to 14° and cut a 3" radius in the top back corner.

Cut the front and back rail to length. Mark the locations along the back face of the front rail where each seat support will be attached. Attach the seat supports to the front rail with 2½" screws (**photo 2**). Rails should be located 1½" and 19" in front of each end.

Apply exterior-rated wood glue to the bottom face of each notch. Place the front rail in the front leg notches and the back rail in the back leg notches. Keep the ends of the rails flush with the outside faces of the legs. Attach the rails to the legs with screws (**photo 3**).

Adjust the positions of the parts so that the front leg is plumb and the arm support is level. Then attach the back legs to the outside seat supports and the arm support to the front and back legs (**photo 4**).

Cut the table bottom crosspiece to length and width. Attach the back supports to the seat supports with 2½" screws (**photo 5**). In addition, attach the two outside back supports to the arm supports. This completes the assembly of the chair frame.

ATTACH THE SEAT & BACK SLATS
The appearance of your side-by-side chair is greatly influenced by the uniformity and spacing of the back slats and seat slats. The best way to achieve uniform

Attach the rails. The front rails should be attached to the front legs and the back rails are attached to the back legs. Use exterior wood glue and 2½" deck screws.

Attach the supports and legs. Temporarily clamp the parts together in the correct orientation and then drive 2½" screws through the inside faces of the arm supports and seat supports to attach them to the legs.

lengths for the slats is to set a stop block for your power miter saw. Use spacers between the slats to ensure regular gaps. For the ⅛" gaps required here, you can use 16d common nails as spacers.

Cut all of the back slats and seat slats to length (**photo 6**). Sand the ends prior to installation while you still have unrestricted access. Place the slats on the back supports, leaving a ⅛" space between slats. Drill two ⅛"-diameter pilot holes and countersinks through each slat end, centering the holes over the back support. Attach the slats to the supports with

2" screws (**photo 7**). Attach the seat slats to the seat supports, again leaving a ⅛" gap in between the slats.

ATTACH THE TABLE & ARMREST

Cut the table posts, table supports, tabletop planks, and armrests to length. Use a coping saw or jigsaw (an oscillating jigsaw is best) to round the front corners of the outside tabletop planks and armrest. Cut each corner to a 1" radius (roughly the same as a can of tomato paste). Sand the edges smooth with a power sander. Also use the jigsaw to round the back outside corners of the

Attach the back supports to the arm supports using 2½" deck screws. Make sure all screw heads are recessed slightly.

Stop Block

Cut the slats. Set the stop-block attachment on your power miter saw or stand for the correct length. Measure the first slat to make sure the length is correct.

armrests to a 4" radius. Use a compass to mark the 4" radius (slightly larger than a 1-gallon paint can).

Round over the outside edges of the tabletop and armrests with a router and ¼" piloted roundover bit. Attach the crosspiece between the two middle seat supports. Attach the table posts to the inside face of the front rail and front face of the table bottom crosspiece with 2" deck screws. Attach the table supports to the table posts with 2" screws. Finally, attach the tabletop planks to the table supports with 2" screws, leaving a ⅛" space between the planks,

and attach the armrests to the arm supports with 2" screws. Center the pilot and countersink holes over the supports.

Optional: Drill an umbrella posthole through the middle plank (**photo 8**). The typical patio umbrella pole diameter is 1½". For increased comfort, order back cushions and seat cushions. A good size for a back cushion is 3" thick × 19" square. The seat cushions should be around 3" deep × 17" long × 19" wide.

Fasten the slats. Use 16d nails or scraps of wood as spacers for a ⅛" gap. If you're using a cordless drill/driver with adjustable torque, set the clutch at a very low setting to prevent overdriving the screws. Drive two 2" screws through each end of the slat and into the back support.

Drill a hole for the optional umbrella post. Here, the 1½"-dia. posthole is located 8¾" from the back edge of the tabletop (on center) and is centered across the middle plank. A 1½"-dia. hole saw chucked into your drill is the best tool for making the pole hole.

Classic Adirondack Chair

Adirondack furniture has become a standard on decks, porches, and patios throughout the world. It's no mystery that this distinctive furniture style has become so popular. Attractive but rugged design and unmatched stability are just two of the reasons for its timeless appeal, and our Adirondack chair offers these benefits and more.

Unlike most of the Adirondack chair designs you're likely to run across, this one is very easy to build. There are no complex compound angles to cut, no intricate details in the back and seat slats, and no complicated joints. It can be built with basic tools and simple techniques. And because this design features all of the classic Adirondack chair elements, your guests and neighbors may never guess that you built it yourself (but you'll be proud to tell them you did).

We made our Adirondack chair out of cedar and finished it with clear wood sealer. But you may prefer to build your version from pine (a traditional wood for Adirondack furniture), especially if you plan to paint

the chair. White, battleship gray, and forest green are popular color choices for Adirondack furniture. Be sure to use quality exterior paint with a glossy or enamel finish.

Materials ▸

1	2 × 6" × 8 ft. cedar board	Moisture-resistant glue
1	2 × 4" × 12 ft. cedar board	Deck screws (1¼", 1½", 2", 3")
1	1 × 6" × 14 ft. cedar board	⅜ × 2½" lag screws with washers
1	1 × 4" × 8 ft. cedar board	Finishing materials
1	1 × 2" × 12 ft. cedar board	

This straightforward example of an Adirondack chair design is nicely proportioned and very easy to build from dimensional cedar lumber. Bright paint (usually red or forest green) is a common finish for Adirondack chairs. Or, you may choose to apply a clear finish to show off the warm cedar wood (inset photo).

Classic Adirondack Chair

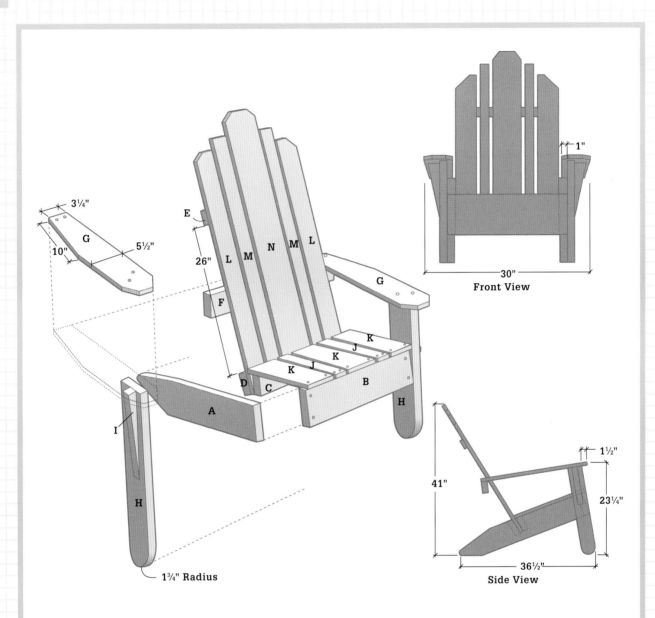

Front View

Side View

Cutting List

Key	Part	Dimension	Pcs.	Material
A	Legs	1½ × 5½ × 34½"	2	Cedar
B	Apron	1½ × 5½ × 21"	1	Cedar
C	Seat support	1½ × 3½ × 18"	1	Cedar
D	Low back brace	1½ × 3½ × 18"	1	Cedar
E	High back brace	¾ × 1½ × 18"	1	Cedar
F	Arm cleat	1½ × 3½ × 24"	1	Cedar
G	Arms	¾ × 5½ × 28"	2	Cedar

Key	Part	Dimension	Pcs.	Material
H	Posts	1½ × 3½ × 22"	2	Cedar
I	Arm braces	1½ × 2¼ × 10"	2	Cedar
J	Narrow seat slats	¾ × 1½ × 20¼"	2	Cedar
K	Wide seat slats	¾ × 5½ × 20¼"	3	Cedar
L	End back slats	¾ × 3½ × 36"	2	Cedar
M	Narrow back slats	¾ × 1½ × 38"	2	Cedar
N	Center back slat	¾ × 5½ × 40"	1	Cedar

Classic Adirondack Chair

MAKE THE LEGS

Sprawling back legs that support the seat slats and stretch to the ground on a near-horizontal plane are signature features of the Adirondack style. Start by cutting the legs to length. To cut the tapers, mark a point 2" from the edge on one end of the board. Then, mark another point 6" from the end on the adjacent edge. Connect the points with a straightedge. On the same end, mark a point 2¼" from the other edge. Then, on that edge mark a point 10" from the end. Connect these points to make a cutting line for the other taper. Cut the two taper cuts with a circular saw. Use the tapered leg as a template to mark and cut identical tapers on the other leg of the chair (**photo 1**).

BUILD THE SEAT

The legs form the sides of the box frame, which supports the seat slats. Where the text calls for deck screw counterbores, drill holes ⅛" deep with a counterbore bit. Cut the apron and seat support to size. Attach the apron to the front ends of the legs with glue and 3" deck screws.

Position the seat support so the inside face is 16½" from the inside edge of the apron. Attach the seat support between the legs, making sure the part tops are flush. Cut the seat slats to length, and sand the ends smooth. Arrange the slats on top of the seat box, and use wood scraps to set ⅝" spaces between the slats. The slats should overhang the front of the seat box by ¾".

Fasten the seat slats by drilling counterbored pilot holes and driving 2" deck screws through the holes and into the tops of the apron and seat support. Keep the counterbores aligned so the cedar plugs used to fill the counterbores form straight lines across the front and back of the seat. Once the slats are

Cut tapers into the back edges of the legs with a circular saw or jigsaw.

Round the sharp slat edges with a router and roundover bit or simply break the edges by sanding with a power sander.

installed, use a router with a ¼" roundover bit (or a power sander) to smooth the outside edges and ends of the slats (photo 2).

MAKE THE BACK SLATS

The back slats are made from three sizes of dimension lumber: 1 × 2, 1 × 4, and 1 × 6. Cut the back slats to length. Trim off the corners on the widest (1 × 6) slat. First, mark points 1" in from the outside top corners. Then, mark points 1" down from the corners on the outside edges. Connect the points and trim along the lines with a saw. Mark the 1 × 4 slats 2" from one top corner in both directions. Draw cutting lines and trim the same way (these are the outer slats on the back).

ATTACH THE BACK SLATS

Cut the low back brace and the high back brace and set them on a flat surface. Slip ¾"-thick spacers under the high brace so the tops of the braces are level. Then, arrange the back slats on top of the braces with ⅝" spacing between slats. The untrimmed ends of the slats should be flush with the bottom edge of the low back brace. The bottom of the high back brace should be 26" above the top of the low brace. The braces must be perpendicular to the slats.

Drill pilot holes in the low brace and counterbore the holes. Then, attach the slats to the low brace by driving 2" deck screws through the holes. Follow the same steps for the high brace and attach the slats with 1¼" deck screws.

MAKE THE ARMS

The broad arms of the chair, cut from 1 × 6 material, are supported by posts in front and the arm cleat attached to the backs of the chair slats. Cut the arms to length. To create decorative angles at the outer end of each arm, mark points 1" from each corner along both edges. Use the points to draw a pair of 1½" cutting lines on each arm. Cut along the lines using a jigsaw or circular saw.

Attach the square ends of the posts to the undersides of the arms, being careful to position the part correctly.

Mark points for cutting a tapered cut on the inside back edge of each arm (see Diagram page 17). First, mark points 3¼" in from each inside edge on the back of each arm. Next, mark the outside edges 10" from the back. Then, connect the points and cut along the cutting line with a circular saw or jigsaw. Sand the edges smooth.

ASSEMBLE THE ARMS, CLEATS & POSTS

Cut the arm cleat and make a mark 2½" in from each end of the cleat. Set the cleat on edge on your work surface. Position the arms on the cleat top edge so the arm back ends are flush with the cleat back, and the untapered edge of each arm is aligned with the 2½" mark. Fasten the arms to the cleats with glue. Drill pilot holes in the arms and counterbore the holes. Drive 3" deck screws through the holes and into the cleat.

Cut the posts to size. Then, use a compass to mark a 1¾"-radius roundover cut on each bottom post corner (the roundovers improve stability). Position the arms on top of the square ends of the posts. The posts should be set back 1½" from the front ends of the arm and 1" from the inside edge of the arm. Fasten the arms to the posts with glue. Drill pilot holes in the arms and counterbore the holes. Then, drive 3" deck screws through the arms and into the posts (**photo 3**).

Cut tapered arm braces from wood scraps, making sure the wood grain runs lengthwise. Position an arm brace at the outside of each arm/post joint, centered side to side on the post. Attach each brace with glue.

Drill counterbored pilot holes in the inside face of the post near the top . Then, drive deck screws through the holes and into the brace (**photo 4**). Drive a 2" deck screw down through each arm and into the top of the brace.

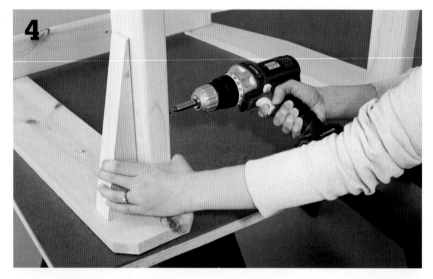

Drive screws through each post and into an arm brace to stabilize the arm/post joint.

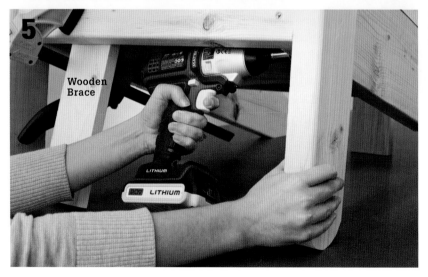

Wooden Brace

Clamp wood braces to the parts of the chair to hold them in position while you fasten the parts together.

ASSEMBLE THE CHAIR

To complete the construction, join the back, seat/leg assembly, and arm/post assembly. Before you start, gather scrap wood to brace the parts while you fasten them.

Set the seat/leg assembly on your work surface, clamping a piece of scrap wood to the front apron to raise the assembly front until the leg bottoms are flush on the surface (about 10"). Use a similar technique to brace the arm/post assembly so the back cleat bottom is 20" above the work surface. Arrange the assembly so the posts fit around the front of the seat/leg assembly and the bottom edge of the apron is flush with the front edges of the posts.

Drill a ¼"-diameter pilot hole through the inside of each leg and partway into the post. Drive a ⅜ × 2½" lag screw and washer through each hole, but do not tighten completely (**photo 5**). Remove the braces. Position the back so the low back brace is between the legs and the slats are resting against the front of the arm cleat. Clamp the back to the seat support with a C-clamp, making sure the low brace top edge is flush with the tops of the legs.

Tighten the lag screws at the post/leg joints. Then, add a second lag screw at each joint. Drill three evenly spaced pilot holes near the top edge of the arm cleat and drive 1½" deck screws through the holes and into the back slats (**photo 6**). Drive 3" deck screws through the legs and into the ends of the low back brace.

APPLY FINISHING TOUCHES

Cut or buy ¼"-thick, ⅜"-diameter cedar wood plugs and glue them into visible counterbores (**photo 7**). After the glue dries, sand the plugs even with the surrounding surface. Finish-sand all exposed surfaces with 120-grit sandpaper. Finish the chair as desired; we simply applied a coat of clear wood sealer.

Drive screws through counterbored pilot holes in the arm cleat, near the top and into the slats. Check to make sure they did not penetrate the back slats on the seat side.

Glue cedar plugs into the counterbores to conceal the screw holes.

Slatted Garden Bench

Casual seating is a welcome addition to any outdoor setting. This lovely garden bench sits comfortably around the borders of any porch, patio, or deck. With a compact footprint, it creates a pleasant resting spot for up to three adults without taking up a lot of space. Station it near your home's rear entry for a convenient place to remove shoes or set down grocery bags while you unlock the door.

The straightforward, slatted design of this bench lends itself to accessorizing. Station a rustic cedar planter next to the bench for a lovely effect. Or, add a framed lattice trellis to one side of the bench to cut down on wind and direct sun. You can apply exterior stain or a clear wood sealer with UV protectant to keep the bench looking fresh and new. Or, leave it unfinished and let it weather naturally to a silvery hue.

Materials ▸

1 2 × 8" × 6 ft. cedar board	1 2 × 2" × 6 ft. cedar board
4 2 × 2" × 10 ft. cedar boards	1 1 × 4" × 12 ft. cedar board
1 2 × 4" × 6 ft. cedar board	Moisture-resistant glue
1 2 × 6" × 10 ft. cedar board	Wood sealer or stain
	Deck screws (1½", 2½")

Graceful lines and trestle construction make this bench a charming furnishing for any garden as well as porches, patios, and decks.

Slatted Garden Bench

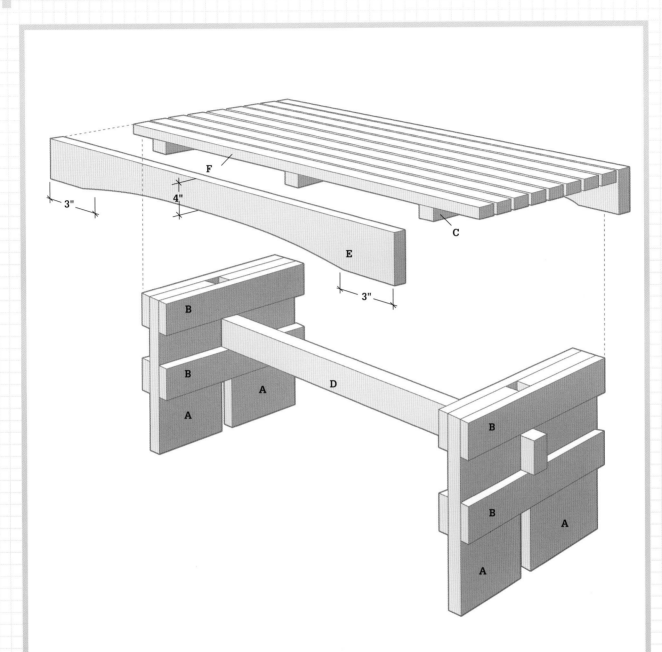

Cutting List

Key	Part	Dimension	Pcs.	Material
A	Leg halves	$1\frac{1}{2} \times 7\frac{1}{4} \times 14\frac{1}{2}$"	4	Cedar
B	Cleats	$\frac{3}{4} \times 3\frac{1}{2} \times 16$"	8	Cedar
C	Braces	$1\frac{1}{2} \times 1\frac{1}{2} \times 16$"	3	Cedar
D	Trestle	$1\frac{1}{2} \times 3\frac{1}{2} \times 60$"	1	Cedar
E	Aprons	$1\frac{1}{2} \times 5\frac{1}{2} \times 60$"	2	Cedar
F	Slats	$1\frac{1}{2} \times 1\frac{1}{2} \times 60$"	8	Cedar

Slatted Garden Bench

BUILD THE BASE

Cut the leg halves, cleats, and trestle to length. Sandwich one leg half between two cleats so the cleats are flush with the top and the outside edge of the leg half. Then, join the parts by driving four 1½" deck screws through each cleat and into the leg half. Assemble two more cleats with a leg half in the same fashion.

Stand the two assemblies on their sides, with the open ends of the cleats pointing upward. Arrange the assemblies so they are roughly 4 feet apart. Set the trestle onto the inner edges of the leg halves, pressed flush against the bottoms of the cleats. Adjust the position of the assemblies so the trestle overhangs the leg half by 1½" at each end. Fasten the trestle to each leg half with glue and 2½" deck screws (**photo 1**).

Attach another pair of cleats to each leg half directly below the first pair, positioned so each cleat is snug against the bottom of the trestle. Slide the other leg half between the cleats, keeping the top edge flush with the upper cleats. Join the leg halves with the cleats using glue and 2½" deck screws (**photo 2**). Cut the braces to length. Fasten one brace to the inner top cleat on each leg assembly, so the tops are flush (**photo 3**).

MAKE THE APRONS

Cut the aprons to length. Lay out the arc profile onto one apron, starting 3" from each end. The peak of the arc, located over the midpoint of the apron, should be 1½" up from the bottom edge. Draw a smooth, even arc by driving a casing nail at the peak of the arc and at each of the starting points. Slip a flexible ruler or strip of thin plywood or hardboard behind the nails at the starting points and in front of the nail at the peak to create a smooth arc. Then, trace along the inside of the ruler to make a cutting line (**photo 4**). Cut along the line with a jigsaw and sand the cut smooth. Trace the profile of the arc onto the other apron and make the cut. Sand the cuts smooth.

Cut the slats to length. Attach a slat to the top inside edge of each apron with glue and deck screws (**photo 5**).

Attach the trestle to the legs, making sure it is positioned correctly against the top cleat bottoms.

Attach the remaining leg half to the cleats on both ends, sandwiching the trestle on all sides.

Attach the outer brace for the seat slats directly to the inside faces of the cleats.

4

Mark the profile cuts on the aprons. Use a flexible ruler pinned between casing nails to trace a smooth arc.

5

Attach a 2 x 2 slat to the top inside edge of each apron using 2½" deck screws and glue.

INSTALL THE APRONS & SLATS

Apply glue at each end on the bottom sides of the attached slats. Flip the leg and trestle assembly and position it flush with the aprons so that it rests on the glue of the two slatted bottoms. The aprons should extend 1½" beyond the legs at each end of the bench. Drive 2½" deck screws through the braces and into both slats.

Position the middle brace between the aprons, centered end-to-end on the project. Fasten it to the two side slats with deck screws. Position the six remaining slats on the braces using ½"-thick spacers to create equal gaps between them. Attach the slats with glue and drive 2½" deck screws up through the braces and into each slat (**photo 6**).

APPLY FINISHING TOUCHES

Sand the slats smooth with progressively finer sandpaper, up to 150-grit. Wipe away the sanding residue with a rag dipped in mineral spirits. Let the bench dry. Apply a finish of your choice—a clear wood sealer protects the cedar without altering the color.

6

Attach the seat slats with glue and 2½" deck screws. Insert ½"-thick spacers to set gaps between the slats.

Knockdown Garden Bench

Snoopy shoppers at your local home center will never guess you're building a garden bench when they spot your cart full of materials for this project. That's because the materials for this garden bench are more typical for a backyard deck. Concrete foundation blocks and beefy dimensional lumber may suggest decks, but here they are combined to create a contemporary, Eastern-influenced garden bench. Featuring interlocking joinery (in the finest Asian tradition) and minimal use of metal fasteners, this bench is reminiscent of the post-and-beam construction featured in many ancient Japanese timberframe structures.

The precast concrete piers, designed to hold a deck undercarriage, are dressed up with stain to function as tapered concrete bench legs. The seat is made from deck posts and typical joist lumber (4 × 4s and 2 × 10s). You only need a few power tools to build this bench—a circular saw, jigsaw, and drill/driver. A couple of additional tools can speed up the construction: a 12" miter saw, because of its capacity to cut 4 × 4s in a single pass, and a router to round over the cut edges.

The sturdy combination of crossing half joints and hefty parts creates a very solid bench. But it's also a very heavy bench. Fortunately, this type of joinery also eliminates the need for many fasteners, making it easy to disassemble the bench into pieces so you can move it around your yard as you please and reassemble it quickly and easily.

Materials ▸

1	2 × 6" × 8 ft. cedar board	4	Precast concrete deck piers
2	2 × 8" × 8 ft. cedar boards		2½" exterior-rated screws
1	2 × 10" × 8 ft. cedar board		Exterior wood stain
4	4 × 4" × 8 ft. cedar boards		Concrete stain

Because the principal parts of this unique garden bench fit together with no mechanical fasteners, it can be disassembled and moved around your yard with little effort.

Knockdown Garden Bench

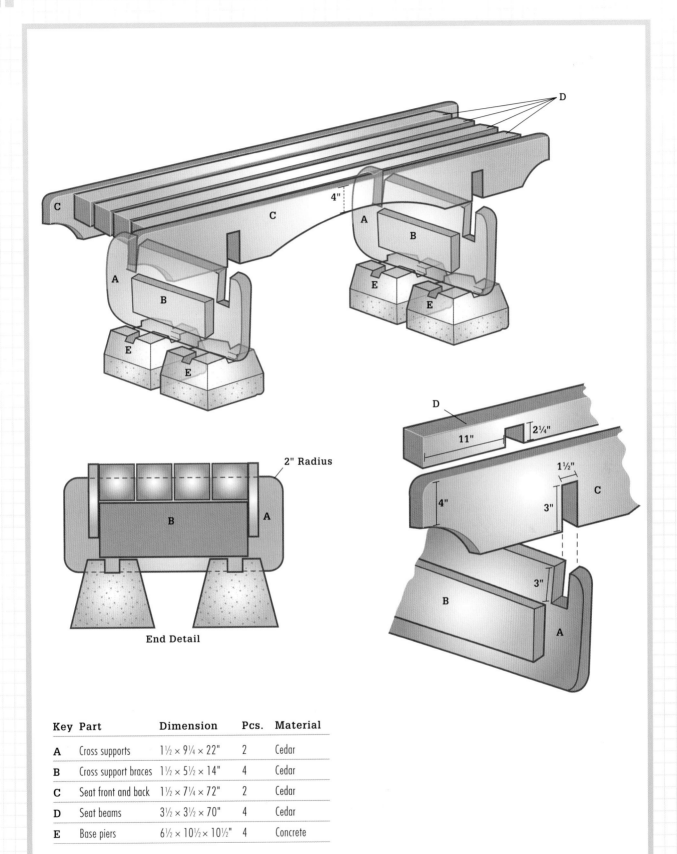

End Detail

Key	Part	Dimension	Pcs.	Material
A	Cross supports	1½ × 9¼ × 22"	2	Cedar
B	Cross support braces	1½ × 5½ × 14"	4	Cedar
C	Seat front and back	1½ × 7¼ × 72"	2	Cedar
D	Seat beams	3½ × 3½ × 70"	4	Cedar
E	Base piers	6½ × 10½ × 10½"	4	Concrete

Knockdown Garden Bench

MAKE THE CROSS SUPPORTS

The cross supports are the notched end pieces that support the seat beams. Cut them to length from 2 × 10 stock. Also cut the cross support braces to length from 2 × 6 stock (these sandwich the cross supports, to prevent the cross supports from rocking). Outline the notches that will hold the front and back onto the cross supports. Drill ⅜"-diameter starter holes for the jigsaw blade, located inside one corner of each notch area. Cut out the notches with a jigsaw (**photo 1**). Scribe 2" radius lines on the outside corners of the cross supports, and cut along the radius lines with a jigsaw. Sand the corner radius cuts smooth, and round over the outside edges of the cross supports with a router and ¼"-radius piloted roundover bit (**photo 2**).

MAKE THE SEAT FRONT & BACK

Cut the seat front and back pieces to length and width from 2 × 8 stock. These parts need to be cut with multiple profiles, including roundovers on the top, scallops on the bottom, and notches to mate with the notches in the cross supports. First, mark the outlines of the notches that will fit over the cross supports. Drill ⅜"-diameter jigsaw blade starter holes at an inside corner of each notch. Next, cut out the notches with a jigsaw.

Draw a concave, 6" radius line on each bottom corner of each front and back part to create cutting lines for decorative scallops with refined profiles. Draw a 2"-radius roundover line (convex) at each top corner. Sand the cuts smooth and round over the outside edges of the seat front and back pieces with a router and ¼"-radius roundover bit.

The front and back parts also have shallow arcs cut into the bottoms. To lay out these arcs, mark a center point (end to end) 4" down from the top of each workpiece and then drive a screw halfway into each center point. Mark the end points of the arc (19½" from each end) and then bend a 40" long flexible piece of scrap wood or metal over the screw to form the arc profile. Trace the arc profile (**photo 3**). Next, cut along the radius and arc profile lines, and then sand the arcs smooth. Ease the edges with your router and roundover bit.

Cut the notches in the cross supports. Drill a starter hole for your jigsaw blade in one corner of each notch. Clean up the edges of the notch with a chisel, if necessary.

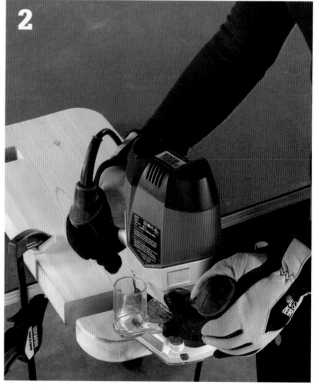

Round over the part edges. Ease the outside edges of the cross supports with a router and ¼" roundover bit. Leave the edges of the cross-support notches square.

3

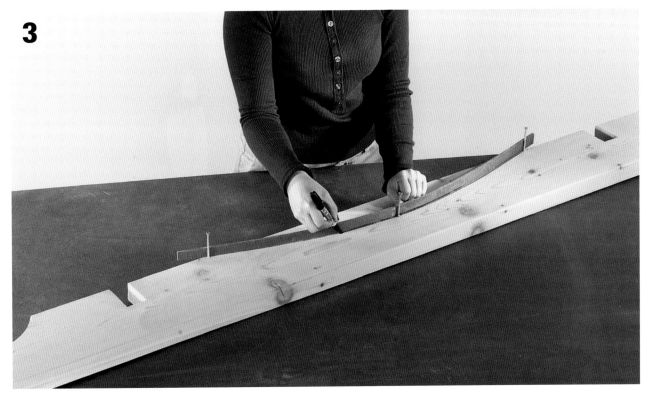

Draw the bottom profile arcs. Bend a scrap piece of wood or metal across a screw or nail to form the arc profile along the bottom edges of the front and back. Trace the arc with a marker.

Precast Concrete Piers ▸

Precast concrete piers are designed for use with platform-style decks that are not attached to a structure. Individual piers measure roughly 8" high and are 11" square at the base. They weigh 45 pounds each. The cast top channels are sized to accept standard 2× dimensional lumber. If you will not be moving the bench around, it's a good idea to prepare a few inches of compactable gravel as a base for each pier to help with stability and drainage.

MAKE THE SEAT BEAMS

The space between the seat front and back is filled with seat beams cut from 4 × 4 stock. This helps keep the weight (and cost) of the project down, compared to using solid 2 × 8s all the way across. Cut the seat beams to length and width. Clamp the seat beams together and mark the notch edge lines across the tops of all four beams. Set your circular saw blade depth to 2¼" and make several crosscuts between the notch layout lines to remove waste material (**photo 4**). Smooth the saw kerf edges remaining in the notch bottoms (**photo 5**) with a chisel and wood mallet (don't use a hammer).

STAIN THE BENCH PARTS

Apply exterior-rated wood stain to all of the wood parts. Redwood and cedar tones are traditional colors, but for a look that's more appropriate to the design, try using a dark stain color. A penetrating, semi-transparent wood stain is easy to apply and gives the wood a durable finish.

The concrete piers can also be stained with concrete stain to blend in better with the wood bench parts. Apply a concrete stain to all surfaces of each of the concrete base piers (**photo 6**).

ASSEMBLE THE BENCH

Position the top edge of each cross support brace between the cross support notches and 2¼" below the top edge of the cross support. Attach the cross support braces with 2½" exterior screws (**photo 7**). These are the only mechanical connections you need to make.

Place the four concrete piers in the location where the bench will be set up. Position the piers in pairs that are approximately 3 feet apart. Place one support brace across each side pair of concrete piers. Place the seat front and back on the cross supports. Shift the concrete piers and cross supports until the notches align. Place the seat beams between the front and back pieces (**photo 8**). Adjust the parts so that all notches seat fully on the adjoining parts.

Cut notches into the seat beams. Remove waste material from the notch area by making multiple kerf cuts with a circular saw set to 2¼" cutting depth.

Smooth out the notches. Use a sharp wood chisel and mallet to clean up the ridges and edges left in the notch bottom after cutting the kerf.

6

Color the parts. Apply a coat of dark concrete stain to the precast concrete piers. Follow the stain manufacturer's instructions for application and dry time. Stain the wood parts a matching or complementary dark wood tone with exterior wood stain.

7

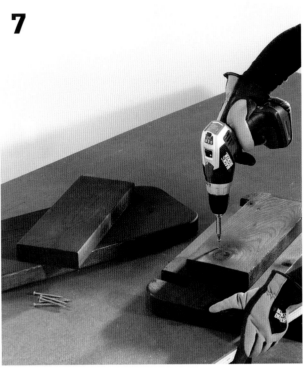

Make the cross support assemblies. Attach the cross support braces on each side of the cross support using 2½" deck screws. Drill ⅛" pilot holes for the screws to minimize the chance of wood splitting.

8

Assemble the bench. Transport the parts to the location where the bench will be installed. Set the supports onto the piers and then position the bench into the notches in the supports. Adjust the component positions until all of the notches are fully seated.

Sling-Back Adirondack

Named for the region of New York State where this classic design originated about 100 years ago, the Adirondack chair is an iconic piece of American outdoor furniture. Through the years countless Adirondack variations have been built, all featuring the trademark wide arms, slanted seat, and slanted backrest that define the style. The version shown here combines those tried-and-true frame proportions with the laid-back comfort of a sling-back canvas beach chair to create an Adirondack chair that borrows from multiple design sources.

The parts are fastened with stainless steel screws. Stainless steel is an excellent material for outdoor use because it does not corrode or stain wood, but it is softer than hardened steel so it's necessary to drill a pilot hole for every screw to prevent stripping the head or breaking the shaft. Stainless steel finish washers (sometimes referred to as decorative washers) are used under the heads of all exposed screws.

The most unique feature of this chair is the canvas seat. Select a material that is weather resistant and will not stretch. The top and bottom edges of the canvas are exposed, so they must be hemmed (a custom tailor or interior designer can do this for you). A simple straight-stitch hem is all that is required. The hemmed canvas is secured between two wood rails and can be easily removed for storage, cleaning, or replacing.

Materials ▸

4 ¾ × 5" × 8 ft. white oak boards	2 ¼"-dia. × 3½" machine screws
1 60 × 50" canvas (10 ounce)	14 ¼"-dia. finish washers
Wood screws (1¼", 2")	14 ¼"-dia. washers
No. 10 finish washers	14 ¼"-dia. locknuts
12 ¼"-dia. × 3" machine screws	

Adirondack chairs are classic backyard furnishings. No two designs are exactly alike, but the form is instantly recognizable even when it has a unique feature like the canvas seat on this interpretation.

Sling-Back Adirondack

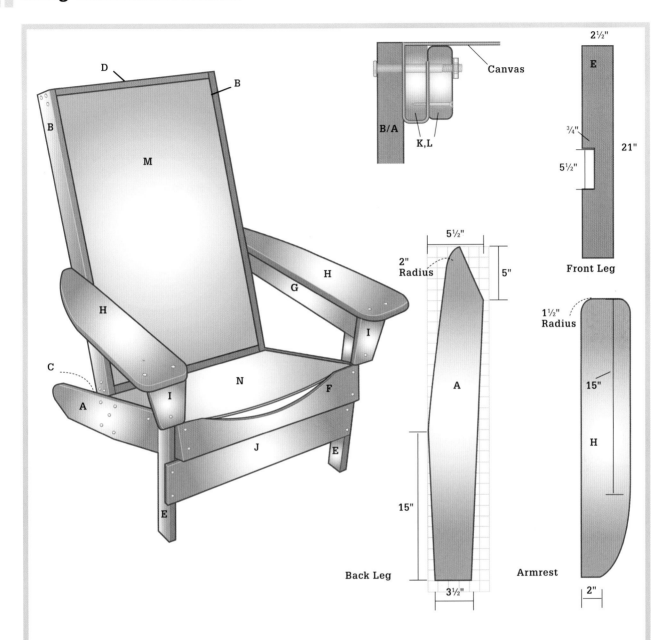

Canvas

B/A

K,L

2½"

E

¾"

5½"

21"

Front Leg

5½"

2"
Radius

5"

A

15"

3½"

Back Leg

1½"
Radius

15"

H

2"

Armrest

Cutting List

Key	Part	Dimension	Pcs.	Material
A	Back legs	¾ × 5 × 36"	2	White oak
B	Backrests	¾ × 4 × 40"	2	White oak
C	Back leg braces	¾ × 2½ × 22½"	2	White oak
D	Backrest braces	¾ × 2½ × 21"	2	White oak
E	Front legs	¾ × 2½ × 21"	2	White oak
F	Front leg brace	¾ × 5½ × 25½"	1	White oak
G	Armrest supports	¾ × 2½ × 26"	2	White oak

Key	Parts	Dimension	Pcs.	Material
H	Armrests	¾ × 5½ × 28"	2	White oak
I	Corbels	¾ × 4 × 7"	2	White oak
J	Front rail	¾ × 5½ × 24"	1	White oak
K	Back canvas rails	¾ × 2 × 33¾"	4	White oak
L	Seat canvas rails	¾ × 2 × 16"	4	White oak
M	Back canvas	33½ × 37¾"	1	Canvas (10 ounce)
N	Seat canvas	32 × 17"	1	Canvas (10 ounce)

Sling-Back Adirondack Chair

CUT THE PARTS

Cut all of the wood chair parts to length first and then rip-cut them to width on a table saw or with a circular saw and straightedge cutting guide (**photo 1**). If you are using random-width, rough-sawn hardwood, square it and plane it to thickness before cutting it to length. Rip-cut all parts that share the same width at the same time: the armrests and front rails are 5½" wide; the back legs are 5" wide; the backrests and corbels are 4" wide; the back leg braces, backrest braces, front legs, and armrest supports are all 2½" wide; and the back and seat canvas rails are 2" wide. Draw the back leg outline on each back leg blank (**photo 2**). Use the construction drawing (page 33). Cut along the back leg layout lines with a jigsaw.

Clamp the front legs together face-to-face and use a router and ½"-diameter straight bit to cross-cut the notch that holds the front rail in the front leg (**photo 3**). Clamp stop blocks to the legs at a distance from the notch edges equal to the distance from the edge of the router bit to the edge of the router base plate.

Draw the armrest shape on the armrests (see drawing, page 33). The arc runs from a point on the back edge that is 2" from the inside edge to a point on the outside edge that is 15" from the front edge. The front corners are 1½"-radius. Use a jigsaw to cut along the armrest layout lines. Miter-cut the back end of the armrest supports to 27°.

The final frame parts to cut are the corbels that support the outside edge of the armrest. Cut the two corbels to length and then draw the arc profile on each corbel and cut along the arc line with a jigsaw.

ASSEMBLE THE FRAME

Sand all faces of every workpiece smooth before beginning the assembly process. Attach the backrests to the back legs with 1¼" stainless steel screws (**photo 4**). The backrest should be square with the top edge of the back half of the back leg. Attach the backrest braces to the backrests with 2" stainless steel screws and finish washers (**photo 5**).

Clamp the front leg brace to the front legs, keeping both legs perpendicular to the brace. Drill two countersunk pilot holes through each side of the brace and into the legs. Attach the brace to the legs with 2" stainless steel screws and finish washers. Clamp the

Dimension your lumber. If you purchased sanded-four-side (S4S) stock, you will only need to rip it to the correct widths after you cut the parts to length.

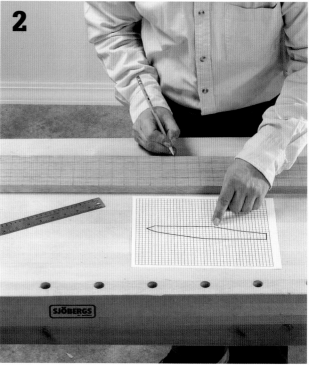

Lay out the parts. Use the back leg layout pattern on the construction drawing as a reference for marking the outline of the back legs on the back leg blanks.

armrest supports to the front legs. The front and top edges of the front brace are flush with the front and top edges of the front legs. Drill two countersunk pilot holes and attach the parts with 1¼" stainless steel screws and finish washers. Hold the front leg assembly upright and place the back legs on the front leg brace. Adjust the back leg assembly until the angled back edge of the arm support is flush with the back edge of the backrest and the front leg is plumb. Clamp the armrest support to the backrest and attach the leg assemblies with 1¼" stainless screws (**photo 6**). Attach the back leg braces to the back legs with 2" stainless steel screws and finish washers. Drill two countersunk pilot holes through each back leg and into each brace.

Clamp the corbel to the front of the front leg and armrest support. Align the top and inside edges of the three parts. Drill one countersunk pilot hole through the corbel and into the front leg. Drill a second countersunk pilot hole through the corbel and into the end of the armrest support. Attach each corbel with two 2" stainless steel screws and finish nails (**photo 7**). Attach the armrests to the armrest supports with three 2" screws. Attach the front rail to the front edges of the back legs with 2" screws. Apply an exterior wood finish to the frame.

Cut the leg notches. Clamp a straightedge to each side of the front leg notch layout lines to function as stops for your router. Cut the front leg notch in several passes with a router, lowering the bit with each pass.

Join the legs and backrest. First, clamp the backrests and the back legs together. Drill two pilot holes through the backrest and into each back leg. Drive 1¼" stainless steel screws with finish washers.

Install the backrest braces. Space the backrest braces 33¾" apart with the top backrest brace flush with the top of the backrests and the backs flush.

ATTACH THE CANVAS SEAT & BACK

The sling-style seat and back canvas panels are secured to the frame by rolling one side of the canvas around one rail and then sandwiching that rail between a second rail and the backrest. Machine screws secure the rails to the backrest. Cut the seat and back canvas rails to length if you have not already cut them. Cut the canvas seat and back to size, keeping the factory-seamed edges in the exposed position when possible. With the right side on a table, fold up ¼" of material along one long side of the canvas and then press. Fold the fabric over again ½" and press for a finished, straight edge. Hand- or machine-stitch a ⅜" hem. Repeat for the other side. With the seat canvas still right side down on a table, align one of the seat canvas rails on top

of the canvas so the canvas top edge is centered lengthwise under the rail. Roll the rail and canvas back onto the fabric two full turns (**photo 8**). Clamp another seat canvas rail on top of the fabric with edges flush. Connect the rails with three 1¼" screws (**photo 9**). Repeat the process of rolling the canvas and attaching the second rail for the other lower edge of the seat canvas.

Clamp the seat canvas rails and canvas to the back legs with the fronts of the canvas rails flush against the front rail. Drill ¼"-diameter pilot holes through the front legs, back legs, and seat canvas rails. Attach the canvas rails with ¼"-diameter machine screws, finish washers, and lock nuts (**photo 10**). Repeat the same process to attach the back canvas to the back canvas rails and then to the backrests (**photo 11**).

Attach the armrest supports. Drive two 1¼" screws through the inside faces of the back legs and two 1¼" screws through the inside faces of the backrests. Locate these screws 1" from the bottom edge of the back legs and 1" from the back edge of the backrests.

Attach the corbels. Drive two 2" screws through the top of the corbel and into the armrest support. Drill a pilot hole for each screw.

8

Wrap the seat rail by rolling the top and bottom edges of the seat canvas around one of the seat canvas rails. The canvas sides should be hemmed by this point if they are not factory edges.

9

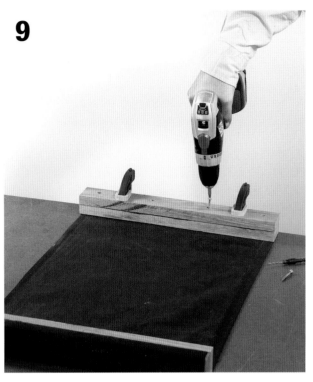

Secure the canvas between rails. Sandwich the canvas between the two rails and fasten the rails together with screws. Drill pilot holes and countersink the holes for each screw.

10

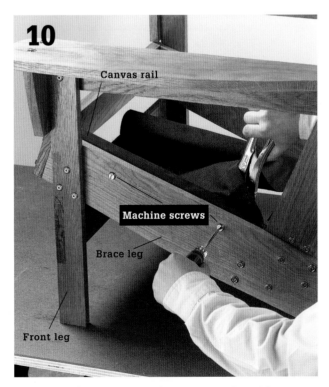

Canvas rail

Machine screws

Brace leg

Front leg

Attach the front canvas rails. Run one 3½" machine screw through the front leg, back leg, and seat canvas rails. Run two 3" machine screws through the back leg and canvas rails.

11

Attach the back canvas rails. Use four 3" machine screws per side to attach the back canvas rails to the backrest.

Porch Swing

A beautiful evening outdoors gets a little better when you're sitting and enjoying it from a porch swing. The gentle, rhythmic motion of the swing is a relaxing coda to any stressful day.

Essentially, a porch swing is a garden bench with chains instead of legs. Like garden benches, swings can be built to suit just about any style. Also like garden benches, too often the style of a porch swing comes at the expense of comfort. In fact, if you were to test each of the thousands of porch swing designs in existence, you might be amazed to discover how many are simply not comfortable. This porch swing was designed with both style and comfort in mind. It sits a bit deeper than many other versions and the back is pitched at just the right angle. Another key to its comfort is that the back rails don't extend all the way down to the seat slats, creating open space that is ergonomically important.

Despite the custom appearance of this porch swing, it is actually built from common ⅞" cedar boards, ⁵⁄₄" cedar deck boards, and cedar 2× lumber.

This porch swing can be hung from eyehooks in a porch ceiling that features sufficient structural framing, including joists that are no smaller than 2 × 8. Or, you can hang it in a variety of locations from a freestanding porch swing stand. The swing stand shown on pages 46 to 51 is designed to complement this swing.

Materials ▸

2 1 × 6" × 8 ft. cedar boards	Eyebolts (exterior):
1 ⁵⁄₄" × 12 ft. cedar deck board	2 @ ⅜ × 3½"
	2 @ ⅜ × 6½"
4 2 × 4" × 8 ft. cedar	8 ⅜"-dia. washers
Deck screws (2½", 3")	Finishing materials
	4 ⅜"-dia. locknuts

This cedar swing is roomy enough for two but compact enough to hang from either a stand or a front porch ceiling. Made of cedar, it is lightweight yet durable and moisture-resistant.

Porch Swing

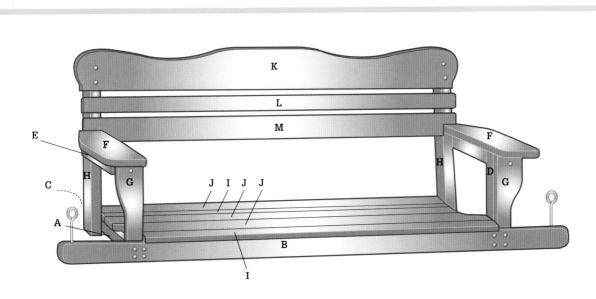

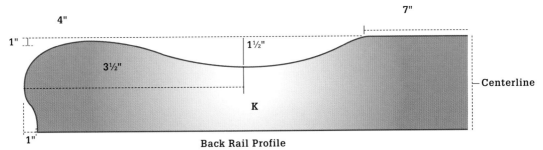

Back Rail Profile

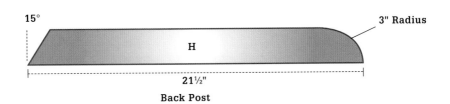

Back Post

Cutting List

Key	Part	Dimension	Pcs.	Material	Key	Part	Dimension	Pcs.	Material
A	Seat supports	1½ × 3¼ × 17½"	3	Cedar	H	Back posts	1½ × 3 × 21½"	2	Cedar
B	Front rail	1½ × 3 × 68"	1	Cedar	I	Seat slats	⅞ × 2⅜ × 48"	2	Cedar
C	Back rail	1½ × 2½ × 48"	1	Cedar	J	Seat slats	⅞ × 5 × 48"	3	Cedar
D	Front posts	1½ × 2½ × 11¾"	2	Cedar	K	Top back rail	⅞ × 5½ × 54"	1	Cedar
E	Arm supports	1¼ × 2 × 22"	2	Cedar	L	Middle back rail	⅞ × 2 × 52"	1	Cedar
F	Armrests	1¼ × 5½ × 24¼"	2	Cedar	M	Bottom back rail	⅞ × 3 × 52"	1	Cedar
G	Arm fronts	1¼ × 3¼ × 9¼"	2	Cedar					

Porch Swing

BUILD THE SEAT FRAME

Make the workpieces for the seat supports by cutting three 17½" lengths of 2 × 4. Cedar is shown here; you can also use treated pine if you want a natural wood finish or untreated SPF (spruce, pine, or fir) if you plan to paint the swing. Lay out the seat-support profile on one of the seat support pieces (**photo 1**) using the diagram on page 39 as a reference. The seat support is scooped on the top edge so the seat slats follow a comfortable flow. At the low point in the middle of

each support, the thickness of the part drops to 1¾". At the back end the part should be 2½" from top to bottom and at the front end it should peak at 3¼" and then drop down slightly over the last inch. Plot the profile so the tops of the part follow straight lines that conform to the width of the slats that will rest on them. The back edge of the part should be mitered at 15° to follow the backrest angle. Cut along the layout line with a jigsaw and then use the first seat support as a template to trace the profile onto the remaining

Lay out the parts. Plot the seat support profile onto one of the seat support workpieces using the dimensions given on page 39 as a reference.

Cut the front rail end profiles. Use a compass to draw the front rail end radius and cut along these lines with a jigsaw. Sand the cuts smooth.

Seat rail

2" Radius

1" Radius — Top

Bottom

two seat supports. Also use the jigsaw to cut out the second and third seat supports. Gang the seat supports together with clamps and sand the profiles all at the same time so they are exactly the same.

Make the seat front rail by cutting a 2 × 4 to 68" long and rip-cutting ¼" off each edge to remove the rounded edges, leaving a workpiece that's 3" wide. On the front face of the front rail first mark a 2" radius on the bottom corners and then draw a 1" radius on the top corners. Cut along the corner radius lines with a jigsaw (**photo 2**). Make the seat back rail by cutting a 2 × 4 to 48" in length and then rip-cutting it down to 2½" wide. Attach the seat supports to the seat front and back rails with 3" deck screws (**photo 3**).

ATTACH THE BACK & ARM SUPPORTS

Cut a pair of 11¾" lengths of cedar 2 × 4 and rip-cut these pieces to 2½" wide to make the front posts. Drill counterbored pilot holes and attach the front posts to the front rail and outside seat supports with 2½" deck screws (**photo 4**). *Note: Counterbore pilot holes for all structural joints.* If you're looking to save a bit of time, consider attaching the seat slats with screws driven through pilot holes that are countersunk only.

Join rails and seat supports. Drive two 3" deck screws through the front rail and into the front ends of the seat supports. Also drive one 3" screw through the back rail and into the back end of each seat support. Apply exterior glue to the mating parts first to reinforce the joints.

Attach the front posts. Drive two 2½" deck screws through the side of the front post and into the outside seat supports. Drive two 2½" deck screws through the front rail and into the front posts.

Next, cut two 21½" lengths of 2 × 4 and rip them to 3" wide, and then miter-cut the bottom ends to 15° to make the back posts. Draw a 3" radius on the back top corners of each back post and cut along the radius line with a jigsaw. Attach the back posts to the outside seat supports with 2½" screws (**photo 5**).

Cut one 22" length from a ¾ deck board (actual thickness is 1" to 1¼") and rip-cut that piece into two 2"-wide pieces to make the two arm supports. Attach the arm supports to the front and back posts with 2½" screws (**photo 6**). Cut two 9¼" pieces of the ¾ deck board to

make the arm fronts. Lay out the arm front profile on each piece and cut the profiles with a jigsaw. Attach the arm fronts to the front posts with 2½" deck screws.

ATTACH THE BACK RAILS & SEAT SLATS

Cut two 24¼" pieces of ¾ deck boards to make the armrests. Lay out the armrest profile on each deck board and cut the boards using a jigsaw. The backside edge should have a curved taper of 1" starting 7" from the end. The armrests should be rounded at a 1" radius on both front corners. Cut four 48" long pieces of ⅞ × 5½"

Attach the back posts. Clamp the pieces together and drive two 2½" deck screws through each back post and into the outside seat supports.

Attach the arm supports. Drive two 2½" deck screws through each end of the arm supports and into the front and back posts. Then attach the arm front with two 2½" deck screws.

(nominal 1 × 6) boards to make the seat slats. Rip-cut three of the boards to 5" wide and then rip-cut the fourth deck board into two 2⅜"-wide pieces.

Cut a 54" piece of ¾ deck board to make the top back rail. Make a template of one-half of the top back rail on a piece of cardboard according to the profile drawing on page 39. Cut the template out with scissors or an X-acto knife. Trace the template onto each half of the top back rail (**photo 7**). Then, cut along the layout line with a jigsaw. Sand smooth. Cut a 52" piece of ¾ deck board to make the middle

and bottom rails. Rip-cut this piece into one 2"-wide board and one 3"-wide board. Use a router and ¼" roundover bit to ease the edges of the armrests, seat slats, and back rails (**photo 8**). Attach the armrests, seat slats, and back rails with 2½" deck screws (**photo 9**).

FINISH THE SWING
Although you may choose to leave the swing unfinished if it is made of a good exterior wood, such as cedar or redwood, most people prefer to apply a top coat or even

7

Lay out the back rail profile. Use the information on page 39 to make a cardboard template of half of the top back rail. Use this template to lay out the first half of the top back rail profile and then flip the template to lay out the second half.

an exterior wood stain and a top coat. Protecting the wood not only allows the wood tone to retain its color, it also minimizes the raised wood grain effect that occurs when water soaks into unprotected wood. The raised grain is not uncomfortable in and of itself, but it can lead to splintering.

Before applying your finish of choice, sand all of the wood surfaces up to 150 grit using a pad sander. Do not use an aggressive sander, such as a belt sander. Cut or buy wood plugs from the same species as the swing wood. Glue the plugs into the counterbored holes at screw locations. Once the glue has set, trim the plugs flush with the wood surface using a flush-cutting saw, or simply sand the tops down so they are even with the surrounding wood surface. Then, wipe down the entire project with a rag dipped in mineral spirits or denatured alcohol, wait for the wood to dry, and then apply your finish. If you have access to an HVLP sprayer, it is an excellent choice for applying the finish smoothly and quickly. Two or three light coats will yield much better results than one or two heavier coats.

8

Ease the edges. Round over all edges of the armrests, back rails, and the top edges (smooth face) of the seat slats. Use a router with a ¼" radius roundover bit to make these profile cuts.

9

Finish the assembly. Attach the armrests, seat slats, and back rails with 2½" deck screws.

HANGING THE SWING

Install the four ⅜"-diameter eyebolts that will be fastened to the hanging chains or ropes (**photo 10**). Of these two options, chains take a bit longer to install but they won't need adjusting once they're set, and you don't have to tie and retie knots. Porch swing chains can be purchased as kits from hardware stores and from online sellers. Each kit contains a pair of chain assemblies with two swing chains, which consist of a Y-fitting that connects to an S-hook at the end of a single chain dropping from the ceiling or stand. Make sure the chain you buy is of sufficient strength and rated for outdoor usage. If you are using rope, choose rope that won't shrink or stretch (such as ⅝"-diameter nylon rope).

Two bolts are attached through the front rail and two bolts are attached through the back edges of the armrests and back posts. Hang the porch swing from chains or ropes so that the front edge is approximately 16" off the ground. The back edge of the swing should be level with the front edge or slightly lower. Adjust the hanging height to suit the primary users.

10

Prepare for hangers. Drill ⁷⁄₁₆"-dia. guide holes for each ⅜" eyebolt. Fasten the eyebolts with washers and locknuts.

Porch Swing Stand

What good is a porch swing if you don't have a place to hang it? Porch swings originally hung from the ceilings of covered porches, but you don't need a porch to enjoy a porch swing in your outdoor living space. Instead, you can build this attractive porch swing stand to hold your swing. It will look great in a garden, yard, or on a deck. And the total height is low enough to fit under most raised porches or decks. In fact, unless you're sure that your ceiling has the structural strength to handle a swing, this stand is probably a better option.

This swing stand is designed to hold up to a 4-foot-wide porch swing. The only tools you need to build it are a power miter saw or circular saw, jigsaw, and drill/driver. The design is simple enough to build in a day, but the speed of construction doesn't result in any lack of strength. The cross braces and gussets that reinforce the 4 × 4 legs and 4 × 6 top beam give this stand more than enough strength to hold two adults

(do not exceed). The only modification you may need to make to the plan is to match the distance between the eyebolts in the stand to the dimension between your porch swing's hanging chains or ropes.

Materials ▸

1 2 × 6" × 10 ft. cedar board	3" deck screws
1 2 × 8" × 12 ft. cedar board	Lag bolts (hot dipped or stainless steel):
4 4 × 4" × 8 ft. cedar boards	8 @ ⅜ × 5"
1 4 × 6" × 8 ft. cedar board	12 @ ⅜ × 6½"
	20 ⅜" lock washers
	20 ⅜" nuts
	2 ½ × 6" eyebolts

This sturdy stand made from cedar timbers is designed to support the swing project shown on pages 38 to 45. But if you like the stand, its design is neutral enough to support any other swing or seat that you buy, build, or already own.

Porch Swing Stand

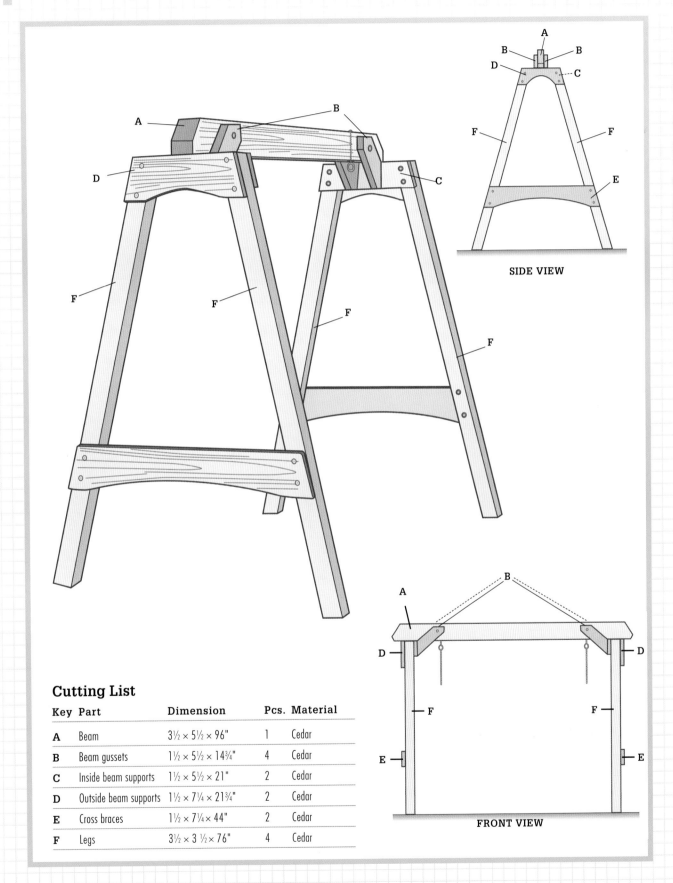

SIDE VIEW

FRONT VIEW

Cutting List

Key	Part	Dimension	Pcs.	Material
A	Beam	3½ × 5½ × 96"	1	Cedar
B	Beam gussets	1½ × 5½ × 14¾"	4	Cedar
C	Inside beam supports	1½ × 5½ × 21"	2	Cedar
D	Outside beam supports	1½ × 7¼ × 21¾"	2	Cedar
E	Cross braces	1½ × 7¼ × 44"	2	Cedar
F	Legs	3½ × 3 ½ × 76"	4	Cedar

Porch Swing Stand

CUT THE PARTS

Cut each 76"-long 4 × 4 leg with parallel 14° miters at the ends (**photo 1**). You need a 10" or 12" power miter saw for enough capacity to cut the legs in a single pass. Be sure to provide ample support for the workpiece, including the cutoff portion. If you don't have a miter saw, mark the angled cutting lines with a protractor or speed square, and cut them with a circular saw or handsaw. Cut the two 44"-long cross braces from a piece of 2 × 8. Miter-cut each end to 14°.

The bottom edge of the cross brace features a decorative arc profile. Draw this arc using a flexible strip of wood (such as 1"-wide strip of ¼" lauan plywood) as a gauge. Mark points on the workpiece that are 4" from the outside edges of the long side of the cross brace. At each mark, tap two small nails into the face of the cross brace near the edge. Tap a third nail centered across the length of the brace and 2" up from the bottom to mark the apex of the arc. Flex a thin scrap of wood against the nails to create a smooth

Cut the stand legs to length. If you have a 10" or 12" power miter saw, you should be able to make the 14° end cuts in one pass. Be sure the end of the workpiece is supported.

Trace the cross-brace arcs. Flex a thin piece of wood or metal against two nails to act as a template for laying out the arc profile on the leg cross braces.

arc profile. Trace the arc with a pencil (**photo 2**) and then remove the nails and cut along the line with a jigsaw.

Miter-cut the 14° ends of the two 21"-long 2 × 6 inside beam supports to length. Miter-cut the 14° of the two 21¾"-long 2 × 8 outside beam supports. Use the same method that you used to create the arc on the cross braces to create an arc along the bottom edge of the outside beam supports.

Cut the beam gussets 14¾" long. Make two marks 3½" in from each end along the top edge of each gusset, and draw a 45° line from each mark to the outside end of the gusset. Then, draw a second 45° line from the outside edge down to the bottom edge of the gusset (**photo 3**). Cut off the corners of each gusset on these marked cutting lines.

The top beam is an 8-foot long 4 × 6 timber. Miter-cut the top corners of the beam to 45°, starting 3½" in from each end of the beam.

ASSEMBLE THE STAND

To attach the gussets to the inside beam supports, first mark the center of each beam support and then measure out 1¾" from the center to designate the

Make the gussets. Draw 45° cutting lines at ends of the beam gussets using a try square as a guide. Trim along the cutting lines.

Attach the gussets. Bore counterbore holes and guide holes for bolts, washers, and nuts through the beam supports, cross braces, and legs. Drive ⅜ × 6½" lag screws with washers to secure the gussets.

positions of the inside edges of the gussets. Draw alignment lines on these marks, perpendicular to the top and bottom edges of the beam supports. Position your drill ¾" to the outside of these lines and bore ³⁄₁₆"-diameter guide holes through the beam supports. Hold the gussets in position and drill ⅛" pilot holes in the ends of the gussets using the beam pilot holes as a guide. Attach the gussets to the beam supports with 3" deck screws.

Lay the legs on a flat surface. Position the outside beam support and cross brace under the legs. Then, position the inside beam support and gusset assembly on top of the legs. Clamp the legs between the beam supports and clamp the cross brace to the legs. Drill two 1⅛"-diameter × ½" deep counterbore holes and ⁷⁄₁₆"-diameter guide holes through each joint and attach the parts with ⅜"-diameter × 5" and ⅜"-diameter × 6½" bolts (**photo 4**).

Raise the leg assembly. Position the beam on the beam supports so it fits in between the gussets. Clamp the beam in place and then drill counterbores and guide holes through the joints, just as you did for the leg assembly. Fasten the

beam with ⅜"-diameter × 6½" bolts secured by washers and locknuts (**photo 5**).

The chain or rope that supports the swing will be fastened to an eyebolt that runs down through the beam. Drill two ⁹⁄₁₆"-diameter vertical pilot holes through the center of the beam, spaced the same measured distance as there is between your swing's hanging chains or ropes. To avoid creating a place for water to pool, a counterbore hole is not drilled for the nuts that fasten the eyebolts. Fasten two ½"-diameter × 6" eyebolts with lock washers and nuts to the beam (**photo 6**).

INSTALL THE STAND & HANG THE SWING
The swing stand should be placed on level ground. A porch swing is not intended to swing fast or in a long arc, like a play swing does, so there is no need under normal use to anchor the stand to the ground. Hang the porch swing so the top front edge of the seat is approximately 16" off the ground (**photo 7**). The back edge of the swing should be level with the front edge or slightly lower. Adjust the hanging height to suit the primary users.

5

Attach the beam. Drill counterbores for washers on both gussets and drill guide holes for ⅜"-dia. x 6½"-long lag bolts. Insert the bolts and secure with lock washers and nuts.

6

Install eyebolts on the beam. Fasten ½"-dia. eyebolts to the beam with washers and locknuts.

7

Hang the swing. Use chains (preferred) or rope to hang the porch swing from the eyebolts in the swing stand beam. The front edge of the swing seat should be roughly 16" off the ground, and the swing should be level or tilted slightly backwards when at rest.

Recyclables Bench

Few areas in your home are better suited for a sturdy bench than porches, entryways, breezeways, and even patios and garages that are located next to an entry door. The reasons are pretty obvious: it's convenient to have a place to sit while removing shoes or boots, and a flat, raised surface is perfect for setting down groceries and packages while fumbling around for the house keys. Along with providing a seating option, this bench has a flip up lid and is sized to hold grocery bags of recyclables so you can keep them out of the house and out of sight until curbside pick-up day.

The principal design flair on this project is created by the scalloped rim rails and vertical columns running along the faces and sides. With a subtle Grecian architectural theme, the look imparts a bit of elegance to the sturdy wood box and lid. The parts also provide structural support, allowing for thin front and side panels that keep down the weight and cost while allowing slightly more interior storage space.

Because this bench is painted, it can be built with inexpensive construction-grade lumber even if it is destined for porch, patio, or some other exposed or partially exposed area.

Materials ▸

4 1 × 4" × 8 ft. clear pine boards	1 ¾" × 4 × 8 ft. AB plywood
2 1 × 2" × 8 ft. clear pine boards	3 2½" brass butt hinges
6 1 × 6" × 10 ft. clear pine boards	¼"-dia. dowels
	#00 biscuits
	Deck screws

Indoor/outdoor benches that combine seating and storage are readily available for purchase today, but the typical model in stores has a bleak appearance that's much more about utility than design appeal. This storage bench employs some classical styling elements for an appearance that makes no concessions to utility.

Recyclables Bench

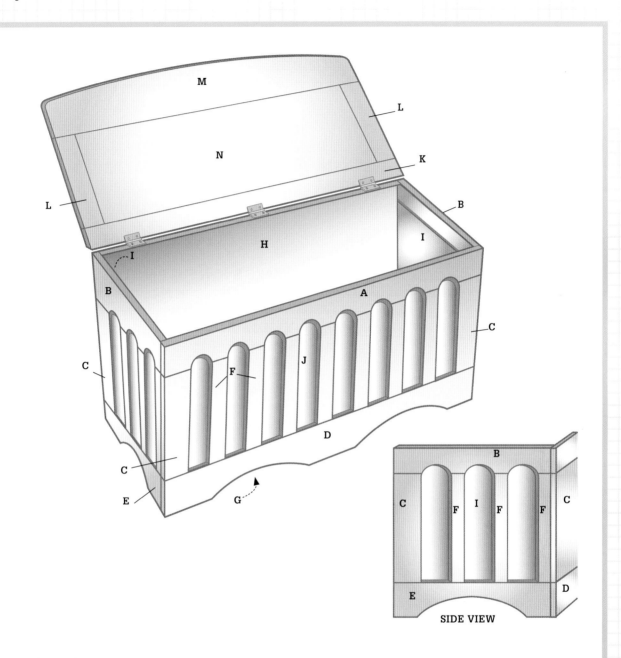

SIDE VIEW

Cutting List

Key	Part	Dimension	Pcs.	Material
A	Front top rail	¾ × 3½ × 40½"	1	Pine
B	Side rails	¾ × 3½ × 16½"	2	Pine
C	Corner boards	¾ × 3 × 12"	4	Pine
D	Front base rail	¾ × 5½ × 40½"	1	Pine
E	Side base rails	¾ × 5½ × 16½"	2	Pine
F	Filler stiles	¾ × 1½ × 12"	13	Pine
G	Bottom panel	¾ × 15¾ × 39"	1	AB plywood

Key	Part	Dimension	Pcs.	Material
H	Back panel	¾ × 21 × 39"	1	AB plywood
I	Side panels	¼ × 13 × 12"	2	AB plywood
J	Front panel	¼ × 13 × 38"	1	AB plywood
K	Lid back rail	¾ × 3½ × 41"	1	Pine
L	Lid side rails	¾ × 3½ × 10"	2	Pine
M	Lid front rail	¾ × 5½ × 41"	1	Pine
N	Lid panel	¾ × 10 × 34"	1	AB plywood

Recyclables Bench

MAKE THE PROFILED RAILS

The top rails and base rails for this bench feature decorative cutouts and curves that should be cut before the bench frame is assembled. The top rails have a series of half-circles separated by 1½" of square-end material that mates with the tops of the 1 × 2 filler stiles. The best way to make the half-round cutouts is to cut full circles in a workpiece and then rip-cut that piece down the center. For the top rails, a piece of 1 × 8 SPF (spruce/pine/fir) is wide enough to make both the sides and the top. Cut a 1 × 8 to about 48" long and then draw a centerline from end to end. Lay out 3"-diameter circles along the centerline so the equators of the circles are 1½" apart on the centerline (start in the center and work out toward the ends, leaving slightly more than 3" of uncut wood at each end). Chuck a 3"-diameter hole saw in a drill and carefully cut the circles (**photo 1**). If you have a drill press, use it here.

After the holes are cut, set up a table saw to rip-cut the workpiece along the centerline. If you do not have a table saw, use a circular saw and a straightedge cutting guide. Cut along the centerline (**photo 2**). Then, trim the ends of one ripped workpiece so they are exactly 3" out from the outer edges of the circular cutouts. Cut the side top rails from the other half of the workpiece (**photo 3**). Each side rail should have 3" of uncut material at the back and 1½" at the front.

Cut the 1 × 6 stock for the base rails to length and lay out the arcs according to the dimensions on page 53. The arcs essentially create leg forms at the ends of each rail and in the middle of the front rail. Use a jigsaw to cut out the arcs (**photo 4**) and then sand them so they are smooth. Cut the corner boards and the filler stiles to length.

MAKE & JOIN THE PANEL ASSEMBLIES

Join the rails, corner boards, and stiles to create a front panel assembly and two side panel assemblies. Because of the width of the top and base rails, there are several better options than screws to connect the

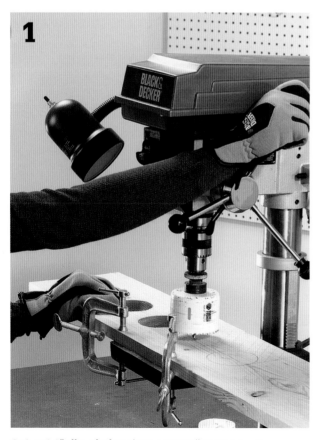

Cut out 3"-dia. circles along a centerline on a 1 × 8 workpiece to make the top rails. Use a 3" hole saw to cut the wood.

Rip-cut the rail workpiece along the centerline to create two workpieces with half-round cutouts. Use one for the front top rail and the other to make the side top rails.

horizontal rails to the vertical corner boards and filler stiles. If you own or have access to a pocket screw jig, pocket screws can be used to make the connections. Otherwise, use dowels to reinforce the joints. You can use a dowel jig or dowel points for this, or you can rely on math and marking.

To join the horizontal and vertical parts with dowels, start by using a drill press (if you have one) to drill ⅜"-diameter × ¾" deep dowel holes in the bottom edges of the top rails (**photo 5**). Clamp a straightedge guide to your drill press table to ensure that the holes are a uniform distance in from the front edges of the workpieces. The holes should be centered on each 1½" shoulder where it will meet a spacer stile. Use a pair of evenly spaced dowels to secure each corner board. After the dowel holes are drilled into the rails, clamp all of the stiles and corner boards together edge-to-edge with the ends flush. Use the same drill press setup to drill dowel holes in the ends of the clamped parts (**photo 6**) making sure the dowel hole above each spacer stile location is centered. *TIP: If your drill press doesn't have enough throat capacity to drill these*

dowel holes, you may be able to do it by orienting the table vertically and drilling them individually instead.

Apply a small amount of exterior glue into each dowel hole, and make the dowel joints to complete the assembly. Use a bar clamp or pipe clamp to draw the parts together, if necessary. Once the glue has dried, join the front assembly to the side assembly with glue and 2½" countersunk wood screws. Make sure the top and bottom edges are flush. Cut the back panel to size from ¾" plywood and attach it to the backs of the side assemblies with glue and 2½" countersunk wood screws. Cut the bottom panel to size and install it in the base of the bench so the top of the panel is ¼" below the tops of the base rails using glue and countersunk 2½" wood screws (**photo 7**). You could also use biscuits and a plate joiner or pocket screws to make these connections.

Cut the front panel and side panels to size from ¼"-thick plywood. If you decide to use a two-tone painting scheme, paint the frame and the panels separately using two or three thin coats of exterior trim paint. Once the paint has dried, apply a thin bead of exterior-rated adhesive to the backs of the filler

Trim the scalloped rails to length so the correct amount of uncut materials is left at each end.

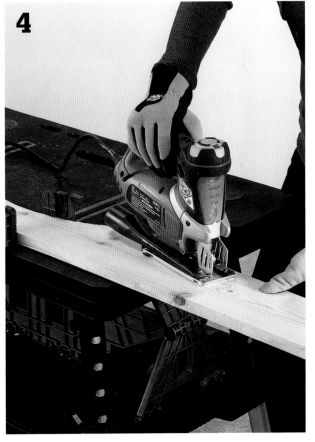

Make the 2"-deep arc cutouts on the bottoms of the rails to create the feet shapes.

stiles and corner boards and then position the panels behind the front and side assemblies, centered so any reveals are even around the perimeters of the panels. Press on the panels to set them in the adhesive and then staple them or drive ¾" brads to reinforce the joints.

MAKE & ATTACH THE LID

The lid for this storage bench is made from ¾" plywood that's framed with solid wood. To make it this way, you need to employ either a biscuit joiner, a pocket screw jig, or a dowel jig. A simpler alternative is to cut the entire lid to the finished dimensions from ¾" exterior plywood, and fill the voids in the plywood edges with wood filler before painting.

Cut the lid frame parts from 1 × 4 and 1 × 6 stock. Trace the profile for the front edge into the 1 × 6 using the dimensions on page 53 as a guide. Cut the lid panel to size from ¾" AB plywood (or another high-quality grade). Join the back and side lid rails using dowels, biscuits, or pocket screws and glue; then attach the lid panel to the inside edges of the three-sided frame using the same joinery techniques. Attach the front lid rail to the front ends of the side rails and the front edge of the lid panel **(photo 8)**. Sand the lid smooth after the glue dries and fill any holes or voids with wood filler. Paint all project parts with exterior paint. Attach the lid with three 2½ × 2½" exterior-rated butt hinges **(photo 9)** or, if you prefer, a piano hinge. Add optional lid supports to prevent slamming and other hardware as you see fit.

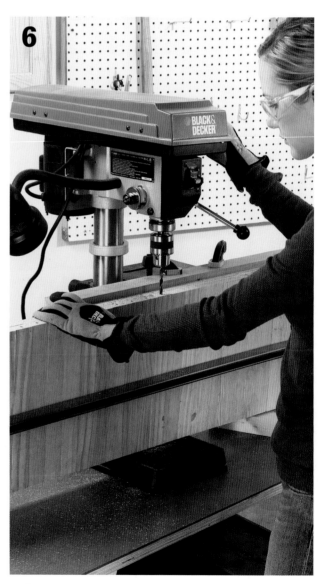

Drill dowel holes in the top and bottom rails to make dowel joints with the filler stiles and the corner boards.

Drill mating dowel holes in the top and bottom ends of the filler stiles and the corner boards. Gang the parts together edge to edge to ensure a uniform setback from the front faces.

Install the base panel using glue and counterbored screws. The top of the base panel should be ¼" below the tops of the bottom rails on all sides.

Make the bench lid by capturing the plywood lid panel between the back and side lid rails and then adding the front lid rail.

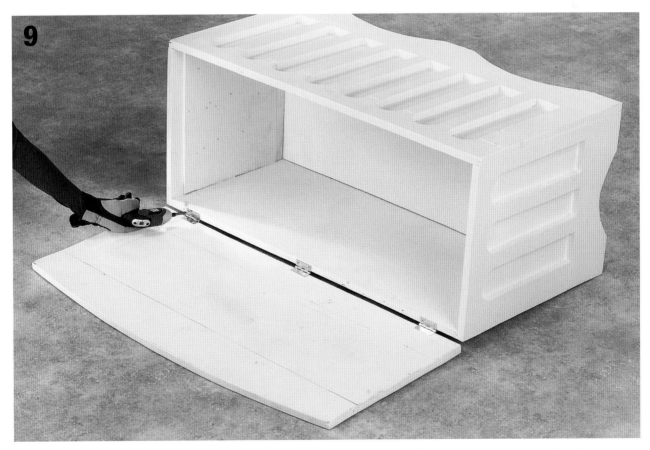

Attach the lid with hinges. Add any additional hardware you may want, such as lid support hardware or chest handles.

Luxury Sun Lounger

Reclining in comfort on a summer afternoon—that's all the motivation most people will need to build this wood sun lounger. It features four recline positions so you can select a comfortable back angle whether you plan to read a book, take an afternoon nap, or bag some serious rays. Fashioned from mahogany for high-end nautical appeal, the lounger features two pullout trays for beverages or books. Mahogany is naturally rot resistant, but it will last longer (and resist staining better) if it is coated with an exterior sealer. But the parts that make this lounger are made from stock ¾"-thick and 1½"-thick lumber so you can choose to build it from just about any exterior-grade lumber, such as cedar, redwood, or white oak.

Most of the parts for this lounger are rip-cut to width—a task that's easiest to accomplish with a table saw, but can also be done with a circular saw and straightedge. All of the exposed, sharp edges are eased with a router and roundover bit. If you don't have a router, you can use a power sander, a block plane, or even hand-sand them.

Materials ▸

2 ¾ × 1½" × 8 ft. mahogany boards	10 ¼" brass flat washers
9 ¾ × 3½" × 8 ft. boards	4 ¼" brass locknuts
2 ¾ × 5½" × 10 ft. boards	½"-dia. × 27" rod
2 1½ × 3½" × 8 ft. boards	2 8"-dia. wheels
1 ¾"-dia. × 24" hardwood dowel	6 ½" galvanized washers
Brass screws (1¼", 2½")	½"-dia. aluminum rod
36 No. 10 brass finish washers	1 ½"-dia. × 19½" CPVC tubing
4 ¼"-dia. × 2" brass machine screws	2 ½" push caps

Made of rich mahogany and dressed up with solid brass hardware, this sun lounger has a nautically inspired appearance that is right at home poolside.

Luxury Sun Lounger

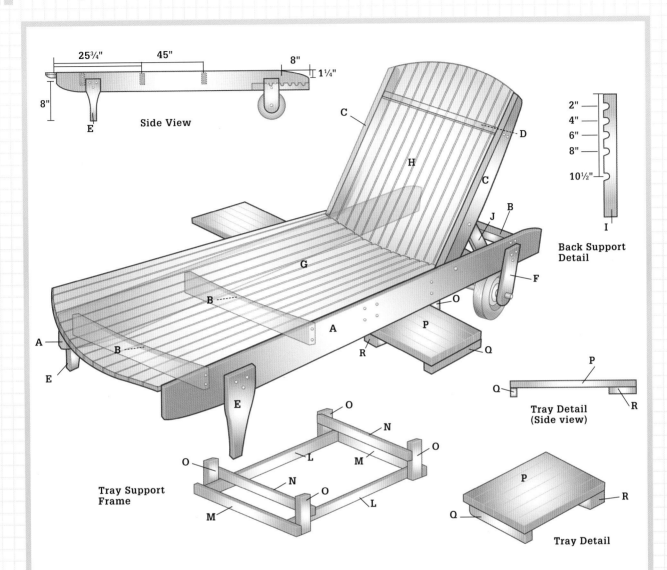

Side View

Back Support Detail

25¾" 45" 8" 1¼"

8"

E

2"
4"
6"
8"
10½"

I

C
D
H
C
B
J
F
O
P
R
Q

G
B
A
B
E
E

O
N
O
L
M
N
O
M
L

Tray Support Frame

P
Q
R

Tray Detail (Side view)

P
R
Q

Tray Detail

Cutting List

Key	Part	Dimension	Pcs.	Material
A	Base rails	¾ × 5½ × 77"	2	Mahogany
B	Base stretchers	1½ × 3 × 24"	4	Mahogany
C	Back rails	¾ × 3 × 30"	2	Mahogany
D	Back stretchers	1½ × 3 × 22"	2	Mahogany
E	Front legs	¾ × 4 × 12"	2	Mahogany
F	Back legs	¾ × 4 × 10¼"	2	Mahogany
G	Base slats	¾ × 1¾ × 51"	13	Mahogany
H	Back slats	¾ × 1¾ × 31½"	12	Mahogany
I	Back support rails	¾ × 1⅝ × 15"	2	Mahogany
J	Back support arms	¾ × 2 × 15"	2	Mahogany
K	Back support rod	¾" dia. × 23¾"	1	Oak dowel

Optional Pull-out Trays

Key	Part	Dimension	Pcs.	Material
L	Tray frame sides	¾ × 1½ × 24"	2	Mahogany
M	Tray frame ends	¾ × 1½ × 13½"	2	Mahogany
N	Tray frame crosspieces	¾ × 1½ × 13½"	2	Mahogany
O	Tray frame supports	¾ × 1½ × 5½"	4	Mahogany
P	Tray slats	¾ × 1¾ × 12"	12	Mahogany
Q	Tray fronts	¾ × 1½ × 10¾"	2	Mahogany
R	Tray backs	¾ × 3½ × 10¾"	2	Mahogany

Luxury Sun Lounger

BUILD THE BASE FRAME

Begin construction of the sun lounger by making the base frame. Achieving strong joints and perfectly square corners at this stage helps to ensure that your project fits together as designed. Cut the base rails and back rails to length and width. Use a piece of cardboard to make a template of the curved profile (8" long and 1¼" deep) that's cut into the ends of the rails (see drawing, page 59). Trace the curved profile onto the bottom front corner and the top back corner of each base rail and onto the top (back) end only of the seat back rails (**photo 1**). Use a jigsaw to cut along the curved lines (**photo 2**) and then smooth the cuts with a power sander. Round over the top edges of the base rails with a router and ¼"-radius roundover bit (**photo 3**) or ease them with sandpaper.

Cut the front legs to length and width. Use the same curved-profile template that was used for the base and back rails to trace two mirror-image curves on the bottom corners of each front leg (**photo 4**). Use a jigsaw or band saw to cut along the curved lines.

Preparing Your Stock ▸

The sun lounger seen here is designed so it can be built easily with common dimensional lumber found at any home center. Depending on your location, that would include cedar, redwood, or cypress along with treated and untreated SPF (spruce/pine/fir). In some cases, you can find select, sanded hardwoods in standard dimensions at your building center. A well-stocked lumberyard will have much greater selection of dimensioned lumber suitable for exterior projects, such as white oak, mahogany, teak, and ipê. But if you intend to build any project with hardwood, you greatly expand your species options and save significantly on your materials costs by milling your own stock. The most inexpensive way to buy hardwood is in random widths and lengths. Most often, lumber sold this way has been planed or sawn to a uniform thickness that's a bit thicker than standard dimensions. For example, ⁴⁄₄ ("four quarter") stock is a very common size that is readily planed down to standard ¾" thickness with a surface planer.

In addition to thickness, rough stock must also be squared. This is typically done with a stationary jointer. You run the best edge through the jointer until it is flat and then make a parallel rip cut along the other edge. The squared stock can be run through a planer to create smooth, flat surfaces that will achieve the desired thickness.

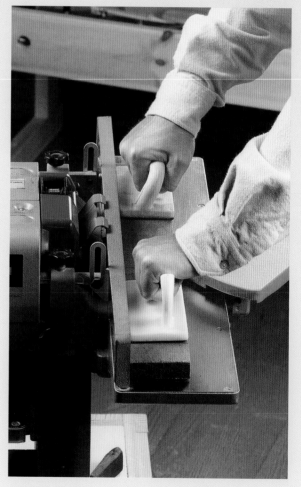

Narrow stock can be flattened on the face with a jointer, but for wider stock you need a power planer. Dressing, squaring, and dimensioning random-width lumber is time-consuming but saves a lot of money on material costs versus pre-milled stock.

Cut the back legs to length and width. Draw a 2"-radius half-circle on the bottom of each leg. Cut along the half-circle line with a jigsaw. Cut the base stretchers to length and width. To mark the curves on the stretchers, bend a flexible 24" long piece of scrap wood (a 1" wide strip of ¼"-thick lauan plywood is a good choice) or metal to create the arc along the top edges of the base stretchers (**photo 5**). Trace the arc on three of the base stretchers (the rearmost base stretcher remains flat). Cut along the arc lines on each base stretcher with your jigsaw or band saw.

Attach the base rails to the base stretchers with 2½" screws and finish washers. Attach the legs to the base rails with exterior wood glue, 1¼" exterior-rated screws, and decorative, rounded finish washers (we used brass hardware but stainless steel is also a good choice). Drill three ⅛"-diameter pilot holes through the legs before driving each screw (**photo 6**).

BUILD THE BACK FRAME

Cut the back rails to length and width. Trace the curved profile on the top back corner of each back rail. Cut along the curve on each back rail. Round over the top edges of the back rails. Cut the back stretchers to length and width. Bend a flexible 24"-long piece of scrap wood or metal to create the arc along the inside

Draw the end profile onto the rails. Using a cardboard template, trace the smooth curve onto the ends of each part, as shown in the drawing, on page 59. Draw the curved profile on a piece of heavy cardboard. Cut along the profile line to make the template. This template allows you to trace the curved profile onto the parts.

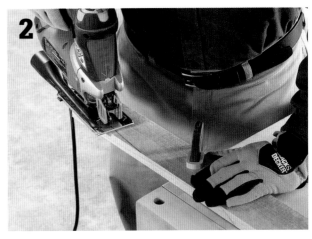

Cut the curves. Use a jigsaw or band saw to cut the curved profiles on the ends of the base rails and on one end of each back rail. Use a sander to remove any blade marks and smooth the edges.

Round-over the edges of the base rails with a router and ¼" piloted roundover bit. Use a sharp bit and avoid stopping in one place to prevent burning the wood.

Trace the curve profile on the bottom corners of the front legs. Flip the template to create symmetrical curves.

edge of the back stretchers. Trace the arc on both of the back stretchers. Cut along the arc line of both back stretchers. Attach the back rails to the back stretchers with 2½" exterior-rated screws (**photo 7**).

ATTACH THE BASE & BACK SLATS

Rip-cut ¾ × 3½" boards to make two 1¾"-wide slats from each board. Cut the base and back slats to length and width from this stock. Round-over the long edges of each slat with a router and ¼"-radius piloted roundover bit. Evenly space the base slats across the base stretchers with the foot ends of the slats extending 3" beyond the foot ends of the base rails. Drill countersunk pilot holes in each slat, centering each hole across the slat and base stretcher. Attach the base slats to the base stretchers with countersunk 1¼" exterior-rated screws (**photo 8**).

Repeat the same process to attach the back slats to the back stretchers. The top edges of the back slats extend 3" beyond the top edges of the back rails. Use a string and pencil as a trammel to draw a 24" radius across the ends of the base and back slats (**photo 9**).

Lay out the stretcher arcs. Tap a finish nail 1" down from the top edge of a base stretcher. Use this nail as a flex point for bending the strip of wood to make the arc on the base stretchers. Drive two more nails near the ends of the curve to help hold the shape. Cut out and sand along the curve and use this stretcher as a template for tracing arcs on the other two stretchers.

Fasten the back legs to the base rails with brass screws and finish washers.

Cut off the slat ends along the radius line. Sand the cut edges smooth and then round-over the ends of the slats.

ATTACH THE BACK, BASE & ADJUSTABLE BACK SUPPORT

Cut the back support rail to length and width. Mark the center of each notch (the notches are calibrated to create multiple backrest position settings). Drill a ¾"-diameter hole that is centered on each notch layout line and located ½" from the top edge. Make two cuts through the top of the back support rail to open up the top of each notch (**photo 10**). The back cut is made perpendicular to the top edge so that the support bar does not slide out of the notch when you lean on the back. The front cut is beveled slightly forward so that the support bar slides out when the back is raised. Attach the support rails to the base rails with 1¼" screws.

Cut the back support arms to length and width. Draw 1"-radius half-circles at each end of the support arms. Cut along the radius lines. Drill a ¾"-diameter

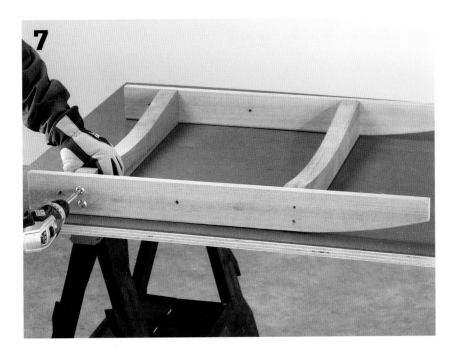

Attach back rails to back stretchers. Use 2½" screws (brass is seen here) and finish washers. The top edges of the back stretchers are flush with the top edges of the back rails.

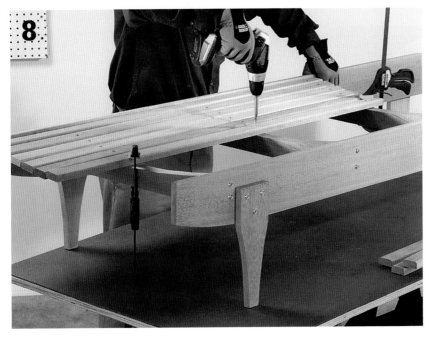

Attach the base and back slats. Drill ⅛"-dia. countersunk pilot holes centered across each slat and stretcher, and fasten with 1¼" screws (do not use decorative washers here).

hole on one end of the arm and a ¼"-diameter hole at the other end. Drill ¼"-diameter holes through the back rails where the support arms will be attached. Attach the support arms to the back rails with ¼ × 2" machine screws and locknuts. Place a flat washer between the support arm and back rail and place a finish washer under the screw head.

Cut the back support bar to length and slide it through the ¾"-diameter holes in the support arms. Place the back assembly on the flat support rails, leaving a ½"-wide space between the base slats and back slats. Drill the ¼"-diameter pivot hole through the base rails and back rails. Attach the base rails to the back rails with ¼ × 2" machine screws and locknuts (photo 11).

BUILD THE PULL-OUT TRAYS

The optional pull-out trays are a useful feature that you'll enjoy. To make and install them, start by cutting all tray parts to length and width. Round-over the top edges of the tray slats. Attach the tray slats to the tray front and back with countersunk 1¼" screws. Assemble the tray frame sides, ends, and supports with 1¼" screws. Place the trays on the tray frame sides and then attach the tray crosspieces to the tray supports with 1¼" screws. Position the tray frame

Draw the slat cutoff profile. To mark the profile on the attached slats, measure 24" from the edge of the middle slat and then use a string and pencil as a trammel to draw the 24"-radius line across the slat ends.

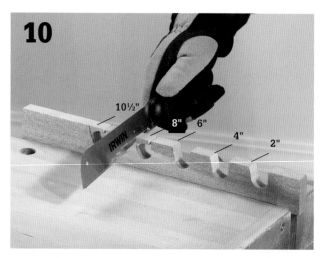

Create the back support notches. After drilling a ¾"-dia. hole at each notch location, make a pair of cuts down from the edge and remove the waste wood to complete each notch.

Mount the back assembly. Attach the back and base with two ¼" machine screws. Insert a washer as a spacer between the base rail and the back to keep them from binding when the back pivots and is raised or lowered.

Install the pull-out trays. Place the trays on the tray frame sides and attach the tray frame crosspieces to the supports, keeping the crosspieces ⅛" above the tray slats.

and tray assembly against the inside face of the base rails with the tops of the frame supports 3⅛" above the bottom edge of the base rails. Attach the frame by driving 1¼" screws through the base rails and into the edge of the frame supports (**photo 12**).

ATTACH THE WHEELS

The sun lounger wheels allow you to easily move the lounger around to follow the sun or just get it out of the way. It is rather heavy, and pulling and dragging it around constantly will shorten its lifespan. Drill the ⅝"-diameter holes for the axle through the back legs. Slide the ½" aluminum rod axle through the holes, fitting flat washers and a piece of ½"-diameter CPVC over the axle and between the wheels (**photo 13**). Secure the wheels on the axle with ½" push caps (**photo 14**).

Install the axle. Slip the aluminum rod into a CPCV plastic tube sleeve and insert into the guide holes in the wheels.

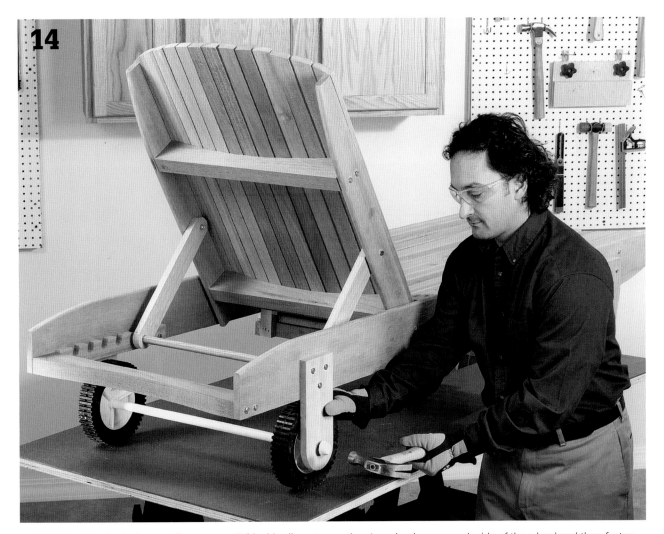

Install the wheels. Make sure the spacers (½" inside-diameter washers) are in place on each side of the wheel and then fasten flanged push caps onto the ends of the rod to secure the wheels to the axle.

Trellis Seat

Spice up your patio or deck with this sheltered seating structure. Set it in a secluded corner to create a warm, inviting outdoor living space.

Made of lattice and cedar boards, our trellis seat is ideal for conversation or quiet moments of reading. The lattice creates just the right amount of privacy for a small garden or patio. It's an unobtrusive structure that is sure to add some warmth to your patio or deck. Position some outdoor plants along the top cap or around the frame sides to dress up the project and bring nature a little closer to home. For a cleaner appearance, conceal visible screw heads on the seat by counterboring the pilot holes for the screws and inserting cedar plugs (available at most woodworking stores) into the counterbores.

Materials ▸

1 4 × 4" × 6' cedar	4d galvanized casing
2 2 × 8" × 8' cedar	nails
5 2 × 4" × 12' cedar	finishing materials
1 1 × 6" × 10' cedar	Note: measurements
11 1 × 2" × 8' cedar	reflect the actual
2 ½" × 4 × 4' cedar	size of dimension
lattice	lumber
Moisture-resistant	*Cut one each: 32",
glue	49", 63"
1¼", 2", 2½" and 3"	
deck screws	

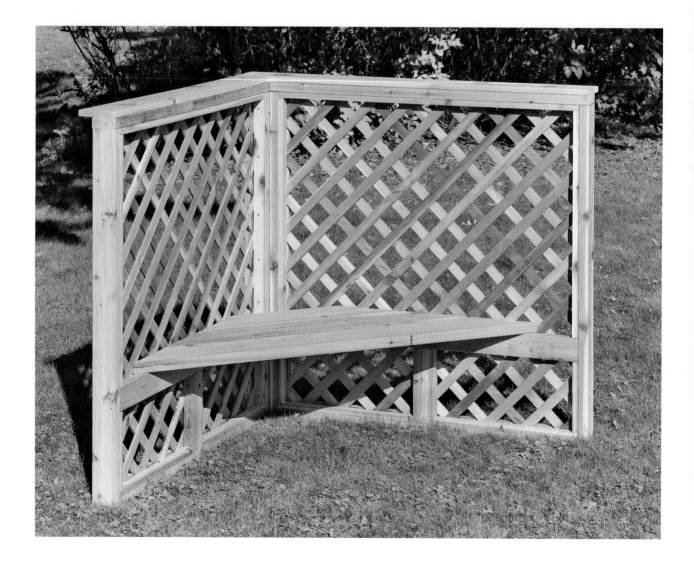

Trellis Seat

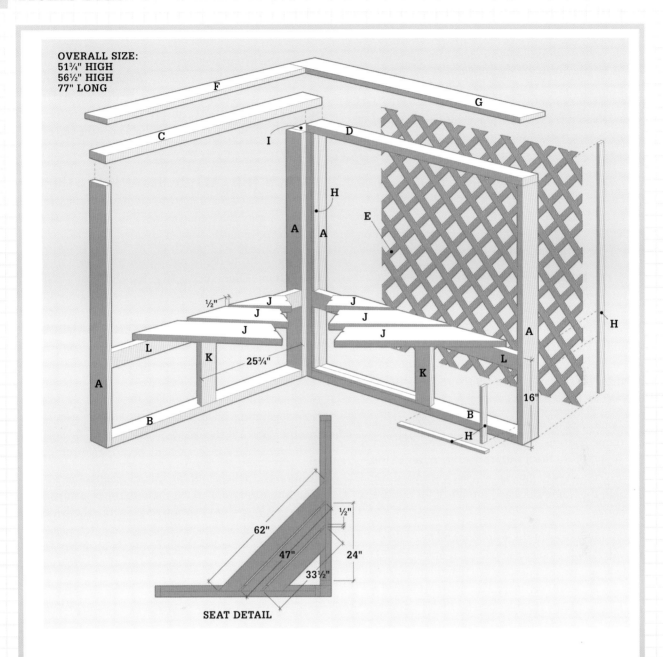

OVERALL SIZE:
51¾" HIGH
56½" HIGH
77" LONG

½"

J

J

J

J

J

J

J

J

F

C

I

D

G

H

A

A

A

E

H

A

L

K

25¾"

A

B

B

L

K

16"

H

SEAT DETAIL

62"

47"

33½"

½"

24"

Cutting List

Key	Part	Dimension	Pcs.	Material	Key	Part	Dimension	Pcs.	Material
A	Frame side	1½ x 3½ x 49½"	4	Cedar	H	Retaining strip	¾ x 1½" cut to fit	22	Cedar
B	Frame bottom	1½ x 3½ x 48"	2	Cedar	I	Post	3½ x 3½ x 49½"	1	Cedar
C	Long rail	1½ x 3½ x 56½"	1	Cedar	J	Seat board	1½ x 7¼ x *	3	Cedar
D	Short rail	1½ x 3½ x 51"	1	Cedar	K	Brace	1½ x 3½ x 11"	2	Cedar
E	Lattice	½" x 4 x 4'	2	Cedar	L	Seat support	1½ x 3½ x 48"	2	Cedar
F	Short cap	¾ x 5½ x 51"	1	Cedar					

Trellis Seat

MAKE THE TRELLIS FRAME.

Cut the frame sides (A), frame bottoms (B), long rail (C), short rail (D), braces (K) and seat supports (L) to length. To attach the frame sides and frame bottoms, drill two evenly spaced ³⁄₁₆" pilot holes in the frame sides. Counterbore the holes ¼ " deep, using a counterbore bit. Fasten with glue and drive 2½" deck screws through the frame sides and into the bottoms.

Drill pilot holes in the top faces of the long and short rails. Counterbore the holes. Attach the long and short rails to the tops of the frame sides with glue. Drive deck screws through the rails and into the ends of the frame sides. The long rail should extend 3½" past one end of the frame (**photo 1**).

Mark points 22¼" from each end on the frame bottoms to indicate position for the braces. Turn the frame upside down. Drill pilot holes in the frame bottoms where the braces will be attached. Counterbore the holes. Position the braces flush with the inside frame bottom edges. Attach the pieces by driving 3" deck screws through the frame bottoms and into the ends of the braces.

Position the seat supports 16" up from the bottoms of the frame bottoms, resting on the braces. Make sure the supports are flush with the inside edges of the braces. Attach with glue and 3" deck screws driven through the frame sides and into the ends of the seat supports.

Attach the braces to the seat supports by drilling angled ³⁄₁₆" pilot holes through each brace edge. Drive 3" deck screws toenail style through the braces and into the top edges of the seat supports (**photo 2**).

JOIN THE TRELLIS FRAMES TO THE POST.

Cut the post (I) to length.

Attach the two frame sections to the post. First, drill pilot holes in the frame sides. Counterbore the holes. Drive evenly spaced 3" deck screws through the frame sides and into the post (**photo 3**). Make sure the overhang of the long rail fits snugly over the top of the post.

ATTACH THE LATTICE RETAINING STRIPS.

Cut the lattice retaining strips (H) to fit along the inside faces of the trellis frames (but not the seat supports or braces).

Nail the strips to the frames, flush with the inside frame edges, using 4d galvanized casing nails (**photo 4**).

CUT AND INSTALL THE LATTICE PANELS.

Since you will probably be cutting through some metal fasteners in the lattice, fit your circular saw with a remodeler's blade. Sandwich the lattice panel between two boards near the cutting line to prevent the lattice from separating. Clamp the boards and the panel together, and cut the lattice panels to size. Always wear protective eyewear when operating power tools.

Position the panels into the frames against the retaining strips, and attach them to the seat supports with ¹¹⁄₄" deck screws (**photo 5**). Secure the panels by cutting retaining strips to fit along the outer edges of the inside faces of the trellis frame. Nail strips in place.

Attach the long rail at the top of one trellis frame with a 3½" overhang at one end to cover the post

Drive deck screws toenail-style through the braces and into the seat supports

BUILD THE SEAT.

Cut the seat boards (J) to length. On a flat work surface, lay the seat boards together, edge to edge. Insert ½"-wide spacers between the boards

Draw cutting lines to lay out the seat shape onto the boards as if they were one board (see diagram, page 67, for seat board dimension). Gang-cut the seat boards to their finished size and shape with a circular saw.

Attach the seat boards to the seat supports with evenly spaced deck screws, maintaining the ½"-wide gap. Smooth the seat board edges with a sander or router.

INSTALL THE TOP CAPS.

Cut the short cap (F) and long cap (G).

Attach the caps to the tops of the long and short rails with deck screws (**photo 6**).

APPLY FINISHING TOUCHES.

Brush on a coat of clear wood sealer to help preserve the trellis seat.

TIP: Fabricated lattice panels are sold at any building center in standard ¾" thickness. For our trellis seat project, we found and used ½"-thick lattice panels. If you cannot locate any of the thinner panels, use ¾"-thick lattice, and substitute ½"-thick retaining strips at the backs of the trellis frames.

Fasten the trellis frames to the post at right angles

Nail 1 × 2 retaining strips for the lattice panels to the inside faces of the trellis frames.

Fasten the lattice panels to the seat supports with 1¼" deck screws, then attach outer retaining strips.

Attach the long and short caps to the tops of the trellis frames. The long cap overlaps the long rail and the post.

Dining & Entertaining Projects

Perhaps the most popular backyard activities are cooking and eating. In fact, throwing backyard barbecues and preparing summertime meals for the family are the primary reasons we acquire most of our yard furnishings. Picnic tables and patio tables are the heart of your outdoor entertaining accommodations, and you'll find several interpretations here. The Cedar Patio table offers sturdiness, a spacious top, and rich wood tones. The trestle-type table with a pair of matching benches is flexible, comfortable, and low-maintenance, thanks to the composite decking used. The outdoor tea table and chairs sets an Eastern tone that is at once contemporary and classic. For ambitious outdoor cooks, investigate the rolling Patio Prep Cart with built-in refrigerator compartment, or the Pitmaster's Locker—a vertical cabinet with a locking door for fuel and grilling accessory storage.

In this chapter:

- Trestle Table and Benches
- Cedar Patio Table
- Teahouse Table Set
- Folding Table
- Occasional Table
- Children's Picnic table
- Traditional Picnic Table
- Patio Prep Cart
- Pitmaster's Locker
- Timberframe Sandbox

Trestle Table and Benches

This modified picnic table-and-bench set combines the tried-and-true dimensions and durability of a classic picnic table with the style and structure of a traditional trestle dining table. It is built with common exterior lumber. The version seen here uses pressure-treated pine to do the structural work of the base frames, but it has a modern twist. For the tabletop and seat tops it employs low-maintenance composite deck boards. The composite deck boards provide a surface that's easy to clean and requires little long-term maintenance. Composite boards are quite a bit heavier than wood, so you might not want to use them if you foresee a need to move your table frequently.

Trestle tables share one principal defining feature: a pair of end leg frames that support a horizontal beam (the trestle). Today, the most common trestle leg tables are the manufactured metal leg folding tables found in almost all schools, hotel banquet rooms, and other commercial settings. But trestle leg construction isn't new; it has been used in table designs for centuries. Early versions were built with large, solid slab-wood legs that were braced with a center stretcher. The stretcher and trestle legs were typically joined by a through-mortise-and-tenon joint that was secured with a pin or key that fit through the tenon.

This outdoor table design reflects the style of those early wood trestle tables. The legs are made from multiple boards instead of a single slab, and the stretcher locks to the leg boards in notches instead of with a through-mortise-and-tenon joint.

Materials ▸

1	1 × 2" × 8 ft. pine board	1	2 × 10" × 8 ft. pine board
9	2 × 4" × 8 ft. boards	6	⅝" × 12 ft. composite deck boards
1	2 × 8" × 10 ft. pine board		Deck screws (2", 2½")

A classic picnic table gets a modern makeover by replacing the wood tabletop and seat boards with low-maintenance composite decking.

Trestle Table and Benches

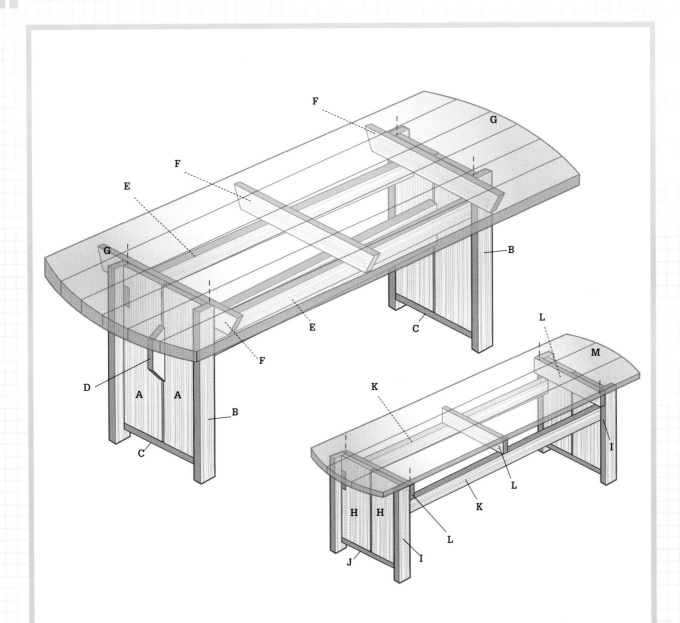

Cutting List

Table

Key	Part	Dimension	Pcs.	Material
A	Inside legs	$1\frac{1}{2} \times 8\frac{3}{4} \times 27"$	4	PT Pine
B	Outside legs	$1\frac{1}{2} \times 2\frac{1}{2} \times 28\frac{3}{4}"$	4	PT Pine
C	Bottom leg rail	$\frac{3}{4} \times 1\frac{1}{2} \times 18"$	2	PT Pine
D	Middle stretcher	$1\frac{1}{2} \times 8\frac{3}{4} \times 52"$	1	PT Pine
E	Side stretchers	$1\frac{1}{2} \times 3 \times 48"$	2	PT Pine
F	Cross supports	$1\frac{1}{2} \times 3 \times 30"$	3	PT Pine
G	Tabletop planks	$1\frac{1}{4} \times 5\frac{1}{2} \times 72"$	6	Decking

Benches (2)

Key	Part	Dimension	Pcs.	Material
H	Inside bench legs	$1\frac{1}{2} \times 6 \times 14\frac{1}{4}"$	8	PT Pine
I	Outside bench legs	$1\frac{1}{2} \times 2\frac{1}{2} \times 16"$	8	PT Pine
J	Bottom bench leg rails	$\frac{3}{4} \times 1\frac{1}{2} \times 12\frac{1}{2}"$	4	PT Pine
K	Side stretchers	$1\frac{1}{2} \times 3 \times 55"$	4	PT Pine
L	Cross stretchers	$1\frac{1}{2} \times 3 \times 15\frac{1}{2}"$	6	PT Pine
M	Seat planks	$1\frac{1}{4} \times 5\frac{1}{2} \times 72"$	6	Decking

Working with Composites ▶

Decking and other building materials made with composite are becoming increasingly popular and are available in a much greater range of sizes, shapes, and colors than they were even a couple of years ago. In fact, composite 2 x 4s that can perform light structural duty are even beginning to hit the market. For any outdoor building project, composites present a number of unique design options. If you are attracted by the low-maintenance qualities of composites and would like to try using them in one of your building projects, as in this trestle table project, you should know a few things about it and how its workability compares to wood.

The basic ingredients in composites are wood dust and plastic resin. This combination gives it some of the look and feel of wood, but little of the structural strength. The plastic makes the material essentially impervious to water damage, hence its popularity as decking. However, because it does contain wood fiber composite, it is susceptible to mold and mildew if you don't clean it regularly.

You can use just about any conventional carpentry tool on composite. However, avoid very fine blades as they can clog up. If you're using a 7¼" circular saw, look for a 40-tooth framing blade. For a 10" power miter saw, use a 60-tooth carbide-tipped blade; for a 12" saw use an 80-tooth blade. For jigsaws, use a 12-TPI (tooth-per-inch) blade.

Composite material does not respond well to sanding. Even coarse sandpapers tend to clog up almost immediately, and the edges of material like decking scratch easily when sanded. For these reasons it's worth taking the time to make your initial cuts as smooth as possible. For the cleanest possible cuts, use a router and straight bit with either a cutting template or a pattern-following sleeve.

Composites can be difficult to get smooth when they're cut. Sanding (left) yields only gummed up papers and a messy edge. Saws (middle) work fine, but avoid blades that are either too fine or too rough. A router and straight bit (right) will yield a perfectly smooth cut but require multiple passes.

Trestle Table and Benches

CUT THE TABLE PARTS

Cut four 27"-long pieces of 2 × 10 and then trim off the edges to make the four 7¼"-wide inside legs. Use a table saw or circular saw to rip-cut these pieces to width. Clamp the four inner legs together face to face with the ends and edges flush. Draw lines to designate the top and bottom of the notches that hold the middle and side stretchers. Use a router and straight bit to cut out the waste material inside the notch outlines. Clamp a straightedge on each side of the notch layout lines at a distance that is equal to the distance between the edge of the bit and the edge of the router base (**photo 1 and photo 2**). These guides will function as stops for the router base. Cut the notches for the middle stretcher

½" deep by 6¾" long and the notches for the side stretchers 1½" deep by 3" long. The tops of both notches should be 3" down from the top of the leg. Cut the notches by making multiple passes with the router, lowering the bit after each pass (**photo 3**). Do not attempt to remove more than ¼" of material (in thickness) in a single pass.

Cut four 28¾" long pieces of 2 × 4 and then trim approximately ½" off the long edges ½" per edge to make the four 2½"-wide outer legs. Cut the two bottom leg rails to length. Cut one 52" long piece of 2 × 10 and then trim approximately ¼" off the long edges to make the 8¾"-wide middle stretcher. Use a miter saw or jigsaw to cut each corner to a 30° miter. Make the cuts 1" in from the ends (**photo 4**).

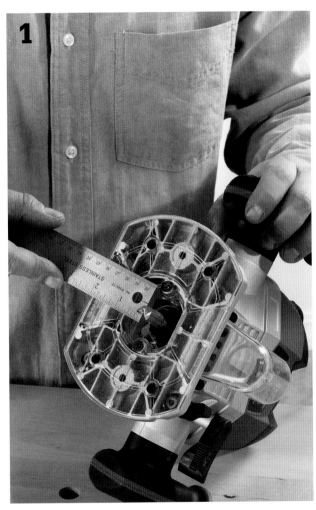

Measure the router bit setback. So you know where to place the straightedge cutting guides to cut the notches with your router, measure the distance from the edge of the straight bit to the outside edge of the base plate.

Gang-cut the stretcher notches into the legs. Clamp a straightedge guide on each side of the notch layout lines so the distance from the blocks to the notch layout line equals the router bit setback distance.

Cut two 48"-long pieces of 2 × 4 and then trim approximately ¼" off the long edges to make the 3"-wide side stretchers. Cut three 30"-long pieces of 2 × 4 and then trim approximately ¼" off the long edges to make the 3"-wide cross supports. Cut 30° miters in the ends of the crosspieces **(photo 4)**.

Sand all of the wood parts to prepare for finishing. Apply an exterior finish to all of the frame parts. In this case a solid-color deck and siding stain was used. Solid color stains are available in a wide range of colors. It looks almost like paint after it is applied, but it doesn't peel as it ages so it is easier to reapply and maintain than paint. Finally, cut the tabletop planks to length. Cut 12-foot deck boards in half to make the 6-foot tabletop and seat top planks.

ASSEMBLE THE TABLE

Begin the assembly of the table by attaching one of the inside legs to the middle stretcher using two 2½" screws.

3

Finish clearing the notches. Don't try to remove all of the waste material from the notches in one pass. Start with a ¼" bit depth and then lower the bit ¼" after each pass.

4

1"-deep by 1½"-wide notches for lap joint with legs

Trim the middle stretcher. Use a miter saw to trim off each corner at a 30° angle. Make the cuts 1" in from the ends.

Attach one of the cross supports to the inner leg with two 2½" screws (**photo 5**). Attach the second inside leg to the cross support with two 2½" screws and toe-screw it into the middle stretcher with one screw (**photo 6**). Repeat the inside leg and cross support assembly sequence to build the other leg assembly. Fit the side stretchers into the notches on the sides of the inside legs and secure them with two 2½" screws at each joint.

Attach the outside legs to the inside legs with three 2½" screws each (**photo 7**). Attach the bottom leg rail to the bottom of the inside legs with four 2" screws. Clamp the middle cross support in position on the middle stretcher and side stretchers. Drill a ⅜"-diameter × 1½"-deep counterbored hole in the top of the cross support and over the center of the stretchers. Then, drill a 3⁄16" pilot hole the rest of the way through the cross support. Attach the cross support to the stretchers by using an extended driver bit or a hand screwdriver to drive a 2½" screw through each pilot hole and into the side stretcher (**photo 8**).

Join the supports and legs. Attach one of the cross supports to the inner leg that has already been attached to the middle stretcher.

Secure the middle stretcher to the leg assemblies. Attach the second inner leg to the cross support and toe-screw this leg into the middle stretcher.

Add outside legs to the leg assemblies. Attach an outside leg to the outer edge of each inside leg. The tops of the inside and outside legs must be flush.

Attach the middle cross support. Drill a deep counterbored hole halfway through the middle cross support and drill a pilot hole through the rest of the cross support. Secure with screws.

Attach the composite tabletop planks to the cross supports with 2" composite decking screws (these are specially designed to minimize "mushrooming" of the composite material around the screw head). Drive two screws in each board, centered over the cross supports.

To make arcs for trimming lines on the ends of the tabletops, measure and mark a point 45" in from each end of the table and centered from side to side. These marks will act as the pivot points for drawing the radius curves on the tabletop ends. Tie a string to a pencil or marker and then measure 45" of string out from the writing utensil. Hold the string on each pivot point and sweep the pencil or marker across the tabletop, keeping it perpendicular at all times. This

will create a radius line (**photo 9**). Cut carefully along the trim lines with a jigsaw and 12-tooth-per-inch blade (**photo 10**). Also draw 3"-radius lines at each corner and then cut along the radius lines. Use a router and ¼" roundover bit to ease the radius edges on the ends of the top boards.

BUILD THE BENCHES

The bench part dimensions are different than the table part dimensions, but the construction process is basically the same. The only notable difference is that the benches do not have a middle stretcher. Cut the bench parts and build the benches using the same steps and techniques that were used to build the table (**photo 11**).

9

Mark the end curves on the tabletop. Use a 45"-long string or wood strip as a compass (more accurately, as a trammel) and a pencil to mark the 45" radius cutting lines on the ends of the tabletop boards.

10

Cut the curves. Use a jigsaw and 12-TPI blade to cut the arc at the ends of the tabletop. Be careful to make clean cuts, as composite material is virtually impossible to sand.

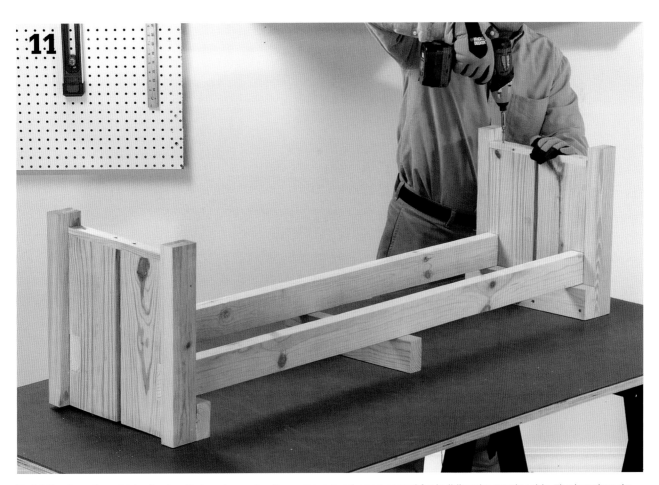

11

Build the benches. Make the trestle benches using the same procedure you used for building the trestle table. The benches do not have a middle stretcher.

Cedar Patio Table

In these days of plastic-resin or aluminum-and-bubble-glass patio furniture, it is refreshing to encounter a nice beefy patio table made of solid wood. With a massive base of 4 × 4 cedar, this square patio table definitely has a surplus of sturdiness. Also boasting warm wood tones, this all-cedar patio table is roomy enough to seat six and strong enough to support a large patio umbrella. The construction process for this table is very straightforward. The legs and cross braces are cut from solid 4 × 4 cedar posts and then they are lag-screwed together. The lag screw heads are countersunk below the wood surface. If you can find them at your local building center, buy heartwood cedar posts. Heartwood, cut from the center of the tree, is valued for its density, straightness, and resistance to decay. Also, take care when selecting the 1 × 4 cedar boards used to make the tabletop. Look for boards that are free of large knots and fairly consistent in tone. Most dimensioned cedar sold at building centers is rough on one face. Either plane the rough faces smooth or face them inward when you install them in this project. Because it's used for an eating surface, apply a natural, clear linseed-oil finish.

Materials ▸

3	4 × 4" × 8 ft. cedar boards	Moisture-resistant glue
3	2 × 2" × 8 ft. cedar boards	Deck screws (2", 3")
2	1 × 4" × 8 ft. cedar boards	20 ⅜ × 6" lag screws with washers
4	1 × 6" × 8 ft. cedar boards	Finishing materials

This patio table blends sturdy construction with rugged style to offer many years of steady service.

Patio Table

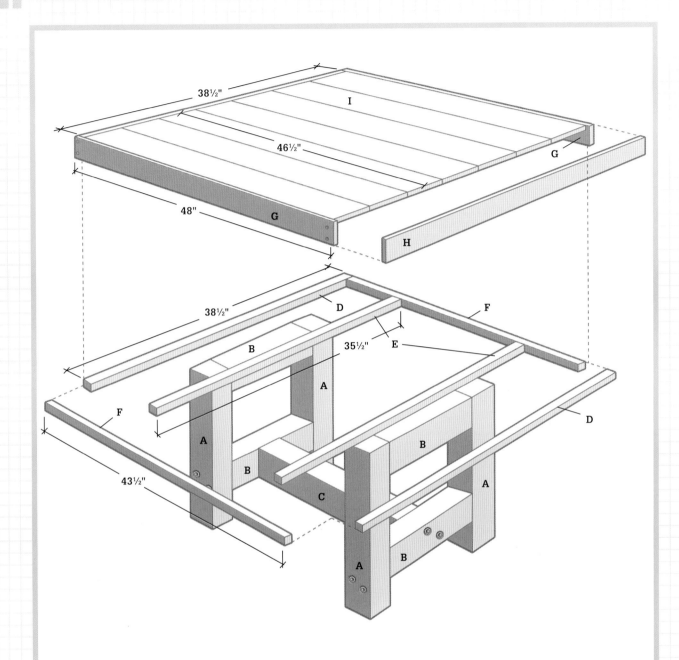

Cutting List

Key	Part	Dimension	Pcs.	Material
A	Legs	3½ × 3½ × 27¼"	4	Cedar
B	Stretchers	3½ × 3½ × 20"	4	Cedar
C	Spreader	3½ × 3½ × 28"	1	Cedar
D	End cleats	1½ × 1½ × 38½"	2	Cedar
E	Cross cleats	1½ × 1½ × 35½"	2	Cedar

Key	Part	Dimension	Pcs.	Material
F	Side cleats	1½ × 1½ × 43½"	2	Cedar
G	Side rails	¾ × 3½ × 48"	2	Cedar
H	End rails	¾ × 3½ × 38½"	2	Cedar
I	Top slats	¾ × 5¼ × 46½"	7	Cedar

Cedar Patio Table

MAKE THE LEG ASSEMBLIES

Cut the legs, stretchers, and spreader to length. Measure and mark 4" up from the bottom edge of each leg to mark the positions of the bottom edges of the lower stretchers. Test-fit the legs and stretchers to make sure they are square. The top stretchers should be flush with the top leg ends. Carefully position the pieces and clamp them together with pipe clamps. The metal jaws on the pipe clamps can damage the wood, so use protective clamping pads.

Drill ⅞"-diameter × ⅜"-deep counterbores positioned diagonally across the bottom end of each leg and opposite the lower stretchers (**photo 1**). Drill ¼" pilot holes through the counterbores and into the stretchers. Unclamp the pieces and drill ⅜" guide holes for lag screws through the legs, using the pilot holes as center marks. Apply moisture-resistant glue to the ends of the stretchers. Attach the legs to the stretchers by driving lag screws with washers through the legs and into the stretchers. Use the same procedure to attach the spreader to the stretchers.

ATTACH CLEATS & RAILS

Cut the side rails and end rails to length. Drill two evenly spaced, ⅛" pilot holes through the ends of the side rails. Counterbore the holes ¼" deep to accept plugs using a counterbore bit. Apply glue and fasten the side rails to the end rails with 2" deck screws.

Cut the end cleats, cross cleats, and side cleats to length. Fasten the end cleats to the end rails ¾" below the top edges of the rails with glue and 2" deck screws (**photo 2**). Repeat this procedure with the side cleats and side rails.

CUT & ATTACH THE TOP SLATS

Cut the top slats to length. Lay the slats into the tabletop frame so they rest on the cleats. Carefully spread the slats apart so they are evenly spaced. Use masking tape to hold the slats in place once you achieve the correct spacing (**photo 3**). Stand the tabletop frame on one end and fasten the top slats in place by driving two 2" deck screws through the end cleats and into each slat. Hold or clamp each slat

Counterbore two sets of holes on each leg to recess the lag screws when you attach the legs to the stretchers.

Attach the end cleats to the inside faces of the end rails. Maintain a ¾" distance from the top edge of the rails to the top edge of the cleats.

Install the tabletop slats. Use pencils or dowels as spacers to set even gaps between top slats. Tape the slats in position with masking tape.

Fasten cross cleats to the tabletop for strength and to provide an anchor for the leg assembly.

Attach the tabletop to the table base with 2" deck screws. Do not overdrive the screws.

firmly while fastening to prevent the screws from pushing the slats away from the frame (**photo 4**).

CONNECT THE LEGS & TOP

Turn the tabletop over and center the legs on the underside. Make sure the legs are the same distance apart at the top as they are at the bottom. Lay the cross cleats along the insides of the table legs. Fasten the cross cleats to the tabletop with 2" deck screws. Fasten the cross cleats to the legs with 3" deck screws (**photo 5**).

APPLY FINISHING TOUCHES

Fill screw hole counterbores with cedar plugs or buttons for a more finished appearance. Smooth the edges of the table and legs with a sander or router (**photo 6**). If you want to fit the table with a patio umbrella, use a 1½"-diameter hole saw to cut a hole into the center of the tabletop. Use a drill and spade bit to cut the 1½"-diameter hole through the spreader. Finish the table as desired. Use clear linseed oil for a natural, nontoxic, and protective finish.

Sand the surfaces smooth before you stain or treat the patio table. Use the sander to break sharp edges with a slight roundover.

Teahouse Table Set

Inspired by low teahouse tables, this table-and-stool set looks great on a small urban patio or in a Japanese-style garden. The table height offers a unique perspective on the rest of the surroundings and creates a more intimate setting for a casual dinner or evening tea. And if the idea of crouching down to sit in these stools doesn't appeal to you, then you might still consider building it as a child's table.

This set is relatively easy to build, but it still features several appealing and unique design details. The legs of the table and stools feature reverse tapers, reinforcing the Eastern design influence. The seats are cupped slightly for greater comfort. And, the round tabletop has a chamfered edge.

You can build this table using any exterior grade lumber, and the parts are sized so that you can find all of the materials at most home centers or lumberyards. This version was built out of cedar and stained with a dark brown, solid semitransparent deck stain, giving it the look of dark weathered wood.

A few power tools are needed to build this set. First, you need a saw, such as a miter saw or circular saw, to cut the parts to length. You also need a saw to cut the tapers—a band saw is best for this, but you could also use a jigsaw with a long blade or make two mating cuts with a circular saw. The circular top is easiest to cut with a jigsaw or with a router equipped with a circle-cutting jig. The chamfered edge on the tabletop is an optional detail that requires a router and chamfer bit.

Materials ▸

Table	Stools (4)
3 1 × 8" × 8 ft. cedar boards	4 1 × 4" × 8 ft. cedar boards
2 2 × 4" × 8 ft. cedar boards	5 2 × 4" × 8 ft. cedar boards
1 4 × 4" × 8 ft. cedar board	Deck screws (2", 2½")

Add a touch of Eastern elegance to your patio or transform your gazebo into a teahouse with this simple-to-make table-and-stool set.

Teahouse Table Set

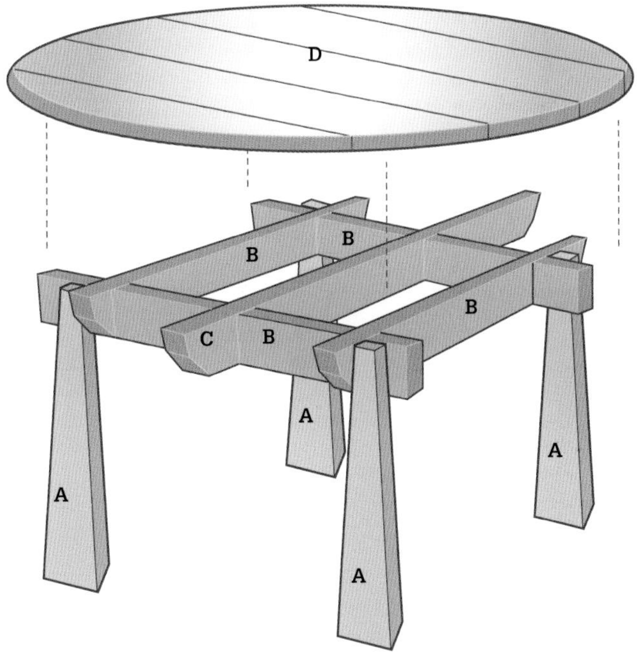

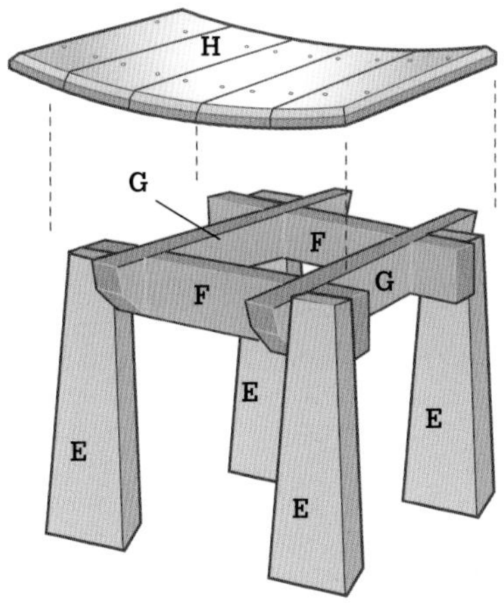

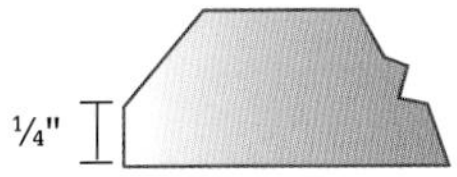

TABLETOP CHAMFER

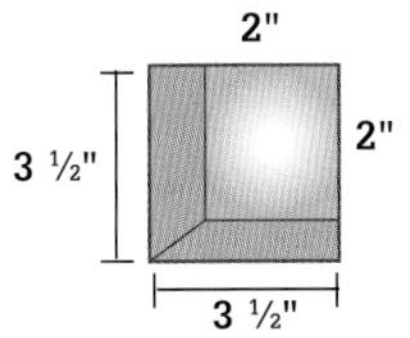

LEG TOP VIEW

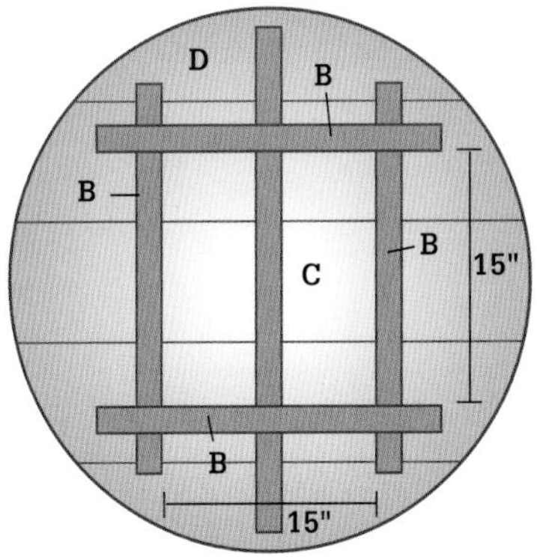

TABLETOP SUPPORT DETAIL

Cutting List

Table

Key	Part	Dimension	Pcs.	Material
A	Legs	3½ × 3½ × 22"	4	Cedar
B	Side supports	1½ × 3½ × 26"	4	Cedar
C	Middle support	1½ × 3½ × 30"	1	Cedar
D	Tabletop planks	¾ × 7¼ × 37"	5	Cedar

Stools (4)

Key	Part	Dimension	Pcs.	Material
E	Legs	1½ × 3½ × 12"	16	Cedar
F	Seat supports	1½ × 3½ × 18"	8	Cedar
G	Seat rails	1½ × 3½ × 12"	8	Cedar
H	Seat planks	¾ × 3½ × 14"	20	Cedar

Teahouse Table Set

BUILD THE TABLE BASE

Begin building the base of the tea table by cutting the leg pieces to length. A 10" or 12" power miter saw can cut through the 4 × 4 in a single pass, but a circular saw requires two joining cuts from opposite sides. Set the saw's cutting depth so it is slightly deeper than one-half the thickness. Cutting with the blade at full depth increases the possibility of uneven cuts.

The table legs are created with reverse tapers—they're wider at the bottom than the top. If you are an experienced woodworker and have a table saw, use a tapering jig to make the parts. A band saw is the next

best bet for making taper cuts. Mark the taper lines on two adjacent sides of each leg (**photo 1**). Cut the tapers with a band saw. Cut the first taper (**photo 2**) and then reattach the taper to the leg with tape, flip the leg, and cut the second taper (**photo 3**). Repeat the taper cuts on all four legs and sand the blade marks smooth.

Cut the side supports and middle support to length. Trim off the bottom corners of each support with 30° miter cuts. The miters should end 1½" in from the ends of the bottom edges (**photo 4**). The table supports fit together with half-lap joints. There

One edge of a straightedge should be on the corner of the leg blank on one end. The other end of the blank should be marked 2" in from the edge. Connect the points to create the taper cutting line.

Make the first taper cut. Using a band saw, place one hand on the tabletop to act as a guide and use your other hand to push and steer the leg through the cut.

are several ways to cut the half-laps notches. In this case, the notches are all spaced 15" apart so it makes sense to cut them all at the same time—a technique referred to as "gang cutting." To gang-cut the supports, mark the center on the bottom face of two of the side supports and the middle support. Also mark the center on the top faces of the two remaining side supports. Clamp the supports together with the center marks facing up and aligned. Next, mark the outsides of the notches on the support that is closest to you and then use a try square or combination square to extend that line across all of the supports (photo 5). Set your circular saw blade to a depth of 1¾". Make cuts along the notch edge layout lines. Align the blade inside the

notch waste area, with the edge of the blade following the layout line.

After cutting the sides of the notches, clean out the rest of the waste material from the notch by making several overlapping cuts with the circular saw (photo 6). Smooth any remaining blade marks on the bottom of the notch with a sharp wood chisel. The two bottom side supports also require a middle half-lap notch to hold the middle support. Clamp the two bottom side supports together and repeat the notch cutting process for the middle notch.

Test-fit the parts to make sure everything fits together and then assemble the table base. First, apply exterior-rated glue to the inside faces of the

Make the second taper cut.
Temporarily reattach the cutoff taper waste piece with masking tape to support the leg on the table. With the leg oriented so the first taper rests on the table, cut the second taper on the adjoining face.

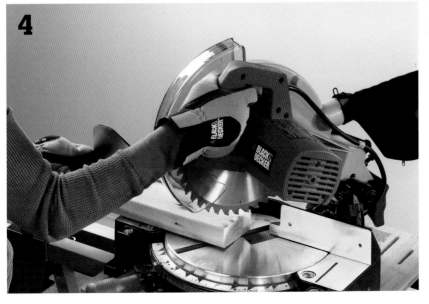

Cut off the bottom corners of the supports. Make marks 1½" in from the ends on the bottom edge of the supports. Align the power miter saw blade with these marks and make 30° miter cuts.

notches. Then, place the top side and middle stretchers in position on the bottom side stretchers. Drive a 2½" screw through the bottom of each half-lap joint. Then, attach the framework to a flat face of each leg (**photo 7**).

MAKE THE TABLETOP

Make the teahouse tabletop as a square and then cut it to round after it is assembled. Cut the tabletop planks to length. Then, mark the center of each plank and attach them in succession to the supports using 2" deck screws. Center each plank across the middle support, leaving a ⅛" gap between the boards. Drill a countersunk, ⅛"-diameter pilot hole for each screw.

To lay out the circular shape for the tabletop, make a compass using a scrap piece of ¼"-thick wood or plywood that is roughly 1½" wide × 20" long. Drill two ⅛"-diameter holes in the scrap, 18⅜" apart. Tap a nail through one of the holes and into the center of the table. *TIP: To find the center, draw straight lines across the tabletop from opposite corners. The point where the lines intersect is the center—provided you were careful and made the top square. Place a pencil tip through the other hole in the scrap wood compass and draw the perimeter of the tabletop* (**photo 8**).

Cut just outside the round tabletop outline with a jigsaw (**photo 9**). Then, use a belt sander to smooth

Lay out the notches. Clamp the stretchers together with the centers aligned. Use a square to extend the notch cut lines across all of the stretchers.

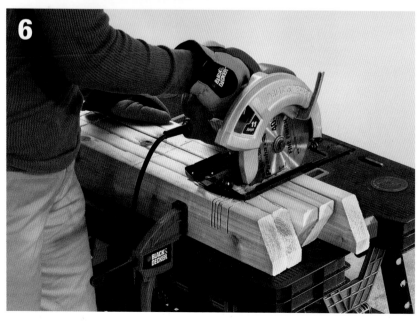

Cut the notch shoulders. Cut the sides of the notch first. Then clean out the middle by making several overlapping cuts.

and shape the wood precisely up to the cutting line. Use a router and 45° chamfer bit to profile the top edge of the table (**photo 10**). Finally, attach the table legs to the tabletop supports with 2½" screws. Drill countersunk pilot holes and drive the screws from the inside faces of the supports.

BUILD THE STOOLS

Make the matching stools. The information on page 85 lists materials and supplies for four stools. Start by cutting the legs to length. Unlike the table legs, the bench legs are only tapered on one side. Make a mark 1½" in from the outside edge of one of the wide faces of the leg. Draw a line from that mark across the wide face down to a point that is 2" up from the opposite bottom corner of the leg (**photo 11**). Cut the tapers with a band saw or jigsaw. Cut the seat supports and seat rails to length. Trim off the bottom corners of the supports with 30° miter cuts. The miters should end 1½" in from the ends of the bottom edge.

Mark and cut the 1½" wide by 1¾" deep notches using the same gang-cutting techniques used to cut the table support notches. Cut the notches in the seat supports as one group and the seat rails as another group. The bottom of the seat arc profile

7

Assemble the base. The framework of the supports is fastened to the legs with 2" screws.

8

Lay out the circular cutting line. Draw the perimeter of the tabletop using an 18⅜" long compass. You can also use a piece of string as a compass.

that is cut in the seat supports is located 1" down from the top edge and is centered across the support side. Tap a finish nail in the bottom point and bend a flexible piece of scrap stock to form the arc profile template. Trace the arc profile on the support (**photo 12**). Cut along the arc line on the first support and then use that support as a template to trace the arc on the other supports.

ASSEMBLE THE LEGS

Attach the supports and rails with glue and screws in the same way that you assembled the table supports. First, cut the seat planks to length. Clamp the seat boards to a flat work surface in groups of five. The boards should be edge to edge with the ends flush. Cut a chamfer profile on both ends of all five boards. Unclamp the boards and rout a chamfer onto the outside edge of each outer board using a piloted chamfer bit (**photo 13**). Space each set of five seat boards evenly across a seat assembly and attach them to the seat supports with 2" screws. Drill a countersunk pilot hole for each screw. Attach the legs to the supports and rails with 2½" screws.

Cut the round tabletop shape. Use a jigsaw to make a rough cut just outside of the cutting line (inset). Then, use a belt sander to remove wood precisely up to the cutting line.

Profile the tabletop edge. Cut a ½" chamfer profile in the top edge of the table with a router and 45° chamfering bit.

Lay out the bench legs. Draw a taper line across one of the wide faces of each leg. Cut along the taper line with a band saw or jigsaw.

Plot the seat support profile. Use a finish nail as a bending point and flex a piece of scrap stock to create an arc template. Clamp the template and trace the profile on the supports.

Cut chamfers in the seat boards. With the workpieces for one complete stool clamped together edge to edge, rout the chamfer profile across the end grain on both ends. The chamfer matches the tabletop edge profile and eliminates sharp edges on the seat.

Folding Table

Sturdy, simple, and portable, this table is the go-everywhere solution for outdoor events that lack stable surfaces on which to place drinks, food, or other essentials. The beauty of this table is that, once folded up, it can be stored in a slim space. You can even keep it under an overhang or in a tool shed outside, although don't be surprised if you become so enamored with it that you bring it indoors.

For an operable folding structure, the construction could not be simpler. You'll find that this doesn't take expert skills and you'll probably only need about a day to construct the table. You also won't have to break the bank; made of ubiquitous pine, the table is relatively inexpensive to put together. Of course, you don't necessarily have to use the wood we've specified. You can always make the table out of cedar and let it age naturally for a wonderfully changeable appearance over time.

Otherwise, you might want to paint or finish the table. Because it doesn't have to be in your yard all the time, a nice coat of your favorite bold hue can add a splash of fun color to your outdoor festivities. A dark stain can help the table blend into a more complex landscape and a clear finish will let the naturally warm look of plain pine shine through.

Materials ▸

5 2 × 4" × 8 ft. pine boards	2 3 × 3" brass butt hinges
6 1 × 6" × 8 ft. pine boards	4 ⅜ × 4½" carriage bolts with lock nuts
3 1 × 4" × 8 ft. pine boards	Wood glue
Deck screws 1¼", 2", 2½"	1"-dia. washers
4 1½ × 6"-long strap hinges	

Sturdy and spacious when set up, this portable table folds up into a small package for convenient storage.

Folding Table

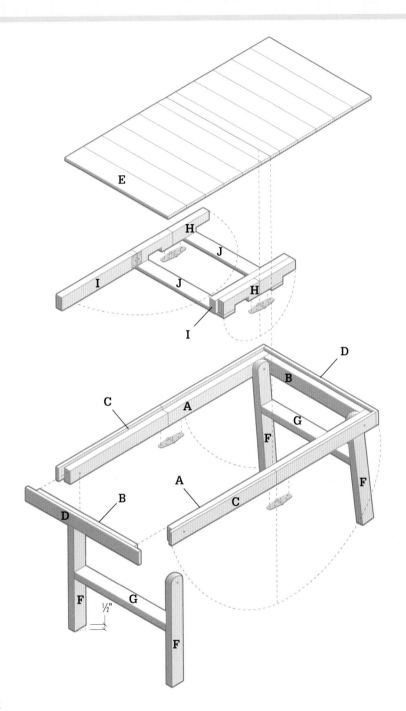

Cutting List

Key	Part	Dimension	Pcs.	Material
A	Side rails	$1\frac{1}{2} \times 3\frac{1}{2} \times 62$"	2	Pine
B	End rails	$1\frac{1}{2} \times 3\frac{1}{2} \times 31\frac{1}{2}$"	2	Pine
C	Side skirts	$\frac{3}{4} \times 3\frac{1}{2} \times 63\frac{1}{2}$"	2	Pine
D	End skirts	$\frac{3}{4} \times 3\frac{1}{2} \times 34\frac{1}{2}$"	2	Pine
E	Slats	$\frac{3}{4} \times 5\frac{1}{2} \times 34\frac{1}{2}$"	11	Pine

Key	Part	Dimension	Pcs.	Material
F	Legs	$1\frac{1}{2} \times 3\frac{1}{2} \times 28\frac{1}{2}$"	4	Pine
G	Stretchers	$1\frac{1}{2} \times 3\frac{1}{2} \times 28\frac{3}{8}$"	2	Pine
H	Cleats	$1\frac{1}{2} \times 3\frac{1}{2} \times 22$"	2	Pine
I	Sweeps	$1\frac{1}{2} \times 3\frac{1}{2} \times 23$"	2	Pine
J	Guides	$\frac{3}{4} \times 3\frac{1}{2} \times 28$"	2	Pine

Note: Measurements reflect the actual size of dimensional lumber.

Folding Table

MAKE THE SIDE SECTIONS

Start by cutting the side rails and skirts. These will create a sturdy support for the slats and, ultimately, for the table. Position a side skirt against each side rail, so that the skirts overhang the rails by ¾" on the long edge. This creates a healthy lip for the slats to sit on.

Center the side skirts on the side rails so that ¾" of the skirt extends at each end (this will be the location of the overlap joints for each end). Clamp the side skirts to the side rails, ensuring that they are perfectly aligned—do not use a skirt or rail that has any bow along its length on edge. Attach the skirts with 1¼" deck screws (you don't need to countersink the holes).

Leave the middle of side skirts and side rails free of screws. Cut these two side assemblies into two equal lengths, sawing at the center of the span. Connect the halves with 6" brass or galvanized strap hinges attached to the bottom edges of the side rail halves, then remove the hinges and unscrew the parts before proceeding.

ATTACH THE END SECTIONS

Cut the end rails and skirts. Position the end rails between the side rails, flush with the side rail ends to create a butt joint with the side rail faces overlapping the end rail ends. Apply glue and drive 2½" deck screws through the side rail faces into the end rails.

Position an end skirt against each end rail, maintaining the ¾"-deep ledge for the slats. With the ends of the end skirts flush with the side rails, drive 1¼" deck screws through the end skirts and into the side rails and end rails. Reattach the side skirts and strap hinges.

ATTACH THE SLATS

Cut the slats to length. Rip-cut one slat in half lengthwise. Position one half of the ripped slat on each side of center cut of the side rail, with no gap (the two parts of the slat will separate when the table is folded).

Attach the slats to the side rails, using glue on the face-to-edge contact area, and securing the slats with 2" deck screws **(photo 1).** Glue and screw the remaining slats evenly spaced down the side rail.

Drill ⅜"-diameter counterbored holes for carriage bolts through each end of the side skirts and side rails for the legs. Center the holes 4¼" in from the ends of the side skirts and 1¾" up from the bottoms of the side rails.

Once the frame is built with the side rails and skirts attached, glue and drill the two halves of the split slat on either side of the center cut through the rail, which allows the table to fold.

MAKE THE LEGS

Cut the legs and stretchers. Cut a 10° miter across the broad face of each leg at one end. At the other end of each leg, use a compass to draw a centered, 1¾"-radius semicircle. Mark the center of the semicircle and drill a ⅜"-diameter hole.

Draw a line across one face of each leg, 14" down from the top. Position the legs in pairs on the work surface. Slide a stretcher between each leg pair with the top faces on the reference lines. Glue and screw the stretchers between the legs with 2½" deck screws.

MAKE THE CLEATS

Cut the cleats. The cleats have 1" notches on one long edge to allow folding. To mark the notches, draw reference lines across one edge of each cleat, 3½", 7¼", and 18½" from one end.

Cut the notches 1" deep from the 3½" line to the 7¼" line, and from the 18½" line to the ends. Cut each cleat in half. Attach the cleat halves with strap hinges.

ATTACH THE SWEEPS AND GUIDES

The sweeps and guides attach to the cleats to form a locking mechanism. Cut the sweeps and guides. Position the guides on the cleats, flush with edges of notches. Attach with glue and 2½" deck screws **(photo 2).**

Turn the tabletop upside down. Position the cleats and guides inside the tabletop so the hinged centers align. Use 1¾"-thick spacers to center the cleats between the side rails. Fasten them to the bottom of the table with glue and 2" deck screws **(photo 3).** Attach 3" brass butt hinges to one end of each sweep, then use the hinges to attach a sweep to one end of each cleat.

APPLY FINISHING TOUCHES

Fasten the legs inside the tabletop, using carriage bolts, washers, and lock nuts **(photo 4).** Check for smooth operation and make any adjustments as necessary for the legs to open smooth and the table to lock in the open position.

Cover the screwheads with wood putty. Sand with 100- or 120-grit sandpaper, and paint or finish as desired.

Align the ends of the guides with the outside edges of the sweeps. These need to be perfectly aligned for the opening mechanism to lock correctly. Glue and screw the guides in place.

With the cleats centered between the side rails, it's an easy task to screw them in place.

Secure the legs in place with carriage bolts, washers, and lock nuts.

Occasional Table

When it comes to outdoor furniture, most of the attention is usually given to big, splashy tables that will seat lots of people or provide abundant space for food next to a grill. But, while there is certainly a need for expansive tabletop space, it's the rare yard or outdoor seating area that can't benefit from at least one more modest accent table. Put a side table next to a lounge or in between two Adirondack chairs and you add a place for drinks, snacks, or the book you're reading.

The table in this project is amazingly simple, but with a few special touches, it's also a stylish accent for your porch, deck, or patio. It is a nicely proportioned structure that will complement patio or deck seating, and is light enough to be moved wherever you need a small table. It is also stable enough to be placed on grass or gravel—so it can go just about anywhere in the yard it might be needed.

The table is made out of cedar so it can be left outdoors all year long, and cedar not only tolerates exposure to the elements, it also ages with a very nice gray patina. Cedar can also be finished clear to maintain the lovely fresh appearance of the wood.

However, you can save some money and craft it out of pine, an especially good choice if you plan on painting the table. If your area of the country experiences harsh weather and you don't intend on moving the table into a garage or shed during winter, you might choose pressure-treated pine.

Materials ▸

2	1 × 3" × 8-ft. cedar boards	1¼" deck screws
9	1 × 4" × 8-ft. cedar boards	Moisture-resistant glue

This sturdy accent table is an easy-to-build addition to your deck furniture. As stylish as it is simple, the design pairs nicely with an Adirondack chair.

Occasional Table

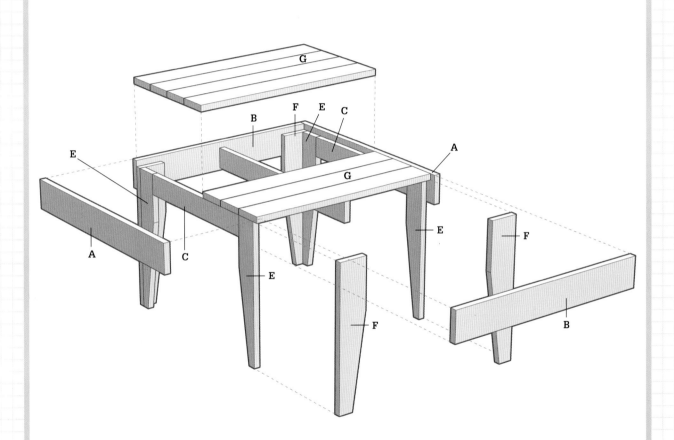

Cutting List

Key	Part	Dimension	Pcs.	Material
A	End aprons	¾ × 3½ × 26½"	2	Cedar
B	Side aprons	¾ × 3½ × 25"	2	Cedar
C	End stringers	¾ × 2½ × 18"	2	Cedar
D	Middle stringer	¾ × 2½ × 25"	1	Cedar

Key	Part	Dimension	Pcs.	Material
E	Narrow leg sides	¾ × 2½ × 17¼"	4	Cedar
F	Wide leg sides	¾ × 2½ × 17¼"	4	Cedar
G	Slats	¾ × 3½ × 25"	7	Cedar

Note: Measurements reflect the actual size of dimensional lumber.

Occasional Table

MAKE THE STRINGERS, APRONS & LEGS

Cut the end aprons and side aprons to length. Because the end aprons overlap the side aprons to form butt joints, the side aprons must be shorter. Mark them on the inside face so that you don't confuse them during construction.

Cut the end stringers and middle stringer to length. Note that these two are different lengths. The middle stringer will provide support that keeps the table sturdy and durable over the long run.

Each leg is formed of two pieces—one narrow and one wide—cut at a taper. The taper adds a bit of visual flair to the table, but the tapers have to be cut correctly or the effect will be ruined. Start by cutting the narrow and wide leg sides to length.

On one wide leg, measure 8¾" down along one edge of the leg side and make a mark. Measure across the bottom end of the leg side 1½" and make another mark. Use a straightedge to connect the two marks to create a leg taper cutting line. Mark cutting lines for tapers on all four wide leg sides (photo 1).

For the tapers on the narrow legs, measure 8¾" down along one edge and make a mark as before. Then measure ¾" across the bottom end and make a mark. Connect the marks to make the taper cutting lines.

Clamp each leg side to the work surface. Cut along the line using a jigsaw or circular saw (photo 2).

ASSEMBLE THE LEGS

The legs must be assembled precisely to maintain the illusion of solid tapered legs in each corner. Apply a ½"-wide bead of moisture-resistant glue on the face of

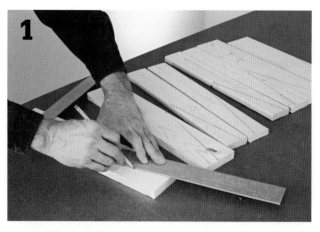

Carefully measure and mark the taper cutting lines for both the wide and the narrow sides of the legs. Work on the wide sides first, and then the narrow, to avoid mixing them up and mis-measuring the cut lines.

A jigsaw is ideal for cutting the taper lines in the legs, although you can also use a circular saw.

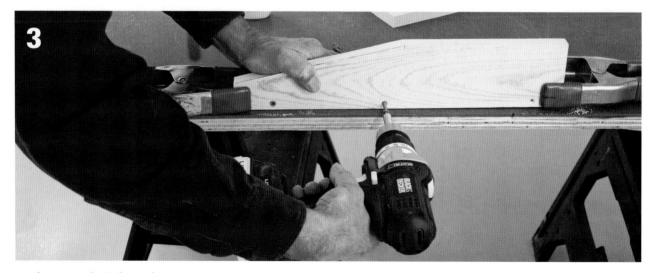

Work on a perfectly flat surface to ensure the leg sides are exactly aligned. Apply a bead of glue where the inside face overlaps the edge of the smaller leg piece, and then drill three countersunk holes and screw the pieces together.

4

Drill two pilot holes at each end and in the middle of each slat, down into the end and middle stringers. Attach each slat with glue and screws at each location.

5

Rounding off the edges of the table gives it a very polished appearance. Cover it with the finish of your choice and the project is complete.

a wide leg side, down along the untapered edge (the mating edge for the other leg piece). Repeat on the untapered edge of a narrow leg side. Join the leg sides together at a right angle to form a leg pair.

Drill and countersink pilot holes for screws to reinforce the joint between the leg pieces. Use three 1¼" deck screws. Glue and screw the rest of the leg pairs in the same manner **(photo 3).** Be careful not to use too much glue or mismatch the legs.

CONSTRUCT THE FRAME

The table frame will securely hold the tabletop slats in place. Work from the outside in by gluing and screwing the side aprons to leg pairs. Carefully align the aprons and legs so that there are no unsightly overlaps or gaps in the frame construction.

Screw the legs to the aprons from the inside of each leg pair to conceal the screw heads. The narrow leg side should face in toward the center of the side apron, and the outside faces of the wide leg sides flush with the side apron ends. The leg pairs' tops should be ¾" down from the side aprons' tops to create recesses for the tabletop slats.

Glue and screw the end aprons to the leg assemblies with the end aprons' ends positioned with the outside faces of side aprons.

Glue and screw the end stringers to the end aprons between the leg pairs. Center the middle

stringer between the end stringers. Use glue and screws to attach the middle stringer to the side aprons, ¾" down from tops to maintain the ledge for the slats.

CUT AND INSTALL THE SLATS

Measure the inside dimension between the end aprons to verify the correct slat length. Measure at different points along the aprons to check that the frame is square and all the slats should be the same length. Cut the slats.

Drill countersunk pilot holes at each end of each slat, down into the middle and end stringers. Glue and screw the slats into the tops of the middle and end stringers, leaving a gap of approximately ¹⁄₁₆" between the slats **(photo 4).**

FINISH THE TABLE

A little easy detailing will give this table a lovely look next to your other outdoor furniture. Smooth all sharp edges by using a router with a roundover bit **(photo 5)** or a power sander with medium-grit (100 to 120) sandpaper. Finish-sand and thoroughly clean the table to remove any sanding residue.

Finish the table with a clear wood sealer or paint it in a color of your choice.

Children's Picnic Table

Picnic tables come in many styles, shapes, and sizes, with one of the sizes being "pint." This downscaled kids' picnic table is a wonderful addition to any backyard where children play. Its light weight allows you to move the table around the yard for impromptu tea parties on the deck or dinner under the trees. Yet its wide footprint makes it extremely stable so your rambunctious little ones won't tip it over.

Constructing this kid-sized picnic table is easy. The trickiest part is probably getting the angles cut correctly at the tops and bottoms of the legs. They should be cut at a relatively shallow 50° angle. If they are cut too steeply the table will be taller and less stable; too shallow and it will be shorter and very difficult to seat oneself in.

With a kids' project such as this it is important that you eliminate any sharp edges and do a thorough job sanding the surfaces smooth and splinter free. The edges of the boards can be "broken" by sanding them lightly so they are not sharp. Or, you can install a roundover bit in your router or laminate trimmer and shape the edges all to the same profile.

The table seen here is built with cedar and coated with a clear, UV-protective sealant. You could also make it from pressure-treated pine and paint it or finish it with a semitransparent deck stain. If you do use treated lumber, be sure to choose hot-dipped lag bolts that are triple-coated to limit corrosion. Or, better yet, use all stainless steel fasteners.

Materials ▸

2 2 × 4" × 6 ft. cedar boards	Deck screws (2½")
3 2 × 6" × 8 ft. cedar boards	16 ⅜ × 3" carriage bolts with nuts
3 2 × 8" × 8 ft. cedar boards	32 washers

This kid-scale table with benches makes picnicking in the backyard even more fun for children. And with its broad legs and low top it is very stable.

Children's Picnic Table

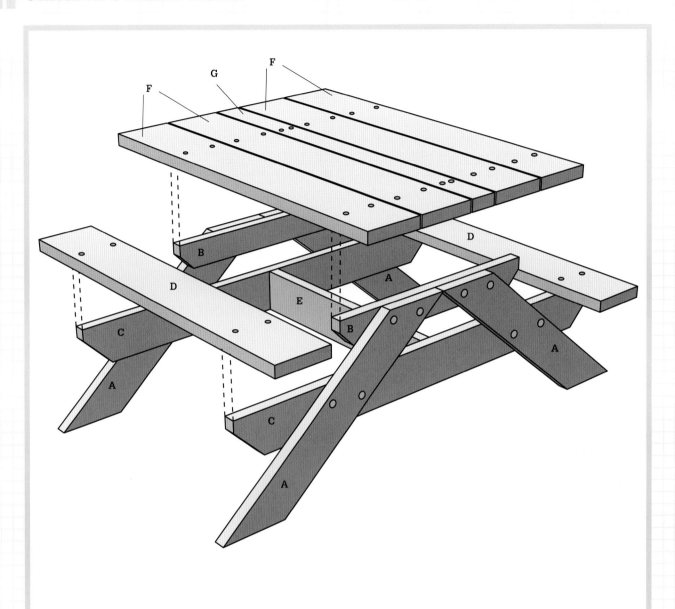

Cutting List

Key	Part	Dimension	Pcs.	Material
A	Legs	$1\frac{1}{2} \times 5\frac{1}{2} \times 32"$	4	Cedar
B	Table supports	$1\frac{1}{2} \times 3\frac{1}{2} \times 29\frac{3}{4}"$	2	Cedar
C	Seat supports	$1\frac{1}{2} \times 5\frac{1}{2} \times 60"$	2	Cedar
D	Seats	$1\frac{1}{2} \times 7\frac{1}{2} \times 48"$	2	Cedar

Key	Part	Dimension	Pcs.	Material
E	Brace	$1\frac{1}{2} \times 5\frac{1}{2} \times 30"$	1	Cedar
F	Tabletops (wide)	$1\frac{1}{2} \times 7\frac{1}{2} \times 48"$	4	Cedar
G	Tabletop (thin)	$1\frac{1}{2} \times 3\frac{1}{2} \times 48"$	1	Cedar

Children's Picnic Table

CUT THE ANGLED LEGS & SUPPORTS

To make the angled legs, use a saw protractor to mark a 50° angle on one end of a 2 × 6 (**photo 1**). Cut the angle using a circular saw. Measure 32" from the tip of the angle, then mark and cut another 50° angle parallel to the first. Do this for all four legs, cutting two legs from one piece of lumber.

Cut the table supports to length. Measure 1½" in from each end of both supports and make a mark. Make a 45° angle starting at the mark and going in the direction of the board end. This relieves the sharp end of the board to prevent injuries and also looks more pleasing. Cut the seat supports to length. Measure 2½" from the ends of both supports, make a mark, and cut a 45° angle to relieve the sharp ends.

ASSEMBLE THE A-FRAMES

Place one of the legs against the tabletop support so the inside edge of the leg is at the centerpoint of the support. Align the top of the leg with the top of the support. Clamp the pieces together. Drill two ⅜" holes through the leg and support. Stagger the holes. To keep the bolts from causing scrapes, recess both the bolt head and nut. Drill 1"-diameter counterbored holes about ¼" deep into the legs and the tabletop supports. Insert a ⅜ × 3" carriage bolt and washer into each hole. Tighten a washer and nut on the end of the bolt using a ratchet wrench. Repeat these steps to fasten the second leg in place. *Note: If your washers are larger than 1", drill a larger counterbore.*

Measure along the inside edge of each leg and make a mark 12½" up from the bottom. Center the seat support over the leg assembly, on the same side of the legs as the tabletop support, with the 45° cuts facing down and the bottom flush with the 12½" marks. Clamp the two pieces together and then drill ⅜" holes with 1"-diameter counterbored holes. Fasten the seat support to the legs using carriage bolts, nuts, and washers (**photo 2**). Repeat this step to assemble the second A-frame.

ATTACH THE TABLETOP & SEATS

Cut the seat boards to length. Stand one of the A-frames upright. Place a seat on the seat support so the seat overhangs the outside of the support by 7½". Align the back edge of the seat with the end of the support. Drill two ³⁄₃₂" pilot holes through the seat into the support and then drive 2½" deck screws. Attach the seat to the second A-frame the same way. Fasten the seat on the other side of the table using the same method.

Cut the brace. Center the brace between the seat supports, making sure they're flush at the bottom. Drill two ³⁄₃₂" pilot holes through the supports on each side, then fasten the brace to the supports using 2½" deck screws. Cut the tabletop boards to length. Place the 2 × 4 tabletop across the center of the tabletop supports, overhanging the supports by 7½". Drill two ³⁄₃₂" pilot holes on both ends of the top board where it crosses the supports. Attach it to the supports with 2½" deck screws.

Place a 2 × 8 tabletop board across the supports, keeping a ¼" gap from the 2 × 4. Drill pilot holes in the end of the board, then insert 2½" deck screws (**photo 3**). Install the remaining top boards the same way, spacing them evenly with a ¼" gap. Allow the outside boards to overhang the end of the tabletop supports.

FINISHING TOUCHES

Sand any rough surfaces and splinters, and round over edges on the seat and tabletop using 150-grit sandpaper. Apply a stain, sealer (foodsafe boiled linseed oil is a good choice), or paint.

Use a saw protractor to mark a 50° angle on the end of the table leg, and then cut the angle using a circular saw.

Fasten the tabletop and seat supports to the legs with carriage bolts. Do not use washers with carriage bolt heads. The washers and nuts are recessed in counterbored holes to prevent injury.

Install the tabletop boards by drilling pilot holes and driving 2½" deck screws. Insert ¼" spacers between boards.

Traditional Picnic Table

Every backyard needs a picnic table, and this one is a classic. The design, with two long built-in benches attached to the sides of an abundant tabletop, can serve many different purposes. It is ideal for outdoor dining, whether you're having an intimate dinner for two or a large birthday party meal. Many people can cram in around the table, and the setup allows for easy access to anything on the table, no matter where you happen to be sitting.

This table design is timeless largely because it is so durable. The picnic table is built to last and will take a lot of abuse. Spills, hot plates full of grilled meat, dropped items and more won't faze this table. But the table remains popular because it is also a handsome form. Simple to build, the look is appealing and seems to fit right in no matter what landscape, patio surface or outdoor area it's assigned to.

It's also adaptable. The traditional material for this type of table is redwood, which will resist rot and the elements quite naturally. You can also go with cedar, which has the same properties and looks just as nice as redwood. Of course, if you'd like to save a bit of money, you can use pine. Nicer woods are best finished in a clear sealer or a light wood stain. Pine is often painted. You can make the legs from pressure treated lumber for greater longevity, but usually this isn't necessary and in any case, PT lumber should not generally be painted.

Materials ▸

1 2 × 6" × 6 ft. cedar board	³⁄₈" × 3" carriage bolts with washers
1 2 × 6" × 10 ft. cedar board	2½" and 3" deck screws
1 2 × 4" × 10 ft. cedar board	

Few pieces of outdoor furniture are so useful—and have such a classic look—as the traditional picnic table with benches on either side.

Traditional Picnic Table

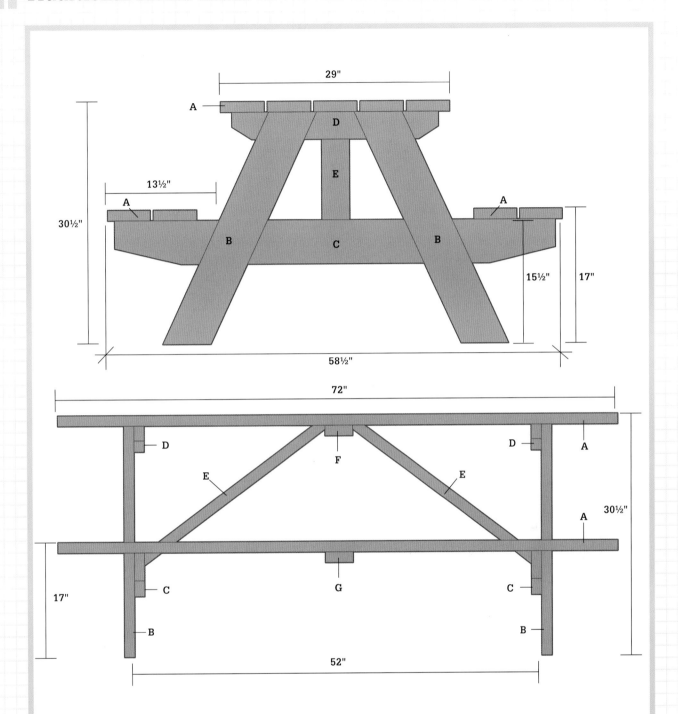

Cutting List

Key	Part	Dimension	Pcs.	Material
A	Slats	1½ × 5½ × 72"	9	2 × 6
B	Legs	1½ × 5½ × 32"	4	2 × 6
C	Seat supports	1½ × 5½ × 57"	2	2 × 6
D	Top supports	1½ × 3½ × 26"	2	2 × 4

Key	Part	Dimension	Pcs.	Material
E	Braces	1½ × 3½ × 30½"	2	2 × 4
F	Top cleat	1½ × 3½ × 26"	1	2 × 4
G	Seat cleat	1½ × 3½ × 10"	2	2 × 4

Traditional Picnic Table

CUT THE LUMBER TO SIZE

The most challenging cuts for the whole table are the legs, which need to be mitered to stand at angles to the table. Make a 25° miter cut across one end of a 2 × 6. Measure 32" from the tip of the angle and cut a second 65° miter parallel to the first **(photo 1).** This makes one leg. Use the first leg as a template for laying out the other legs.

Cut three 2 × 4 tabletop supports 26" long. Measure 1½" from each end of the two end supports, make a mark, and cut a 45° angle. For the flat center support, measure ¾ × ¾" and cut this miter at the bottom of each end.

Cut two 2 × 6 seat supports 57" long. Measure 2½" from the ends of both supports, make a mark, and cut a 45° angle. Cut two 2 × 4 seat stiffeners 10" long.

The bench and tabletop boards don't need to be cut.

ASSEMBLE THE A-FRAME

Mark the centers of the tabletop supports. Measure 2¾" out from this centerline and make another mark. Place one leg against the tabletop support with the inside leg edge aligned with the second mark. Align the angled cut of the leg with the support tops. Clamp the pieces together.

Align the legs and seat and top support on the 2¾" and 15½" marks. Fasten the supports to the legs with a 2½" deck screw at each joint (avoid the bolt locations). Then drill guide holes for the bolts.

Drill two ⅜" holes through the leg and support. Counterbore 1" holes centered over the ⅜" hole about ½" deep into the support **(photo 2).** Insert and tighten a ⅜ × 3" carriage bolt into each hole. Repeat for the second leg.

Use an adjustable square to determine and mark the parallel miter cuts at each end of one leg. Once you've cut the first leg you can use it as a template for laying out the parallel ends cuts on the three remaining legs.

Drill 1"-dia. counterbore holes for the carriage bolts that connect the legs and the supports. When using a spade bit to drill counterbores it is easier if you drill the counterbore before the guide hole that goes all the way through both workpieces.

3

Attach the leg assemblies using carriage bolts, washers, and locking nuts. The legs on each side are assembled before attaching the tabletop and seat boards.

4

Drill countersunk pilot holes for the screws that fasten the tabletop and seat tops to the supports.

Measure along the leg's outside edge and mark 15½" from the bottom. Center the seat support over the leg assembly, on the same side of the legs as the tabletop support, with 45° cuts facing down and the top flush with the 15½" marks. Drill ⅜" guide holes with a 1"-diameter counterbore, and fasten the seat support to the legs using carriage bolts (**photo 3**). Repeat for the second A-frame.

ATTACH THE TABLETOP & SEATS

To make sure you don't strip any screws, drill ³/₃₂" countersunk pilot holes for all the screws.

Stand one A-frame upright. Place a 2 × 6 seat board on the seat support, overhanging the outside of the support by 8½". Align the seat back edge with the end of the support. Attach with 2½" deck screws. Repeat on the opposite side.

Place 2 × 6 tabletop boards across the tabletop supports, overhanging at the ends 8½". Space the boards evenly across the tabletop supports, overhanging the supports by 1½". Fasten the boards with 2½" deck screws (**photo 4**).

Turn the table upside down. Attach a seat stiffener to the underside of each seat at its midpoint, using 2½" deck screws. Attach the tabletop stiffener to the underside of the tabletop at its midpoint, using 2½" deck screws.

Cut two braces 30¼" long, mitering one end 50° and the other at 40°, at intersecting, not parallel, angles. Test fit the braces with the 50° angle against the seat support, and the 40° against the tabletop brace. The tabletop end needs to have the tip of the angle clipped off. Mark and make this cut.

Drill ³/₃₂" countersunk pilot holes and attach the braces with 3" deck screws.

FINISH THE TABLE

Round over the edges of the tabletop and seat tops, to avoid catching on clothing or hurting anyone who bumps the edges. For best results, use a router with a roundover bit to cut the profiles; alternatively, ease all edges with a power sander and 100 grit sandpaper. Sand all surfaces to 120- or 150 grit and apply a clear sealant or stain or paint the table your choice of colors.

Patio Prep Cart

This elegant rolling cook's cart will take your outdoor cooking to a higher level without breaking your bank account. Whether the point is to impress or simply to make your outdoor entertaining a bit more pleasant, setting up an outdoor kitchen that revolves around this clever cart and an ordinary grill is easy. And, because this cart (and most grills) are on wheels, they're easy to move as needed and to roll away into storage.

This cart features 8 square feet of countertop space, a storage cabinet with shelves, and a dedicated place for a refrigerator. The sides are made from 1 × 4 cedar or a similar exterior-grade lumber. Use corrosion-resistant screws to assemble this cart. The screws that attach the siding are driven from the outside, leaving the heads exposed to act as a design feature.

This outdoor kitchen cart employs eight 12 × 12" tiles for the countertop, minimizing the joints in the countertop surface. To simplify construction the tiles are set with construction adhesive (instead of thinset mortar) and the joints between the tiles are filled with exterior caulk (instead of tile grout).

Materials ▸

18 1 × 4" × 8 ft. cedar boards	8 12 × 12" floor tiles
4 2 × 4" × 8 ft. cedar boards	Exterior-rated screws (1¼", 2½")
1 ¾" × 4 × 8 ft. cedar plywood	Lag screws (16 @ ¼" × 1½")
1 ½ × 3" × 5 ft. cementboard	2 3" utility hinges
1 ¾ × 24" × 48 ft. exterior plywood	4 Casters
	1 Door handle
	1 Catch

Both attractive and functional, this rolling cook's cart with space for a refrigerator will make your deck or patio almost as convenient as your kitchen for entertaining friends and family.

Patio Prep Cart

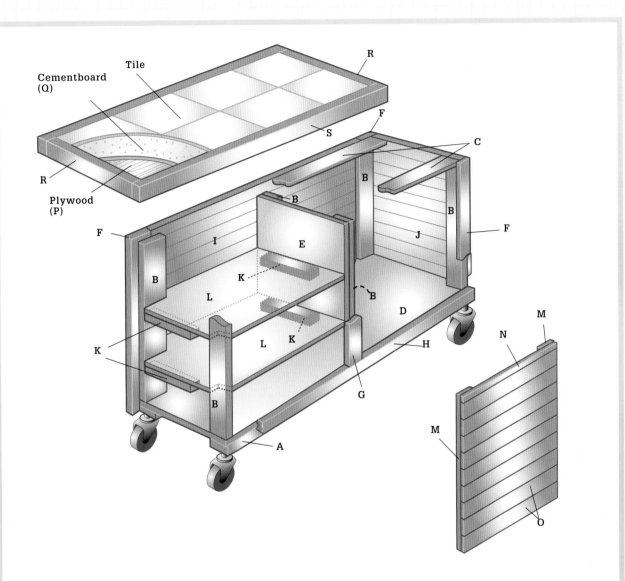

Cutting List

Key	Part	Dimension	Pcs.	Material
A	Bottom supports	$1\frac{1}{2} \times 3\frac{1}{2} \times 46"$	2	Cedar
B	Posts	$1\frac{1}{2} \times 3\frac{1}{2} \times 35"$	6	Cedar
C	Top rails	$\frac{7}{8} \times 3\frac{1}{2} \times 46"$	2	Cedar
D	Bottom panel	$\frac{3}{4} \times 22 \times 46"$	1	Cedar plywood
E	Center panel	$\frac{3}{4} \times 22 \times 35"$	1	Cedar plywood
F	Corner stiles	$\frac{7}{8} \times 2\frac{1}{2} \times 37\frac{1}{4}"$	4	Cedar
G	Front center stile	$\frac{7}{8} \times 2\frac{1}{2} \times 35\frac{3}{8}"$	1	Cedar
H	Front bottom rail	$\frac{3}{4} \times 1\frac{3}{4} \times 42\frac{3}{4}"$	1	Cedar
I	Back siding	$\frac{7}{8} \times 3\frac{1}{2} \times 42\frac{1}{4}"$	10	Cedar
J	Side siding	$\frac{7}{8} \times 3\frac{1}{2} \times 22"$	20	Cedar

Key	Part	Dimension	Pcs.	Material
K	Shelf supports	$\frac{7}{8} \times 1 \times 17"$	4	Cedar
L	Shelves	$\frac{3}{4} \times 19\frac{1}{2} \times 21\frac{3}{4}"$	2	Cedar plywood
M	Door stiles	$\frac{7}{8} \times 3\frac{1}{2} \times 34\frac{1}{2}"$	2	Cedar
N	Top door siding	$\frac{7}{8} \times 1 \times 18\frac{1}{2}"$	1	Cedar
O	Door siding	$\frac{7}{8} \times 3\frac{1}{2} \times 18\frac{1}{2}"$	9	Cedar
P	Worksurface subbase	$\frac{3}{4} \times 24 \times 48"$	1	Ext. plywood
Q	Tile backer	$\frac{1}{2} \times 24 \times 48"$	1	Cementboard
R	Side edging	$\frac{7}{8} \times 1\frac{1}{2} \times 24"$	2	Cedar
S	Front/back edging	$\frac{7}{8} \times 1\frac{1}{2} \times 49\frac{1}{2}"$	2	Cedar

Patio Prep Cart

BUILD THE FRAME

This outdoor kitchen cart is essentially a skeleton of 2 × 4 cedar wrapped in cedar siding and capped off with large tiles. Start by building the skeleton: that is, the frame. Cut the bottom supports, posts, and top rails to length. Cut the bottom panel and center panel to length and width. Attach two of the posts to the center panel with 1¼" screws. Place the center panel and bottom panel on their sides and attach the bottom panel to the posts with 2½" screws (**photo 1**). With the panels on their edges, attach two of the corner posts to the bottom panel. Flip the assembly right-side up and attach one of the top rails to the top of the corner posts and center panel post. Attach the other two corner posts and top rail (**photo 2**). Attach the bottom supports to the bottom panel with 1¼" screws.

INSTALL THE CORNERS, TRIM & SIDING

Cut the corner stiles to length and width. Attach the corner stiles to the corner posts with four 1¼" screws. Drill a countersunk, ⅛"-diameter pilot hole for each screw (**photo 3**). Cut the front-bottom rail to length and width and attach it to the front-bottom support with four 1¼" screws and decorative finish washers.

Cut the side siding and back siding pieces to length. Drill two countersunk pilot holes in each end of each siding board. Space the holes 1" in from the ends and ¾" in from the edges. Attach the siding boards to the corner posts with 1¼" screws, spacing the boards ¼" apart (**photo 4**). Drill a 1¼"-diameter hole near the bottom of the back of the refrigerator section for the power cord to fit through.

INSTALL THE SHELVES

The shelves for this outdoor cart are optional. As shown, they're spaced to allow storage of items of varying height, such as plates and cups. But if you want to store taller items, such as bags of charcoal or a turkey fryer, eliminate the shelves from the plan.

Measure and mark the shelf heights on the inside faces of the left side siding and center divider. Here, the shelves are spaced so the lowest shelf opening is 15" high. The middle opening is 10" high and the top opening is 8" high. The shelf supports are sized so the shelves will not interfere with the front corner posts. Attach the shelf supports with 1¼" screws driven through countersunk pilot holes in the supports and into the cabinet walls. Cut the shelves from ¾"-thick

Attach the bottom panel to the posts. Drive 2½" screws through the underside of the bottom panel and into the ends of the center panel posts.

Install corner posts and top rails. Each top rail should be attached to a corner post and a center panel post with 2½" screws. Drive one screw into each post.

3

Install cornerboards. Attach the corner stiles to the corner posts with 1¼" screws. Align the inside edges of the stiles and posts.

4

Add siding. Drill two countersunk pilot holes through each end of each siding board. Locate the holes 1" from the ends and ¾" from the top and bottom edges. Attach the siding boards with 1¼" screws, spaced with a ¼" gap between boards.

plywood (preferably cedar plywood). Cut 1½ × 3½" notches in the left corners of each shelf board to fit around the posts. Drive a few brads down through the shelves and into the supports to secure them (**photo 5**).

BUILD THE DOOR

Cut the door stiles to length. Cut the door siding to length and the top door siding board to length and width. Drill two countersunk pilot holes in each end of each full-width door siding board. Space the holes 1" in from the ends and ¾" in from the edges. Drill one countersunk pilot hole in each end of the top door siding board. Attach the siding boards to the door stiles with 1¼" screws (**photo 6**).

ATTACH THE WHEELS & HARDWARE

Tip the cabinet upside down and place one caster in each corner (here, 2½" casters are being installed). Mark the caster screw holes and drill ³⁄₁₆" pilot holes for each screw. Fasten the casters with ¼ × 1½" hot-dipped lag screws (**photo 7**). To hang the door, attach zinc-plated or brass hinges (a pair of 3" butt hinges will do) to the door and the left corner post and corner stile (**photo 8**). Also add a handle (an aluminum door pull installed vertically is used here) as well as a latch and strikeplate to hold the door closed.

5

Install the shelves. Attach the shelf supports with screws and then tack the shelves into position with 1¼" brads.

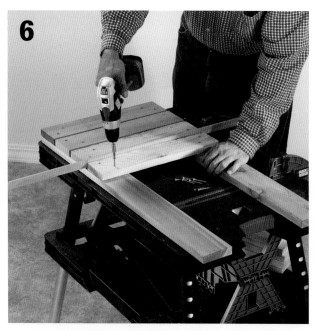

6

Attach the door siding boards to the door stiles. The top door siding board is attached with only one screw in each end.

BUILD & ATTACH THE TOP

The top for this cart features a ¾"-thick plywood subbase that supports a cementboard backer for the tiles (here, eight 12 × 12" porcelain tiles). Cut the plywood subbase to size from exterior plywood and attach it to the top rails with 1¼" deck screws. Cut a piece of tile backer board (here, ½"-thick cementboard) to 24 × 48". Attach the backer board to the subbase with construction adhesive and 1" screws (make sure the screwheads are recessed below the cementboard surface). Attach the tiles to the backer board with construction adhesive (**photo 9**).

Cut the top sides, front, and back edging pieces to length from cedar 1 × 2. Drill countersunk, ⅛"-diameter pilot holes in the edging pieces and attach them to the subbase edges with construction adhesive and brads (**photo 10**). Fill gaps around tile with caulk. Apply a clear, UV-protectant finish to the wood surface and seal the tiles.

7

Attach the casters. Position each caster and drill pilot holes for each caster screw. Attach the casters with ¼ × 1¼" lag screws.

8

Hang the door and install hardware. Fasten the door hinges to the door (or doors if you choose to cover each opening) and then attach the door to the cart frame. Use a ¼" spacer under the door to position it.

Install the tile work surface.
Instead of traditional thinset mortar, exterior construction adhesive is being used because it better withstands temperature and humidity changes.

Attach countertop edging. Made from strips of 1 × 2 cedar, the edging hides the countertop edges and protects the tile. Fill the gaps around the edge tiles and between tiles with caulk.

Pitmaster's Locker

Supplies and accessories for your outdoor grilling and barbecuing have special storage requirements. Some, such as charcoal starter fluid and propane tanks and bottles, are hazardous, flammable chemicals that should be locked safely away outside of the house or garage. Other supplies, such as big bags of charcoal briquettes, turkey fryers, or starter chimneys, are bulky and often dirty or dusty. Additional tools, like grill brushes, thermometers, rib racks, and Texas-size kitchen utensils, are best kept together in a neat area close to your grill. This Pitmaster's Locker addresses all of these concerns in a rugged-looking package that fits in well with today's popular grilling equipment.

The frame for this grill locker is made with solid aluminum angle iron, sold at most building centers. Aluminum is rigid, sturdy, and withstands exposure to the elements very well. It is also relatively easy to drill, which you will appreciate. Because the metals market is fairly volatile, costs for aluminum can run on the high side. But if you buy in volume you can usually save a little money. Our eight pieces of 72" aluminum angle cost us $130 from an Internet seller (this is at a time of high metal costs). If you like this design but want to save some money, you can substitute paintable hardwood, such as poplar, for the frame parts. This requires recalculating the shelf and panel dimensions, however.

The lower shelf of this locker has 24" of height capacity. If you plan to store a 20-pound propane tank on this shelf, you can lower the supports for the middle shelf by 6" and still have enough room for the 17½" tall standard tanks. This creates a middle shelf that has 30" of height capacity (or two shorter shelves).

Materials ▸

8 ¹⁄₁₆ × 1½ × 72" solid aluminum angle	Exterior hasp with padlock
2 ⅜" × 4 × 8 ft. sheet rough cedar siding	3 2 × 2" butt hinges
1 ¾" × 4 × 8 ft. exterior plywood	¼ × ¾" bolts
1 ¼ × ¾" × 8 ft. wood shelf edge	¼" lock nuts
2 1 × 2" × 8 ft. cedar boards	¾" hex-head wood screws
	Aluminum pop rivets

For the serious grill cook (a Pitmaster in barbecuer's parlance), a lockable, dedicated storage locker is the best place to keep tools, fuel, and other supplies organized and safe.

Pitmaster's Locker

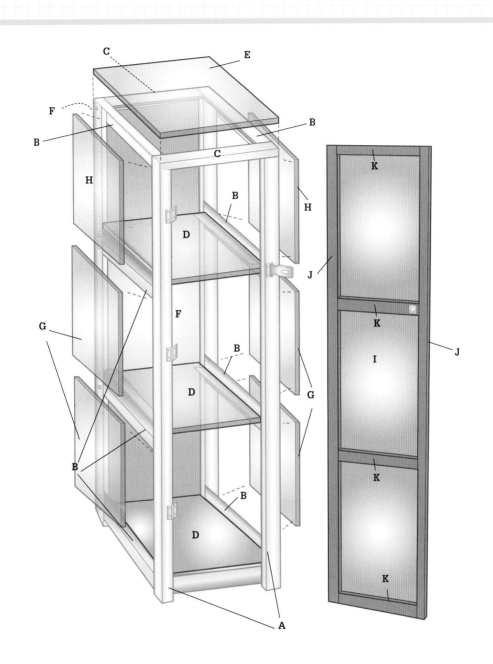

Cutting List

Key	Part	Dimension	Pcs.	Material
A	Frame legs	1/16 × 1 1/2 × 72"	4	Aluminum angle
B	Shelf supports	1/16 × 1 1/2 × 18"	12	Aluminum angle
C	Frame tops	1/16 × 1 1/2 × 18 1/4"	2	Aluminum angle
D	Shelves	3/4 × 17 × 16"	3	Ext. plywood
E	Top*	3/4 × 17 1/2 × 18 1/2"	1	Ext. plywood
F	Back panel	3/8 × 18 × 70"	1	Cedar siding

Key	Part	Dimension	Pcs.	Material
G	Side panels	3/8 × 16 × 23 1/2"	4	Cedar siding
H	Side panels (top)	3/8 × 16 × 21"	2	Cedar siding
I	Door panel	3/8 × 14 × 67"	1	Ext. plywood
J	Door stiles	3/4 × 1 1/2 × 68"	2	Cedar
K	Door rails	3/4 × 1 1/2 × 12"	4	Cedar
L	Top trim (opt.)**	1 × 1" × cut to fit	4	Corner molding

*Exposed edges finished with 1/4 x 3/4" wood shelf edge

**Not shown

Pitmaster's Locker

MAKE THE METAL FRAME

The framework for this locker is built from solid aluminum angle (¹⁄₁₆" thick × 1½" wide each direction). Although aluminum is very rigid, it is also relatively soft and very workable for cutting and drilling. You can easily cut the metal parts for this project with a hacksaw, though keeping the cuts straight can be tricky. *If you have access to a metal cutoff saw, it will save a lot of time—you might consider renting one.* Do not install an abrasive blade in a power miter saw. You can also use a reciprocating saw or a jigsaw with a bimetal blade, as seen here (**photo 1**). Whichever saw you use, clean up and deburr the cut edges with a bench grinder.

Lay out shelf locations on the frame legs with a wax crayon or pencil (avoid permanent markers, as they work but the marks cannot be erased). Install shelf supports between pairs of legs at selected heights. Clamp each support to each leg with a locking pliers. Drill one ¼" guide hole in the middle of each joint (**photo 2**). Use a carbide-tipped twist bit. *TIP: Lubricate the drilling point with a drop of cutting oil before drilling. Add more oil if the metal begins to smoke.*

Once the guide hole is drilled, insert a ¼ × ¾" bolt and add a locknut on the interior side (**photo 3**). Hand-tighten the nut, but wait until the entire frame is assembled and squared before tightening nuts all the way.

After all of the joints are secured with hand-tightened bolts, check the assembly with a framing square and adjust as needed. Begin fully tightening the locknuts. Grasp each nut with a locking pliers and tighten the bolt head with a socket and ratchet or cordless impact driver (**photo 4**).

ADD THE PLYWOOD PANELS & SHELVES

Cut the shelves to size from ¾" thick plywood (use quality plywood such as AB or BC as opposed to sheathing or CDX). Cut the panels from rough-textured cedar siding panels (these come in 4 × 8-foot sheets, usually around ⅜" thick). Sand and stain both faces and the edges of the panels and shelves with exterior stain before installing them.

Attach the back panel, top panel, and side panels in the correct locations with ¾" pop rivets (**photo 5**). Clamp each panel in place and drill guide holes for

Cut the aluminum angle for the frame parts (top) and then deburr the cut ends on a bench grinder (lower). Don't overdo it on the grinder or use a file.

Drill guide holes for bolts. Clamp the part for each joint together with locking pliers and then drill for one ¼" bolt per joint.

Assemble the frame. Secure each frame joint with a ¼ × ¾" bolt and lock nut. If you're able to locate aluminum fasteners use them, otherwise use stainless steel or hot-dipped fasteners.

Assemble the frame by tightening the locknuts onto the bolts. Hand-tighten all nuts first and then check the frame to make sure it is square. Tighten the nuts with a cordless impact driver or a ratcheting socket set.

Attach the panels using aluminum pop rivets driven through guide holes in the frame and the panels.

Hang the door. Attach the hinges to the metal frame first and then attach the other plates to the back of the door on the edge with no shelf edge molding.

the rivets through the frames and the panels. Install the pop rivets from the exterior side of the cabinet. Install the back panel first because it helps to square up the cabinet.

HANG THE DOOR & INSTALL HARDWARE

The locker door is sized to fit in between the metal frame members, and it closes against the slightly recessed shelf edges. It is made from ⅜"-thick siding and framed with 1 × 2 trim. Install three butt hinges to the left leg with bolts and lock nuts. You will probably need to enlarge the screw holes in the hinge plates to accept the ¼"-diameter bolts. After installing all three butt hinges, attach the edge of the door to the free hinge plates (**photo 6**). Test the door. If it works properly, attach the locking hasp. Use exterior-rated wood glue and 1" brass brads to attach ¼"-thick × ¾"-wide wood shelf edge to the front edges of the shelves (**photo 7**).

Make the panels and shelves. Cut the shelves and door to size from exterior plywood and attach wood shelf edge molding to select edges as instructed. Cut the side, back, and top panels from cedar plywood (siding). Stain the parts before installing them in the frame.

Timberframe Sandbox

Building this sandbox requires a good deal more effort than if you simply nailed four boards together and dumped a pile of sand in the middle. The timber construction is both charming and solid. A storage box at one end gives kids a convenient place to keep their toys. The opposite end has built-in seats, allowing children to sit above the sand as they play.

The gravel bed and plastic sheathing provide a nice base for the sandbox, allowing water to drain while keeping weeds from sprouting in the sand. The gravel and liner also keep sand from migrating out of the box. The structure is set into the ground for stability and to keep the top of the pavers at ground level so you can easily mow around them. When your children outgrow the sandbox, turn it into a garden bed.

Materials ▸

14 4 × 4" × 8 ft. cedar boards	Sand
1 1 × 8" × 12 ft. cedar board	Wood sealer/ protectant
2 1 × 6" × 8 ft. cedar boards	Heavy-duty plastic sheeting
2 2 × 2" × 6 ft. cedar boards	2" galvanized screws
Coarse gravel	6" barn nails
	Pavers
	Hinges

If you have small children, a backyard just isn't complete without a sandbox. This version is nicely sized, sturdy, and designed for ease of cleaning.

Timberframe Sandbox

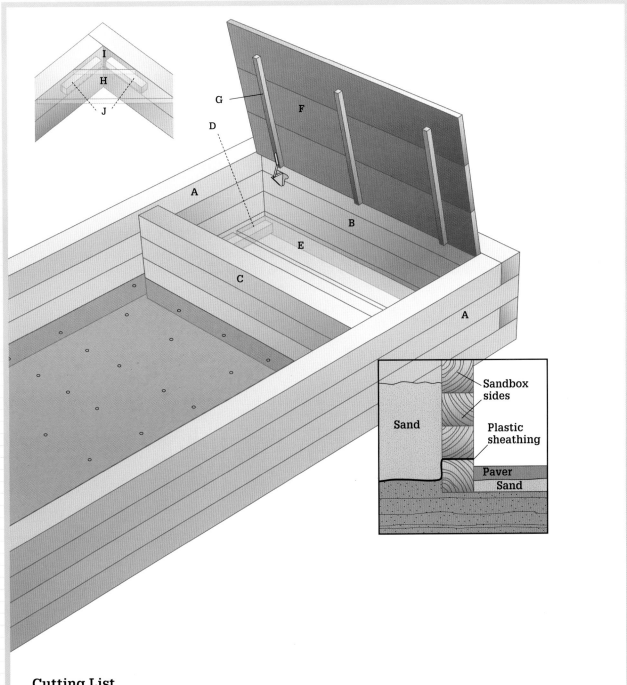

Sandbox sides

Plastic sheathing

Sand

Paver

Sand

Cutting List

Key	Part	Dimension	Pcs.	Material
A	Sandbox sides	3½ x 3½ x 92½"	8	Cedar
B	Sandbox ends	3½ x 3½ x 44½"	8	Cedar
C	Storage box walls	3½ x 3½ x 41"	4	Cedar
D	Floor cleats	1½ x 1½ x 18"	2	Cedar
E	Floorboards	¾ x 5½ x 43"	3	Cedar

Key	Part	Dimension	Pcs.	Material
F	Lid boards	¾ x 7½ x 43½"	3	Cedar
G	Lid cleats	1½ x 1½ x 18"	3	Cedar
H	Bench boards	¾ x 5½ x 18"	2	Cedar
I	Corner bench boards	¾ x 5½ x 7"	2	Cedar
J	Bench cleats	1½ x 1½ x 10"	4	Cedar

Timberframe Sandbox

PREPARE THE SITE
Outline a 48 × 96" area using stakes and strings. Use a shovel to remove all of the grass inside the area. Dig a flat trench that's 2" deep × 4" wide around the perimeter of the area, just inside the stakes and string (**photo 1**).

LAY THE FIRST ROW OF TIMBERS
Cut the side, end, and storage box wall timbers using a reciprocating saw or a power miter saw. Coat the timbers with a wood sealer and let them dry completely. Place the first tier of sides and ends in the trench so the corners on successive rows will overlap one another. Place a level across a corner, then add or remove soil to level it. Level the other three corners the same way. Drill two ³⁄₁₆" pilot holes through the timber sides, then drive 6" barn nails through the pilot holes.

Measuring from the inside of one end, mark for the inside edge of the storage box at 18" on both sides. Align the storage box wall with the marks, making sure the corners are square, and then score the soil on either side of it. Remove the timber and dig a 3" deep trench at the score marks.

Replace the storage box timber in the trench. Its top edge must be ¾" lower than the top edge of the first tier of the sandbox wall. Add or remove dirt until the storage box timber is at the proper height. Drill ³⁄₁₆"-diameter pilot holes through the sandbox sides into the ends of the storage box timber, then drive 6" barn nails through the pilot holes.

Pour 2" of coarse gravel into the sandbox section. Compact the gravel with a hand tamper or simply by stomping on it for a while. Cover the gravel bed section with heavy-duty plastic sheet (**photo 2**). Pierce the plastic with an awl or screwdriver at 12" intervals for drainage.

BUILD THE SANDBOX FRAME
Set the second tier of timbers in place over the first tier and over the plastic, staggering the joints with the joint pattern in the first tier. Starting at the ends of the timbers, drill ³⁄₁₆"-diameter pilot holes every 24", then drive 6" galvanized barn nails through the pilot holes. Repeat for the remaining tiers of timbers, staggering the joints.

Stack the remaining storage box timbers over the first one. Drill ³⁄₁₆"-diameter pilot holes through the

Remove the grass in the sandbox location with a flat-end spade, and then dig a trench for the first row of timbers.

Prepare the base. Lay the first row of timbers, including the wall for the storage box. Fill the sandbox area with a 2" layer of gravel, and cover with plastic sheet or weed blocker.

Build the rest of the sandbox frame, staggering the corner joints. Drill holes and drive barn nails through the holes.

Attach the bench lid using heavy-duty hinges. Install a child-safe lid support to prevent the lid from falling shut.

Install 2 x 2 cleats ¾" from the top of the sandbox to support the seats in the corners. Attach the corner bench boards using galvanized screws.

Place the pavers into the sand base. Use a rubber mallet to set them in place.

sandbox sides into the ends of the storage box timbers, and then drive 6" barn nails into the pilot holes (**photo 3**). Cut the excess plastic from around the outside of the sandbox timbers using a utility knife.

BUILD THE STORAGE BOX FLOOR & LID

Cut the floor cleats and position one against each side wall along the bottom of the storage box. Attach them using 2" galvanized screws. Cut the floorboards and place them over the cleats with ½" gaps between boards to allow for drainage. Fasten the floorboards to the cleats using 2" screws.

Cut the lid boards and lay them out side-by-side, with the ends flush. Cut the lid cleats and place across the lid, one at each end and one in the middle, making sure the end of each cleat is flush with the back edge of the lid. Drill pilot holes and attach the cleats using 2" galvanized screws. Attach the lid to the sandbox frame using heavy-duty child-safe friction hinges (**photo 4**).

BUILD CORNER BENCHES

Cut the bench cleats. Mark ¾" down from the top edge of the sandbox at two corners. Align the top edges of the bench cleats with the marks and fasten them using 2" deck screws.

Cut the corner bench boards to length with a 45° angle at each end. Place it in the corner and attach it to the cleats using 2" screws (**photo 5**). Cut the bench boards to length with a 45° angle at each end. Butt one against the corner bench board, and then attach it to the cleats. Repeat this step to install the second corner bench.

FILL SANDBOX & INSTALL BORDER

Fill the sandbox with play sand to within 4 to 6" of the top. Mark an area the width of your pavers around the perimeter of the sandbox. Remove the grass and soil in the paver area to the depth of your pavers, plus another 2", using a spade. Spread a 2" layer of sand into the paver trench. Smooth the sand level using a flat board. Place the pavers on top of the sand base, beginning at a corner of the sandbox (**photo 6**). Use a level or a straightedge to make sure the pavers are even and flush with the surrounding soil. If necessary, add or remove sand to level the pavers. Set the pavers in the sand by tapping them with a rubber mallet. Fill the gaps between the pavers with sand. Wet the sand lightly to help it settle. Add new sand as necessary until the gaps are filled.

Yard & Garden Projects

Outdoor carpentry projects are not limited to patio tables and garden benches. The projects in this chapter share a common theme: their main purpose is to improve the appearance of your yard.

Yards and gardens do not take care of themselves. So several projects in this chapter are designed to make yard and garden maintenance easier: a clever potting bench with work surfaces at two levels (because potted plants are not one-size-fits-all), a cold frame and more.

There are designs and instructions for several planters and containers: a triple-threat trellis planter for potting, climbing, and hanging; a planter based on a design from the Gardens at Versailles. And for pure decorative fun, we've included a wishing well/ pump house with recirculating water, and a Japanese-inspired luminary.

In this chapter:

- Compost Bin
- Freestanding Arbor
- High-low Potting Bench
- Trellis Planter
- Raised Bed with Removable Trellis
- Versailles Planter
- Jumbo Cold Frame
- Pagoda Lantern
- Firewood Shelter
- Shelter with Swing
- Patio Pergola

Compost Bin

Composting yard debris is an increasingly popular practice that makes good environmental sense. Composting is the process of converting organic waste into rich fertilizer for the soil, usually in a compost bin. A well-designed compost bin has a few key features. It's big enough to contain the organic material as it decomposes. It allows cross-flow of air to speed the process. And the bin area is easy to reach whether you're adding waste, turning the compost, or removing the composted material. This compost bin has all these features, plus one additional benefit not shared by most compost bins: it's very attractive.

Grass clippings, leaves, weeds, and vegetable waste are some of the most commonly composted materials. Just about any formerly living organic material can be composted, but do not add any of the following items to your compost bin:

- animal material or waste
- dairy products
- papers with colored inks
- baked goods
- branches or other pieces of wood

For more infromation on composting, contact your local libary or agricultural extension office.

Materials ▶

4 4 × 4" × 4 ft. cedar posts	1½", 3" galvanized deck screws
5 2 × 2" × 8 ft. cedar boards	Hook-and-eye latch mechanism
8 1 × 6" × 8 ft. cedar fence boards	3 × 3" brass butt hinges (one pair)

Convert organic waste into garden fertilizer inside the confines of this easy-to-make cedar compost bin.

Compost Bin

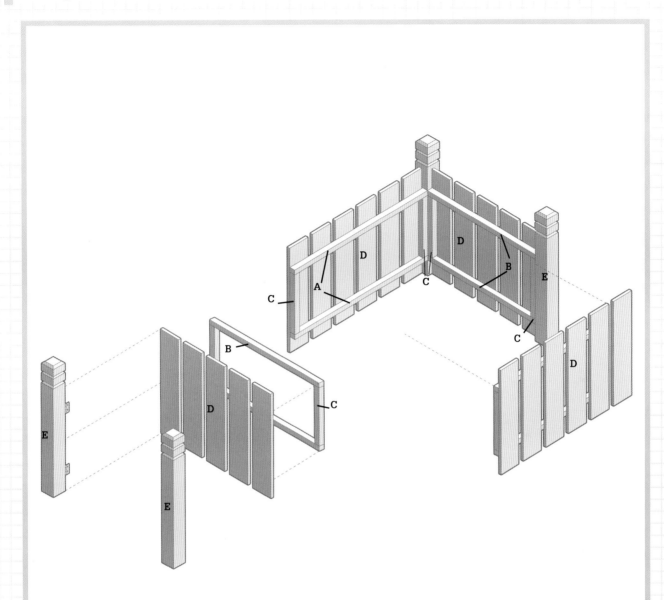

Cutting List

Key	Part	Dimension	Pcs.	Material
A	Side rails	1½ × 1½ × 40½"	4	Cedar
B	End rails	1½ × 1½ × 33½"	4	Cedar
C	Cleats	1½ × 1½ × 15"	8	Cedar
D	Slats	¾ × 5½ × 27"	22	Cedar
E	Posts	3½ × 3½ × 30"	4	Cedar

Compost Bin

BUILD THE PANELS

The four fence-type panels that make up the sides of this compost bin are cedar slats that attach to panel frames. The panel frames for the front and back of the bin are longer than the frames for the sides. Cut the side rails, end rails, and cleats to length. Group pairs of matching rails with a pair of cleats. Assemble each group into a frame—the cleats should be between the rails, flush with the ends. Drill ⅛"-diameter pilot holes into the rails. Counterbore the holes ¼" deep using a counterbore bit. Fasten all four panel frames together by driving 3" deck screws through the rails and into each end of each cleat (**photo 1**).

Cut all of the slats to length. Lay the frames on a flat surface and place a slat at each end of each frame. Keep the edges of these outer slats flush with the outside edges of the frame and let the bottoms of the slats overhang the bottom frame rail by 4". Drill pilot holes in the slats. Counterbore the holes slightly. Fasten the outer slats to the frames with 1½" deck screws (**photo 2**).

When you have fastened the outer slats to all of the frames, add slats between each pair of outer slats to fill out the panels. Insert a 1½" spacing block between the slats to set the correct gap. This will allow air to flow into the bin. Be sure to keep the ends of the slats aligned. Check with a tape measure to make sure the bottoms of all the slats are 4" below the bottom of the panel frame (**photo 3**).

ATTACH THE PANELS & POSTS

The four slatted panels are joined with corner posts to make the bin. Three of the panels are attached permanently to the posts, while one of the end panels is installed with hinges and a latch so it can swing open like a gate. You can use plain 4 × 4 cedar posts for the corner posts. For a more decorative look, buy prefabricated fence posts or deck rail posts with carving or contours at the top.

Cut the posts to length. If you're using plain posts, you may want to do some decorative contouring at one end or attach post caps. Stand a post upright on a flat work surface. Set one of the longer slatted panels next to the post, resting on the bottoms of the slats. Hold or clamp the panel to the post, with the back of the panel frame flush with the inside face of the post. Fasten the panel to the post by driving 3" deck screws through the frame cleats and into the posts. Space screws at roughly 8" intervals.

Stand another post on end, and fasten the other end of the panel frame to it, making sure the posts

Fasten the cleats between the rails to construct the panel frames.

Attach a slat at each end of the panel frame so the outer edges of the slats are flush with the outer edges of the frame.

are aligned. Fasten one of the shorter panels to the adjoining face of one of the posts. The back faces of the frames should meet at the inside corner of the post (**photo 4**). Fasten another post at the free end of the shorter panel. Fasten the other longer panel to the posts so it is opposite the first longer panel, forming a U-shaped structure.

ATTACH THE GATE

The unattached shorter panel is attached at the open end of the bin with hinges to create a swinging gate for loading and unloading material. Exterior wood stain or a clear wood sealer with UV protectant will keep the cedar from turning gray. If you are planning to apply a finish, it's easier to apply it before you hang the gate. Make sure all hardware is rated for exterior use.

Set the last panel between the posts at the open end of the bin. Move the sides of the bin slightly, if needed, so there is about ¼" of clearance between each end of the panel and the posts. Remove this panel gate and attach a pair of 3" butt hinges to a cleat, making sure the barrels of the hinges extend past the face of the outer slats. Set the panel into the opening, and mark the location of the hinge plates onto the post. Open the hinge so it is flat, and attach it to the post (**photo 5**). Attach a hook-and-eye latch to the unhinged end of the panel to hold the gate closed.

Spacing block

Continue to attach slats. The inner slats should be 1½" apart, with the ends 4" below the bottom of the frame.

Stand the posts and panels upright, and fasten the panels to the posts by driving screws through the cleats.

Attach exterior-rated hinges to the end panel frame and then fasten them to the post. Add a latch on the other side of the hinged panel.

Freestanding Arbor

This freestanding arbor combines the beauty and durability of natural cedar with an Asian-inspired design. Set it up on your patio or deck or in a quiet corner of your backyard. It adds just the right finishing touch to turn your outdoor living space into a showplace geared for relaxation and quiet contemplation.

The arbor has a long history as a focal point in gardens and other outdoor areas throughout the world. And if privacy and shade are concerns, you can enhance the sheltering quality by adding climbing vines that weave their way in and out of the trellis. Or, simply set a few potted plants around the base to help the arbor blend in with the outdoor environment. Another way to integrate plant life into your arbor is to hang decorative potted plants from the top beams.

This arbor is freestanding, so it can be easily moved to a new site whenever you desire. Or, you can anchor it permanently to a deck or to the ground and equip it with a built-in seat.

Sturdy posts made from 2 × 4 cedar serve as the base of the arbor, forming a framework for a 1 × 2 trellis system that scales the sides and top. The curved cutouts that give the arbor its Asian appeal are made with a jigsaw, then smoothed out with a drill and drum sander for a more finished appearance.

Materials ▶

7 1 × 2" × 8 ft. cedar boards	#10 × 2½" wood screws
9 2 × 4" × 8 ft. cedar boards	8 ⅜"-dia. × 2½" lag screws
3 2 × 6" × 8 ft. cedar boards	4 6" lag screws
Wood glue (exterior)	Deck screws (2½", 3")
Wood sealer or stain	Finishing materials

Create a shady retreat on a sunny patio or deck with this striking cedar arbor. It can also support a wealth of climbing plants if you so choose.

Freestanding Arbor

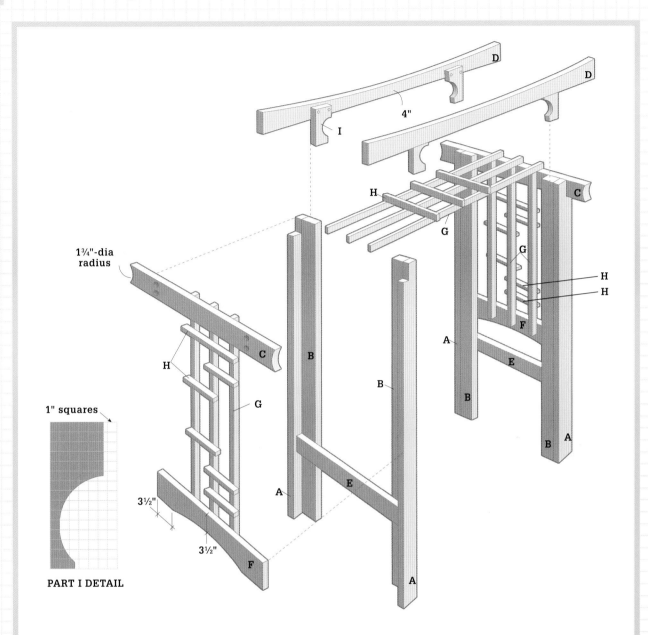

1¾"-dia radius

4"

1" squares

3½"

3½"

PART I DETAIL

Cutting List

Key	Part	Dimension	Pcs.	Material
A	Leg fronts	1½ × 3½ × 72"	4	Cedar
B	Leg sides	1½ × 3½ × 72"	4	Cedar
C	Cross beams	1½ × 3½ × 36"	2	Cedar
D	Top beams	1½ × 5½ × 72"	2	Cedar
E	Side rails	1½ × 3½ × 21"	2	Cedar

Key	Part	Dimension	Pcs.	Material
F	Side spreaders	1½ × 5½ × 21"	2	Cedar
G	Trellis strips	⅞ × 1½ × 48"	9	Cedar
H	Cross strips	⅞ × 1½ × *	15	Cedar
I	Braces	1½ × 5½ × 15"	4	Cedar

*Cut to fit

Freestanding Arbor

MAKE THE LEGS

Each of the four arbor legs is made from two 6-foot-long pieces of 2 × 4 cedar fastened at right angles with 3" deck screws. Cut the leg fronts and leg sides to length.

Position the leg sides at right angles to the leg fronts, with top and bottom edges flush. Apply moisture-resistant glue to the joint. Attach the leg fronts to the leg sides by driving evenly spaced screws through the faces of the fronts and into the edges of the sides (**photo 1**). Use a jigsaw to cut a 3½"-long × 2"-wide notch at the top outside corner of each leg front (**photo 2**). These notches cradle the crossbeams when the arbor is assembled.

MAKE THE CROSSBEAMS, RAILS & SPREADERS

Cut the crossbeams to length and then cut a small arc at both ends of each part. Start by using a compass to draw a 3½"-diameter semicircle at the edge of a strip of cardboard. Cut out the semicircle, and use the strip as a template for marking the arcs (**photo 3**). Cut out the arcs with a jigsaw. Sand the cuts smooth with a drill and drum sander.

Cut two side spreaders to length. The side spreaders fit just above the side rails on each side. Mark a curved cutting line on the bottom of each spreader. To mark the cutting lines, draw starting points 3½" in from each end of a spreader. Make a reference line 2" up from the bottom of the spreader board. Tack a casing nail on the reference line, centered between the ends of the spreader. With the spreader clamped to the work surface, also tack nails into the work surface next to the starting lines on the spreader. Slip a thin strip of metal or plastic between the casing nails so the strip bows out to create a smooth arc. Trace the arc onto the spreader, then cut along the line with a jigsaw. Smooth with a drum sander. Use the first spreader as a template for

Create four legs by fastening leg sides to leg fronts at right angles.

Cut a 2 x 4-size notch in the top of each of the four leg pairs to hold the crossbeams.

Lay out profiles on the ends of the crossbeams. A piece of cardboard acts as a template when you trace the outline for the arc.

Lag-screw the crossbeams to the legs, and fasten the spreaders and rails with deck screws to assemble the side frames.

marking and cutting the second spreader. Cut the side rails to length. They are fitted between pairs of legs on each side of the arbor, near the bottom, to keep the arbor square.

ASSEMBLE THE SIDE FRAMES

Each side frame consists of a front and back leg joined together by a side rail, a side spreader, and a crossbeam. Lay two leg assemblies parallel on a work surface, with the notched board in each leg facing up. Space the legs so the inside faces of the notched boards are 21" apart. Set a crossbeam into the notches, overhanging each leg by 6". Also set a side spreader and a side rail between the legs for spacing.

Drill ⅜"-diameter pilot holes in the crossbeam. Counterbore the holes to ¼" depth using a counterbore bit. Attach the crossbeam to each leg with glue. Drive two ⅜"-diameter × 2½" lag screws through the crossbeam and into the legs (**photo 4**). Position the side spreader between the legs so the top is 29½" up from the bottoms of the legs. Position the side rail 18" up from the leg bottoms. Drill ⅛" countersunk pilot holes into the spreader and rail through

the leg faces. Keeping the legs parallel, attach the pieces with glue and drive 3" deck screws through the outside faces of the legs and into the side rails and spreaders.

ATTACH THE SIDE TRELLIS PIECES

Each side trellis is made from vertical strips of cedar 1 × 2 that are fastened to the side frames. Horizontal cross strips will be added later to create a decorative cross-hatching effect. Cut three vertical trellis strips to length for each side frame. Space them so they are 2⅜" apart, with the ends flush with the top of the crossbeam (**photo 5**).

Drill pilot holes to attach the trellis strips to the crossbeam and spreader. Countersink the holes and drive 2½" deck screws. Repeat the procedure for the other side frame.

CUT & SHAPE TOP BEAMS

Cut two top beams to length. Draw 1½"-deep arcs at the top edges of the top beams, starting at the ends of each of the boards. Cut the arcs into the top beams with a jigsaw. Sand smooth—use a drum sander, if you have one.

ASSEMBLE TOP & SIDES

Because the side frames are fairly heavy and bulky, you will need to brace them in an upright position to fasten the top beams between them. A simple way to do this is to use a pair of 1 × 4 braces to connect the tops and bottoms of the side frames (**photo 6**). Clamp the ends of the braces to the side frames so the side frames are 4 feet apart, and use a level to make sure the side frames are plumb.

Mark a centerpoint for a lag bolt 12¾" from each end of each top beam. Drill a ¼"-diameter counterbored pilot hole through the top edge at the centerpoint. Set the top beams on top of the crossbraces of the side frames. Mark the pilot hole locations onto the crossbeams. Remove the top beams and drill pilot holes into the crossbeams. Secure the top beams to the crossbeams with 6" lag screws.

Cut four braces to length, and transfer the brace cutout pattern from the diagram on page 129 to each board. Cut the patterns with a jigsaw. Attach the braces at the joints where the leg fronts meet the top beams, using 2½" deck screws. To make sure the arbor assembly stays in position while you complete the project, attach 1 × 2 scraps between the front legs and between the back legs

(**photo 7**). Cut and attach three trellis strips between the top beams.

ADD TRELLIS CROSS STRIPS

Cut the cross strips to 7" and 10" lengths. Use wood screws to attach them at 3" intervals in a staggered pattern on the side trellis pieces. You can adjust the sizes and placement of the cross strips but, for best appearance, retain some symmetry of placement. Fasten cross strips to the top trellis in the same manner. Make sure the cross strips that fit across the top trellis are arranged in similar fashion to the side strips (**photo 8**).

APPLY FINISHING TOUCHES

To protect the arbor, coat the cedar wood with clear wood sealer. After the finish dries, the arbor is ready to be placed onto your deck or patio or in a quiet corner of your yard. Because of its sturdy construction, the arbor can simply be set onto a hard, flat surface. If you plan to install a permanent seat in the arbor, you should anchor it to the ground. For decks, try to position the arbor so you can screw the legs to the rim of the deck or toenail the legs into the deck boards. You can buy fabricated metal post stakes, available at most building centers, to use when anchoring the arbor to the ground.

Attach trellis strips to the crossbrace and spreader with deck screws.

Brace the side frames in an upright, level position with long pieces of 1 x 4 while you attach the top beams.

7

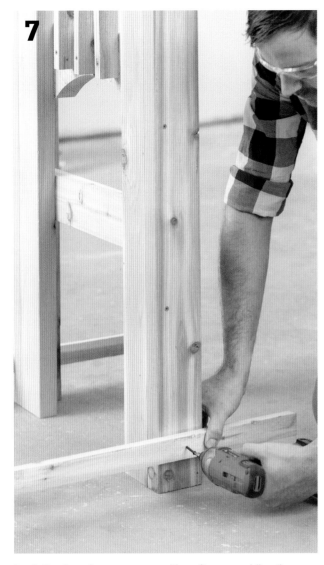

Lock the legs in a square position after assembling the arbor by tacking strips of wood between the front legs and between the back legs.

8

Attach the trellis cross strips to spice up the design and assist climbing plants.

Where to Put Your Arbor ▸

There are no firm rules about arbor placement. It can be positioned to provide a focal point for a porch, patio, or deck. Placed against a wall or at the end of a plain surface, arbors improve the general look of the area. With some thick climbing vines and vegetation added to the arbor, you can also disguise a utility area, such as a trash collection space.

Add a Seat ▸

Create an arbor seat by resting two 2 × 10 cedar boards on the rails in each side frame. Overhang the rails by 6" or so, and drive a few 3" deck screws through the boards and into the rails to secure the seat.

High-low Potting Bench

Working the soil is part of the fun of gardening, but crouching down all day can be exhausting. Many gardening tasks are easier if you can work at a standard workbench height instead of on the ground. That's where a potting bench comes in handy. A potting bench provides a comfortable and efficient place to work on gardening jobs that don't have to happen on the ground.

What makes this potting bench different from most other potting benches is that the work surfaces are at appropriate heights for gardening tasks. The work surface is 30" high, making it easier to reach down into pots. The low work surface is just over a foot high, so you won't have to lift heavy objects such as large pots or bags of soil. In addition to the high-low work surfaces, this bench also features a shelf and hook rail to keep small supplies and tools within reach, yet still off the main work area.

A potting bench gets wet and it gets dirty, so rot- and moisture-resistant materials were chosen to build this bench. The frame is made with pressure-treated pine lumber and the work surfaces are composite deck boards. The composite material provides a smooth surface that will not splinter and is easy to clean.

Materials ▶

1 1 × 2" × 8 ft. PT pine board	4 ⁵⁄₄" × 8 ft. deck boards
2 1 × 4" × 8 ft. PT pine boards	Exterior-rated screws (1¼", 2")
4 2 × 4" × 8 ft. PT pine boards	Cup hooks
1 1¼ × 5½" × 6 ft. PT pine board	

Not all pots are the same height. With two different working heights, this bench is comfortable to use whether you're planting seeds in starter trays or planting a 5-gallon planter with tomatoes.

High-low Potting Bench

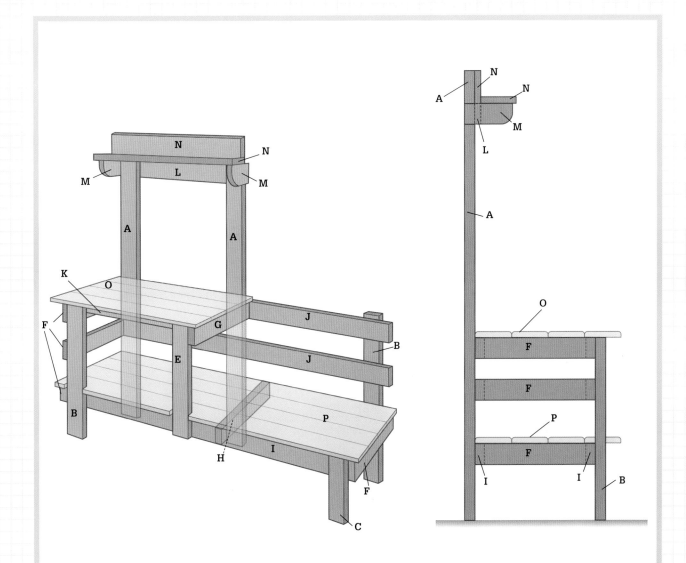

Cutting List

Key	Part	Dimension	Pcs.	Material
A	Long legs	$1\frac{1}{2} \times 3\frac{1}{2} \times 62\frac{3}{4}$"	2	PT pine
B	Mid length legs	$1\frac{1}{2} \times 3\frac{1}{2} \times 29$"	2	PT pine
C	Short leg	$1\frac{1}{2} \times 3\frac{1}{2} \times 12$"	1	PT pine
D	Back strut*	$1\frac{1}{2} \times 3\frac{1}{2} \times 54\frac{1}{4}$"	1	PT pine
E	Front strut	$1\frac{1}{2} \times 3\frac{1}{2} \times 20\frac{1}{2}$"	1	PT pine
F	Outside cross supports	$\frac{3}{4} \times 3\frac{1}{2} \times 22$ "	4	PT pine
G	Middle top cross support	$1\frac{1}{2} \times 3\frac{1}{2} \times 19\frac{3}{4}$"	1	PT pine
H	Middle bottom cross support	$1\frac{1}{2} \times 3\frac{1}{2} \times 16$"	1	PT pine

Key	Part	Dimension	Pcs.	Material
I	Bottom rails	$1\frac{1}{2} \times 3\frac{1}{2} \times 60$"	2	PT pine
J	Back rails	$\frac{3}{4} \times 3\frac{1}{2} \times 60$"	2	PT pine
K	Front rail	$\frac{3}{4} \times 1\frac{1}{2} \times 30$"	1	PT pine
L	Hook rail	$\frac{3}{4} \times 3\frac{1}{2} \times 30$"	1	PT pine
M	Shelf supports	$\frac{3}{4} \times 3\frac{1}{2} \times 7$"	2	PT pine
N	Shelf/shelf back	$1\frac{1}{4} \times 5\frac{1}{2} \times 31\frac{1}{2}$"	2	PT pine
O	High worktops	$1\frac{1}{4} \times 5\frac{1}{2} \times 33\frac{1}{2}$"	4	Deckboards
P	Low worktops	$1\frac{1}{4} \times 5\frac{1}{2} \times 62\frac{1}{2}$"	4	Deckboards

*Not Shown

High-low Potting Bench

CUT THE FRAME PARTS
Cut all of the frame and shelf parts to length. Draw a 3½" radius on the front bottom corner of each shelf support. Cut along the radius lines with a jigsaw or bandsaw (**photo 1**). Sand the profiles smooth. Apply a solid color exterior deck and siding stain to all sides of the frame and shelf parts. Staining these parts isn't mandatory, but it's an opportunity to customize your workbench and the stain will extend the life of the parts.

ASSEMBLE THE FRAME
Attach two back rails and one bottom rail to the long leg, back strut, and back right mid-length leg with

2" deck screws. Check that all of the parts intersect at 90-degree angles. Attach the front rail and one bottom rail to the left front mid-length leg, front strut, and short leg. Connect the back assembly and front assembly by attaching them to the cross supports (**photo 2**).

ATTACH THE WORKTOP PLANKS
Cut the deck boards that will be used to create the work surfaces to length. We used composite deck boards because they require little maintenance and are easy to clean. (See page 74 for more information on working with composites). Place the front deck board for the lower work surface against the backside of the

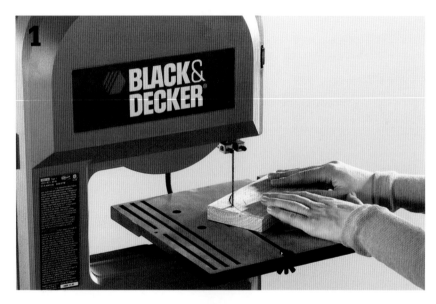

Cut the shelf supports. Use a bandsaw or a jigsaw to make the 3½" radius roundovers on the ends of the shelf supports. Sand smooth.

Assemble the bench frame. Clamp the cross supports to the front and back assemblies. Attach the cross supports with 2" deck screws.

front left leg and front strut. Mark the point where the front leg and strut intersect the deck board. Using these marks, draw the 3¾" deep notch outlines and cut out the notches with a jigsaw (**photo 3**).

Place the top and bottom deck boards on the cross supports, leaving a ¼" space between the boards. Drill two pilot holes that are centered over the cross supports in each deck board. Attach the deck boards with 2" deck screws (**photo 4**). If you are using composite deck boards, use specially designed decking screws.

ATTACH THE SHELF & RACK

Attach the shelf back, shelf hook rail, and shelf supports to the long leg and back strut with 2½" deck screws. Attach the shelf to the shelf supports with 2" deck screws. Fasten the hooks to the shelf hook rail (**photo 5**).

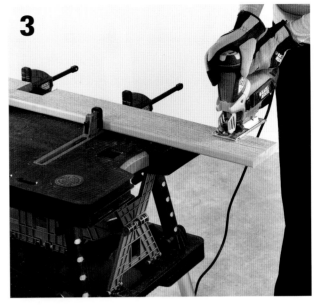

Cut notches. Lay out notches in the front board for the low work surface where the board must fit around the front leg and front strut. Use a jigsaw to cut the notches.

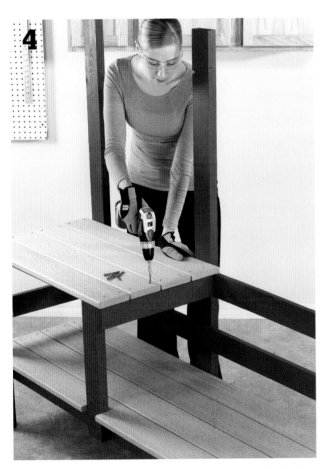

Install the worktop slats. Use composite screws to attach the composite deck boards that create the upper and lower worktops.

Install the shelf and hook rail. Attach the shelf to the shelf supports. Drill pilot holes for each screw to prevent splitting the shelf supports. Once the hook rail is installed twist in the cup hooks.

Trellis Planter

You don't need a large yard—or any yard at all for that matter—to have a garden. Planting in containers makes it possible to cultivate a garden just about anywhere. A container garden can be as simple as a small flowering annual planted in a single 4" pot or as elaborate as a variety of shrubs, flowering plants, and ornamental grasses planted in a large stationary planter.

This planter project combines a couple of different container options to create a larger garden in a relatively small space. The base is an 18 × 30" planter box that is large enough to hold several small plants, a couple of medium-sized plants, or one large plant. It features a trellis back that can be covered by climbing plants.

In addition to the planter and trellis, this project features two plant hangers that extend out from the back posts. Adding a couple of hanging plant baskets further extends the garden display without increasing the space taken up by the planter.

This project is easiest to build with a table saw, miter saw, jigsaw, and drill/driver. If you don't have access to a table saw, use a circular saw or jigsaw and straightedge to rip the 1 × 6 siding boards. An even easier option is to replace the 2¾"-wide siding boards with 3½"-wide 1 × 4s. This modification makes the planter 4½" taller, so you also have to make the front posts 24½" long instead of 20" long and add 4½" to the length of the front posts trim.

Materials ▶

3 1 × 2" × 8 ft. cedar boards	1 ¾ × 4" × 4 ft. exterior plywood
3 1 × 6" × 8 ft. cedar boards	Exterior-rated screws (2", 3")
1 2 × 4" × 10 ft. cedar board	2 ⅜ × 2½" eyebolts
2 4 × 4" × 8 ft. cedar boards	4 ⅜" flat washers
1 2 × 2" × 6 ft. cedar board	2 ⅜" locknuts

This efficient planter combines a box for container gardening with a climbing trellis and a pair of profiled arms for hanging potted plants.

Trellis Planter

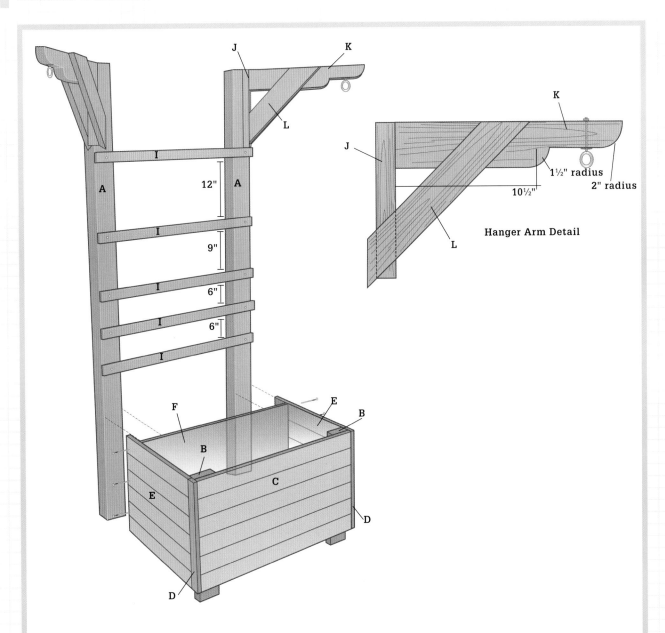

12"

9"

6"

6"

Hanger Arm Detail

1½" radius

2" radius

10½"

Cutting List

Key	Part	Dimension	Pcs.	Material
A	Back posts	3½ × 3½ × 72"	2	Cedar
B	Front posts	1½ × 3½ × 20"	2	Cedar
C	Front siding	¾ × 2¾ × 30"	6	Cedar
D	Front post trim	¾ × 1½ × 18"	2	Cedar
E	Side siding	¾ × 2¾ × 21½"	12	Cedar
F	Back panel	¾ × 18 × 30"	1	Ext. Plywood
G	Bottom supports*	¾ × 1½ × 22¼"	2	Cedar

*Not shown

Key	Part	Dimension	Pcs.	Material
H	Bottom panel*	¾ × 22¼ × 30"	1	Ext. Plywood
I	Climbing rails	¾ × 1½ × 30"	5	Cedar
J	Hanger backs	1½ × 1½ × 12"	2	Cedar
K	Hanger arms	1½ × 3½ × 18"	2	Cedar
L	Hanger braces	1½ × 3½ × 18"	4	Cedar

Trellis Planter

CUT THE BASE PARTS

Cutting the front posts (2 × 4) and back posts (4 × 4) to length is easy. Cutting the hanger parts is a bit trickier, primarily because the plant hangers splay out from the corners of the posts at a 45° angle. The top, outside post corners must be beveled to create flat mounting surface for the hangers. Mark the bevel cut lines on the outside and front faces of the posts (**photo 1**). Tilt the shoe of a jigsaw to 45° and bevel-cut along the layout lines (**photo 2**). Use a handsaw to make a stop cut that meets the bottom of the bevel cut in each back post, forming a shoulder (**photo 3**). Rip-cut some 1 × 6 stock to 2¾" wide (**photo 4**) using a table saw or a circular saw and a straightedge cutting guide. Cut six 30"-long pieces and twelve 21½"-long pieces to make the siding strips.

Also use a circular saw or table saw to cut the bottom and back panels to length and width. Cut 1½"-long × 3½"-wide notches out of the front corners of the bottom panel. Cut the front post trim, bottom supports, and back climbing rails to length from 1 × 2 boards.

ASSEMBLE THE BASE PLANTER

Attach the front siding strips to the front posts with 2" exterior screws. Align the ends of the siding pieces flush with the sides of the front legs. Leave a ¼" space between the siding boards. Drive one screw

Mark the post bevel cuts. The lines at the top of each back post should be drawn 1" out from the corner and should run down the post for 12" long.

Cut the bevels. Tilt the foot of a jigsaw at a 45° angle so it will ride smoothly on the post face and follow the bevel cutting line. Make a bevel cut along the layout line.

through each end of each siding board and into the front legs. Drill a countersunk pilot hole for each screw. Attach the front post trim pieces to the front posts with three or four 2" brad nails or finish nails. Align the front edge of the trim pieces flush with the front face of the front siding. Attach the back panel to the back posts with six 2" screws. Drive three screws into each post.

Attach the back lattice rails to the back posts. Drive one screw through each end of each climbing rail (photo 5). Refer to the construction drawing on page 139 for lattice spacing. Place the front and back assemblies on their sides and install siding on the side that's facing up. The siding boards should be positioned against the front post trim board and flush with the back edge of the back post, spaced ¼" apart.

Attach the siding with 2" screws (photo 6). Flip the project over and repeat the process to attach siding to the other side.

Attach the bottom supports to the front and back legs. The bottom of the front end of the bottom support should be flush with the bottom of the siding. The bottom of the back end of the bottom support should be positioned 2" up from the bottom of the back post. Drive one screw through the front end of the support and into the front leg and two screws into the back legs. Attach the bottom to the bottom supports with four 2" screws—two into each support.

BUILD THE PLANT HANGERS

Cut the hanger backs, hanger arms, and hanger braces to length. Draw the hanger arm profile onto the side of

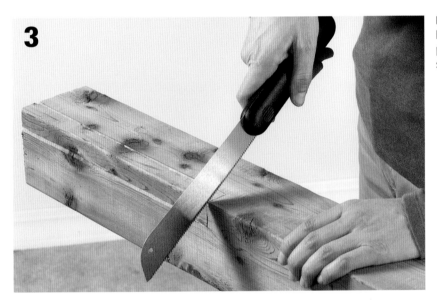

3

Make the shoulder cut. Use a handsaw to cut into the corner of the post to meet the bevel cut, creating a shoulder for the beveled corner.

4

Rip 1 × 6 stock for siding. Using a table saw or a circular saw and cutting guide, rip enough material for the sides and the front to 2¾".

each hanger arm, and use a compass to draw the radius profiles. Profile details are shown on the construction drawings (page 139). Use a jigsaw to cut along the profile layout lines on the hanger arms. Both ends of the hanger brace are mitered at 45°, but the back or bottom end is a compound miter cut, meaning that it has both a miter and a bevel component. Cut the top end 45° miters on all four braces. Then, make compound cuts at the bottom ends of the hanger braces (**photo 7**). Make the cuts so the beveled end faces the post when it is attached.

Drill a ⅜"-diameter hole through the top of each hanger arm. Locate the hole 3" in from the end of the hanger arm. Fasten one eyebolt, two flat washers, and a locknut through each hanger arm. Attach the hanger back to the back end of the hanger arm with two 3" screws. Position a 2 × 2 hanger back and a 2 × 4 hanger arm against the beveled corner of each back post. Drive two 3" screws through the hanger back and into the back posts. Attach the hanger braces to the hanger back and hanger arm with 2" screws (**photo 8**). Make sure the hanger arms remain perpendicular to the posts when you attach the braces.

FILL PLANTER
The planter itself is lined with heavy (at least 4-mil thick) black plastic sheeting. Cut the sheeting pieces

Add the latticework. Attach the horizontal climbing rails to the back posts with countersunk 2" screws. Use one screw at each lattice connection to the posts.

Install siding. Attach the siding to the front and back posts with countersunk 2" screws. After completing one side, flip the project and complete the other side. Then, install siding strips on the front.

that cover the sides, front, and bottom several inches oversized so they overlap in the corners. Cut the back sheeting the same size as the back panel. Attach the plastic to the inside faces of the planter with staples (**photo 9**). Start with the bottom sheet, overlap the sides on the bottom, and then overlap the front over the sides and bottom. Finally overlap the back over the sides, leaving a small gap between the bottom of the back sheet and the bottom sheet to allow water to drain out. Fill the planter with potting soil and add your plants. *TIP: Adding a few inches of gravel to the bottom of the planting compartment allows for better drainage.*

Cut the hanger brace angles. After cutting a flat 45° miter in the top end of the hanger brace, make a compound bevel/miter cut in the bottom end so it will fit flat against the bevel cut in the post.

Install the hanger braces. Clamp the hanger braces to the hanger arms and hanger backs. Attach the hanger braces with 2" screws driven into the hanger back and into the hanger arm. Drive two countersunk screws at each connection.

Line the container. Attach 4-mil black plastic liner with ⅜" stainless steel staples. Overlap the plastic in the corners and leave a small gap along the back bottom edge for drainage.

Raised Bed with Removable Trellis

It's hard to beat PVC plumbing pipe for adding a trellis to a simple raised bed. It's inexpensive and rot-proof and goes together like pieces of a toy construction set. It's also durable, lightweight, and can stand up to just about anything the elements throw at it.

This all-purpose trellis is made almost entirely with PVC parts and is designed to be custom-fit to your raised bed. For a bed with 2× lumber sides, you can secure the trellis uprights to the outside of the bed with metal pipe straps. If the sides of the bed are built with timbers, the trellis simply drops into holes drilled into the tops of the timbers. Of course, you can get much more creative with the configuration if you want to bump up your yield. Add another, identical trellis to the opposite end of a longer raised bed. Or add three—at either end and in the middle—of a really long bed. Making the most of vertical space with a trellis is a great way to grow a lot more vegetables in the same footprint. This can be key if you're looking to put up a lot of vegetables for over the winter.

The trellis as shown is made with 1½-inch PVC pipe and fittings. The parts are friction fit only, so they are not glued together and can easily be disassembled for off-season storage. PVC pipe and fittings are manufactured for a very tight fit; if you push the pipe all the way into the fittings, the joints won't come apart unless you want them to. Separate the joints by twisting the pipe or fitting while pulling straight out. Due to the tight fit, it doesn't help to try to wiggle it loose.

PVC pipe and fittings come in one color: stark white. You may want to paint your trellis to blend in with your garden setting, but this isn't necessary. Once it becomes covered with lush plant growth, the appearance of the pipe will be much less noticeable. Exposure to sunlight somewhat dulls PVC over time, but this doesn't significantly affect its strength.

Materials ▸

2 1½" × 10' PVC pipe	Metal inside corners
2 1½" PVC 90° elbows	Deck screws 1¼", 2½"
2 1½" PVC T-fittings	Tape measure
Heavy jute or hemp twine	Cordless drill and bits
Pipe straps for 1½" PVC (4 screw type)	Hacksaw or miter saw
	Sandpaper
	Scissors or utility knife
	Eye and ear protection
	Work gloves

A raised bed box made from 2 × 6 lumber is used as the base for a sturdy built-in trellis made of PVC tubing. It's the ideal support for heavy climbing plants like beans or cucumbers.

Raised Bed with Removable Trellis

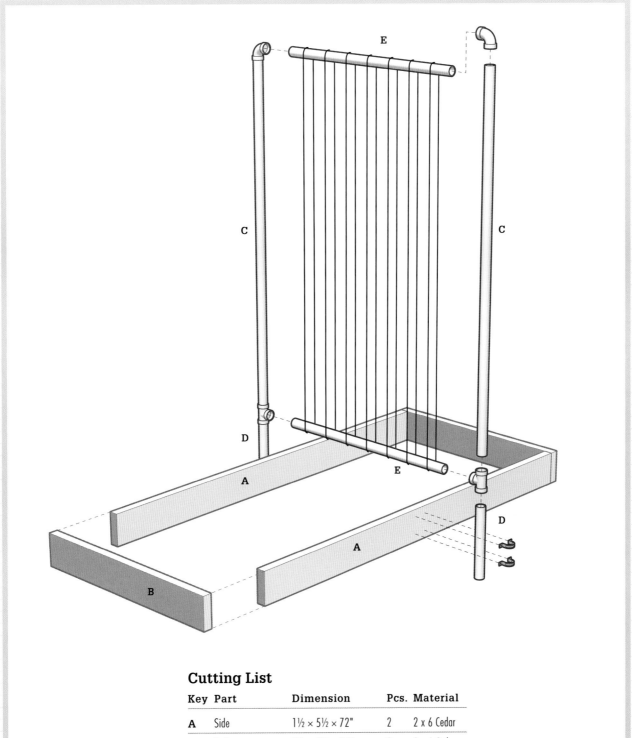

Cutting List

Key	Part	Dimension	Pcs.	Material
A	Side	1½ × 5½ × 72"	2	2 x 6 Cedar
B	End	1½ × 5½ × 36"	2	2 x 6 Cedar
C	Upper vertical	1½ × 60"	2	PVC pipe
D	Lower vertical	1½ × 12"	2	PVC pipe
E	Crosspiece	1½ × 34"	2	PVC pipe

Raised Bed with Removable Trellis

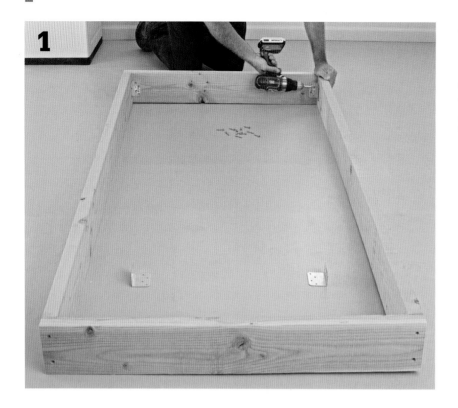

Start by assembling the raised-bed box, reinforcing the joints with metal inside corners. Add a center divider to keep the sides from spreading apart if you decide to make this project longer than 6'. Even if it is shorter, the divider is still a good precaution to help prevent warping.

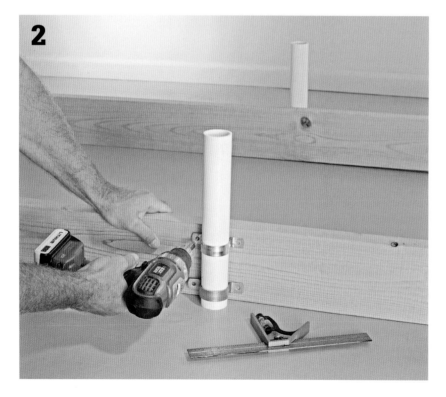

Cut 12"-long pieces of 1½" PVC tubing. Attach them to the outsides of the planter box, near the middle. Use emery paper or sandpaper to remove the burrs and smooth the cut ends of pipe. Draw a perpendicular line where the pipe will go, using a square. Strap the pieces to the outsides with two pipe straps each. Fasten one strap with two screws, but leave the other strap loose until you put the upper vertical PVC on and can check it for plumb.

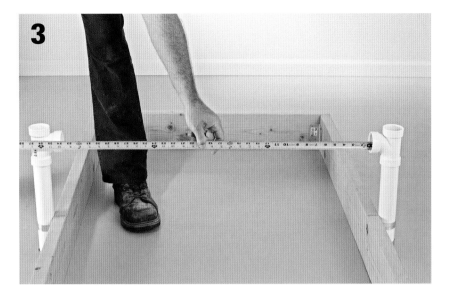

Add a T-fitting to the top end of each pipe. Measure between the hubs of the T-fittings to the insides of the sockets. Cut a piece of 1½" PVC pipe to this length and sand the cut edges smooth; this is the bottom crosspiece. Remove both Ts, fit the piece into the middle hubs of the Ts so the ends of the pipe bottom out in the fittings. Then replace the Ts.

Add the uprights and attach the top crosspiece with elbows. Ensure the pipes are plumb, then secure the bottom straps. Move the planter into your yard or garden, line it with a thick layer of old newspaper or landscape fabric, and fill it with planting medium. Tie jute or hemp twine between the crosspieces so that climbing plants have something to grab onto. When winter comes, you can disassemble the PVC and store it away until spring.

TIP: Raised Box Trellis Options
The basic design of this bed-and-trellis combination lends itself to customization. If, for instance, you want a sturdier trellis to support much heavier plants or stand up to high winds, you can swap the PVC pipes and fittings for metal plumbing pipes and fittings. Better yet, if you want to add a rustic appeal to your unit, you can use copper pipes—just seal the copper so that it doesn't contaminate your plants. The box itself can easily be fabricated from found lumber, or lumber reclaimed from construction sites (just ask the site supervisor or foreman before you go dumpster diving). The only requirement is that the wood you reuse not be treated in any way. Otherwise, free is the best price for a self-sufficient project!

Versailles Planter

Possibly the most famous gardens in the world, the gardens at King Louis XIV's Versailles palace are the birthplace of this famous rolling planter style. Reportedly created by landscape architect Andre Le Notre, the Versailles Planter was originally designed to accommodate the many orange trees that were moved in and out of the orange groves on the grounds. The planter seen here differs in several ways from the classic Versailles model, but anyone who has a historical sense of gardening will recognize the archetypal form immediately.

The classic Versailles planter is constructed from oak slats and is bound together with cast iron straps. Cast iron ball or acorn finials atop the corner posts are also present on virtually every version of the planter. Most of the planters that existed (and still exist) on the Versailles grounds today are considerably larger than the one seen here, with sides as wide as 5 feet, and as tall as 7 feet. These larger models typically have hinged corners so the sides can be removed easily to plant the tree or shrub, as well as to provide care and maintenance. The X-shaped infill on the design seen here is present in some of the Versailles models, but many others consist of unadorned vertical slats.

At 24 × 24", this historical planter can be home to small- to medium-sized ornamental or specimen trees. The trees can be planted directly into the planter or in containers that are set inside the planter. If you wish to move the plants to follow sunlight or for seasonal protection, install the casters as they are shown. Otherwise, the casters can be left out.

Not a gardener? Try building a slatted top for the planter to create a rolling storage bin that, conveniently, is roughly the same height as a patio table. Or even make a few to serve multiple purposes around your yard while maintaining a consistent design theme.

Based on a classic design originated by the landscape architect for Louis XIV's gardens at Versailles, this rolling planter can hold small fruit trees (its original purpose) or be put to use in any number of creative ways in your garden or yard.

Materials ▶

1 4 × 4" × 10 ft. cedar board	4 2 × 2" × 8 ft. treated pine boards
1 4 × 4" × 4 ft. cedar board	1 1 × 6" × 8 ft. cedar board
1 2 × 4" × 8 ft. cedar board board	4 3" casters
1 2 × 6" × 8 ft. cedar board	Deck screws
1 ¾ × 4" × 8 ft. exterior plywood	

Versailles Planter

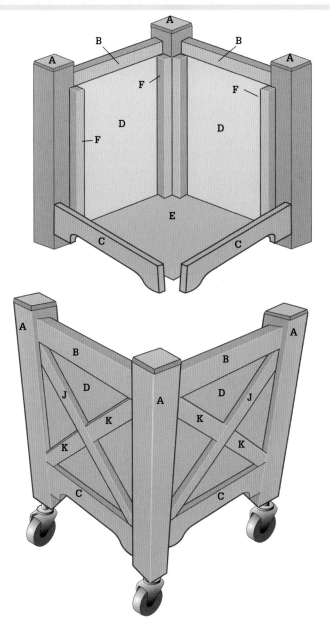

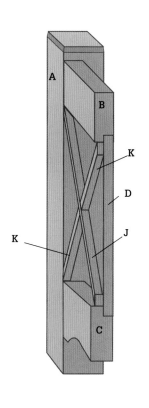

Cutting List

Key	Part	Dimension	Pcs.	Material
A	Corner posts	3½ × 3½ × 30"	4	Cedar
B	Top rails	1½ × 3½ × 17"	4	Cedar
C	Bottom rails	1½ × 5½ × 17"	4	Cedar
D	Side panels	¾ × 17 × 18½"	4	Ext. Plywood
E	Bottom panel	¾ × 17 ×17"	1	Ext. Plywood
F	Corner nailers	1½ × 1½ × 23"	8	PT pine
G	Bottom braces*	1½ × 1½ × 17⅛"	2	PT pine

Key	Part	Dimension	Pcs.	Material
H	Bottom braces*	1½ × 1½ × 14¼"	4	PT pine
I	Blocking*	1½ × 1½ × 7"	3	PT pine
J	X Legs—full	¾ × 2 × 24"	4	Cedar
K	X Legs—half	¾ × 2 × 11"	8	Cedar

*Not shown (see step 4, page 151)

Versailles Planter

MAKE THE BOX

Building the box for the Versailles Planter constitutes most of the work for this project. Start by cutting four 30"-long 4 × 4 cedar posts. Install a ¼" piloted chamfering bit in your router and chamfer all four sides of each post top to create 45° bevels (**photo 1**). You may find that this is easier if you gang all four posts together edge-to-edge and then spin them each 90° after each cut.

Cut the 2 × 2 pressure-treated corner nailers to length and attach them to the inside faces of the posts so the nailers meet at the inside corners. The bottoms of the nailers should be 4" above the post bottoms and the tops should be 3" down from the post tops. Use exterior adhesive and 3" deck screws to attach the nailers.

Prepare a 2 × 4 for the top rails and a 2 × 6 for the bottom rails by cutting a rabbet into each work piece (**photo 2**). Located on the bottom inside edge of the 2 × 4 and the top inside edge of the 2 × 6, the rabbets should be ¾" wide × ¾" deep. You can cut them with a table saw or a router. After cutting the rabbets, cut the rails to length. Lay out the profile on the bottom rails and cut with a jigsaw. Sand smooth.

Cut the side panels from ¾" exterior plywood. Create four side assemblies by attaching the panels in the rabbets on pairs of mating top and bottom rails. Use adhesive and 1¼" deck screws driven through the plywood and into the rails.

Attach the side assemblies to the 2 × 2 nailers on the inside faces of the posts. The top rails should all align 1" down from the post tops. Use adhesive and 3" deck screws driven through the nailers and into the rails. Also drive a few 1¼" deck screws through the panels and into the nailers, making sure to countersink the screwheads slightly so they can be concealed with wood putty (**photo 3**).

Flip the box so it is top-down on your work surface and then install the 2 × 2 bottom braces and blocking. It will work best if you first create the brace grid by end-screwing through the four outer braces and into the inner braces and blocking. Then, attach the four outer braces to the bottom rails with adhesive and 3" deck screws driven every 4" or so (**photo 4**). Now, cut the bottom panel to size. Drill a 1" drain hole every 6" (resulting in nine drain holes). Cut 1½" notches at the corners of the bottom panel using a jigsaw. Set the box with the top up and attach the bottom panel to the braces with adhesive and 1¼" deck screws.

Make the posts. After cutting them to length from 4 x 4 cedar, make a ¼" chamfer cut around all the tops. Gang the posts together for profiling if you like.

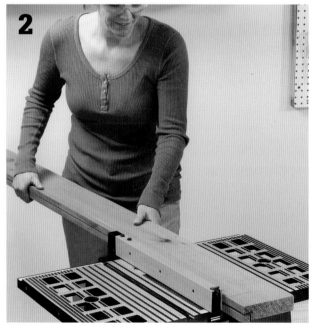

Cut panel rabbets. Make the ¾ x ¾" rabbet cuts in the rail stock using a table saw or router. The rabbets will accept the plywood side panels.

ADD DECORATIVE TOUCHES

Rip-cut an 8-foot-long cedar 1 × 6 into two 2"-wide strips using a tablesaw or circular saw and straightedge guide. Cut the legs of the Xs to length. Cut off the corners of the full-length legs on a miter saw to create arrow shapes. Install the legs between opposite corners of the side panel on the outside faces using construction adhesive and a few 1" brass brads. Cut the half-length X legs with a square end and a pointed end and attach them to the side panels, completing the X shapes **(photo 5)**.

Turn the box back upside down and install 3" exterior-rated casters at the corners of the bottom panel. Flip it onto the casters and attach cedar post cap finials (acorn-shape or round) to the tops of the posts if you wish. Or, leave the tops unadorned. Apply two or three coats of exterior trim paint to the outside of the planter and to the inside at least 6" down from the top. If you will be placing dirt directly into the planter, line it with sheet plastic first. A better idea is to plant your tree or shrub in a square pot and set the pot into the planter. *TIP: If you wish to use the planter form as a patio table, attach some cedar 1× 4 slats to a pair of 17"-long 2 × 4 stretchers and set the top (called a duckboard) onto the planter.*

Attach the side assemblies. First, drive 3" deck screws through the corner nailers and into the rails. Then, drive 1¼" deck screws through the side panels and into the nailers. Reinforce the joints with construction adhesive.

Attach the bottom braces. Assemble the braces into a square grid using adhesive and screws and then attach the whole assembly to the base rails by screwing through the four outer braces that meet the rails.

Make the X shape. The distinctive X shape on the outer surfaces of the side panels is made with 2"-wide strips of cedar that are fastened with adhesive and 1" brass brads.

Jumbo Cold Frame

A cold frame of any size works on the same principle as a greenhouse, capturing sunlight and heat while protecting plants from cold winds and frost. But when your planting needs outgrow a basic backyard cold frame with a windowsash roof, it makes sense to look to the greenhouse for more comprehensive design inspiration. This jumbo version offers over 17 square feet of planting area and combines the convenience of a cold frame with the full sun exposure of a greenhouse. Plus, there's ample height under the cold frame's canopy for growing taller plants.

The canopy pivots on hinges and can be propped all the way up or partially opened to several different positions for ventilating the interior to control temperature. The hinges can be separated just like door hinges (in fact, they are door hinges), so you can remove the canopy for the off season, if desired. Clear polycarbonate roofing panels make the canopy lightweight yet durable, while admitting up to 90 percent of the sun's UV rays (depending on the panels you choose).

The base of the cold frame is a simple rectangle made with 2 × 6 lumber. You can pick it up and set it over an existing bed of plantings, or give it a permanent home, perhaps including a foundation of bricks or patio pavers to protect the wood from ground moisture. For additional frost protection and richer soil for your seedlings, dig down a foot or so inside the cold frame and work in a thick layer of mulch. Because all sides of the canopy have clear glazing, you don't have to worry about orienting the cold frame toward the sun; as virtually all of the interior space is equally exposed to light.

Materials ▸

2 2 × 6" × 6 ft. boards	Roofing screws with EPDM washers
2 2 × 3" × 6 ft. boards	2 3½" exterior-grade butt hinges with screws
1 1 × 2" × 3 ft. board	
1 1 × 1" × 4 ft. board	2 ¼ × 4" eyebolts
1 2 × 4" × 3 ft. board	⁵⁄₁₆ × 3½" stainless steel machine bolts (2 bolts with 8 washers and 2 nuts)
Deck screws 2", 2½", 3"	
5 ½" × 10 ft. thin wall PVC pipes	
2 25 × 96" corrugated polycarbonate roofing panels	2 Heavy-duty hook-and-eye latches
	Outdoor thermometer with remote sensor (optional)
30 × 24" clear acrylic panel	

A cold frame can extend the growing season in your garden to almost—or truly—year round. Use an oversized cold frame like the one in this project and there may be no need to put up vegetables in the fall, because you'll have all the fresh produce you can handle. The hinged canopy is secured with eye hooks when closed to trap heat, but can be propped open for venting to prevent heat buildup.

Jumbo Cold Frame

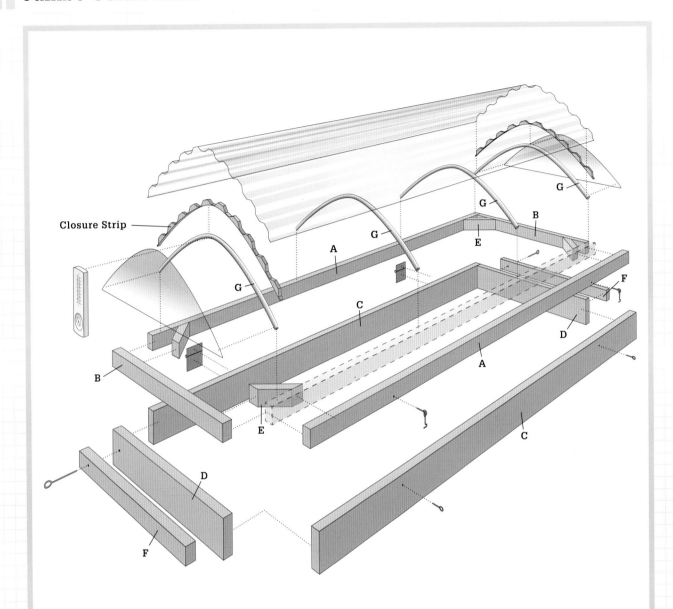

Closure Strip

Cutting List

Key	Part	Dimension	Pcs.	Material
A	Frame sides	$1\frac{1}{2} \times 2\frac{1}{2} \times 94"$	2	Cedar
B	Frame ends	$1\frac{1}{2} \times 2\frac{1}{2} \times 30"$	2	Cedar
C	Base sides	$1\frac{1}{2} \times 5\frac{1}{4} \times 94"$	2	Cedar
D	Base ends	$1\frac{1}{2} \times 5\frac{1}{4} \times 30"$	2	Cedar
E	Frame braces	$1\frac{1}{2} \times 2\frac{1}{2} \times 8"$	4	Cedar
F	Prop sticks	$\frac{3}{4} \times 1\frac{1}{2} \times 30"$	2	Cedar
G	Filler strips	$\frac{3}{4} \times \frac{3}{4} \times 37"$	2	Cedar

Jumbo Cold Frame

BUILD THE BOXES

Making the boxes for this jumbo cold frame is the easiest part of the project. The full box frame is simply a rectangle formed from butt-jointed pieces of 2 × 6.

Cut these pieces to length and then drill pilot holes and fasten the frame end pieces between the frame side pieces with 3" deck screws. Use two screws for each joint. Then, cut the canopy frame pieces to length and join them in the same fashion **(photo 1).**

Stabilize the corners of the canopy frame with 2 × 4 braces cut to 45° angles at both ends. Install the braces on-the-flat, so their top faces are flush with the tops of the canopy frame. Drill pilot holes and fasten through the braces and into the frame with one 2½" screw at each end **(photo 2).** Then, drive one more screw through the outside of the frame and into each end of the brace. Check the frame for square as you work.

MAKE THE CANOPY SUPPORT

The roof (called the canopy here) for this jumbo cold frame is made of clear corrugated plastic roof panels. The clear end caps are made of inexpensive acrylic. These parts are attached to a support framework fashioned from ½"-diameter PVC tubing. Build your framework first and then custom-make the roof and end panels to ensure a good fit all around.

Cut all the frame ribs to 37" long from ½" PVC tubing **(photo 3).** You can cut these easily with a jigsaw, miter saw, hacksaw, or a tubing cutter (a specialty plumbing tool).

Install miter-cut 2x4 braces at each corner of the canopy frame to help prevent it from racking.

Cut the ribs for the canopy support framework from ½" PVC tubing. Make sure you're using flexible PVC and not rigid Schedule 40 PVC.

Assemble the box frames with simple butt joints. The base frame and the canopy frame are rectangles of the same dimensions.

Deck screws driven partway into the top edges of the base frame are used as receptors over which the ribs are fitted.

Use the heads of 2" deck screws as receptors that you can fit the open ends of the tubing ribs onto. Drive the screws in 1" from the outside edges of the base frame and ¾" from the ends, angling the screws at about a 35 to 45° angle toward the center (**photo 4**). Leave about ¾" of the screw exposed. Drive two additional screws on opposite sides of the base frame, 32¼" from each end.

Install the PVC ribs by sliding one end securely onto the angled 2" screw, then bending the tubing until the other end fits over the opposite screw (**photo 5**). Take your time with this, and use a helper if you need. The tension from the bent PVC should be sufficient to hold the ribs in place during assembly of the canopy, but you can wrap a little duct tape around them to hold them steady if they want to spring off of the screws.

CUT THE END PANELS

The roof of the canopy is formed from corrugated plastic roof panels. These are relatively inexpensive and lightweight, which makes the cold frame portable. But they have enough structural integrity to stiffen up the canopy so there is no need to add ties or spreaders between the individual roof ribs.

When making the canopy, use your box frames and ribs to mechanically transfer the shapes and dimensions to the parts before you cut them. Start with the end panels, which can be cut from one 24 × 30" sheet of clear acrylic (sold in the size at most building centers). To mark the sheet for cutting, hold it against one end with the edge flat on the ground. Trace the curving top edge of the end PVC tubing rib onto the acrylic, using a marker (**photo 6**). Cut the clear acrylic along this cutting line with a jigsaw fitted with a plastic-cutting jigsaw blade or any fine-tooth jigsaw blade. Do not install the end panels yet.

INSTALL THE CANOPY PANELS

The framework for the raised bed canopy is sized so a pair of 25 × 96" roof panels (a standard size) will span the framework with enough overlap at the top to create a good seam.

Start installing them by attaching the bottom edge of one of the panels to the outside edge of the base frame, about an inch up from the bottom. Drill ¼" holes along the bottom edge of the panel. These guide holes for the screws need to be at least ½" down from the edge of the 2 × 3 so it will not split.

Locate the holes so they are 2½" from each end. Drill additional holes in the same line, approximately every 16". Attach one panel along the bottom edge by driving a self-sealing roofing screw at each screw guide

Flex the PVC tubing to both ends fit over opposite screws. The tubing should snap back to create tension that holds it in place.

Trace the profile of the end ribs onto a sheet of clear acrylic to create a cutting line for the end panels.

Secure the lower edge of one of the corrugated roofing panels to the base frame. Use self-sealing roofing screws (they have an EPDM rubber gasket).

hole you've drilled **(photo 7)**. *Note: To ensure that the ribs on the corrugated panels overlap snugly at the seam, install one panel first, all the way to the top, and then install the second panel starting at the top and working your way down the opposite side from the first panel.*

Mark and drill ¼" rib guide holes for the next course of screws into the roof panel, 4 to 6" up from the bottom. Locate holes for the ribs so they are 1⅛" and 33¼" from each end (four ribs total). Adjust the PVC ribs until the predrilled holes in the roof panels are centered on the ribs, then predrill each rib through the outer wall with a ⅛" bit. Fasten the panel to the two intermediate ribs **(photo 8)**.

At the ends, insert a plastic closure strip (sold by the roof panel supplier) over the end ribs to fit between the rib and the roof panel and close the voids. Hold the closure strip securely in place and predrill it and the rib wall **(photo 9)**. Attach the panel at each end and continue to secure it with screws, working toward the top.

At the top, lap the second panel over the first so the two panels fit together and make a clean seam. They should overlap so at least two of the panel ridges are covered with a double layer of roof panel. Position the second panel and trim it for width if necessary (it's okay to overlap several ridges instead of cutting). Fasten the second panel using the same screw pattern you used on the first.

ATTACH THE END PANELS

Fit the arc-shaped end panels that you've already cut into the openings at the ends of the canopy. Mark the screw locations. Place the panel on a piece of plywood and predrill screw guide holes with a ¼"-diameter bit to avoid cracking the clear acrylic, which isn't as soft or flexible as the roof panels.

Screw the panels in place with self-sealing roofing screws, hand-tightening with a screwdriver to avoid overdriving them and cracking the clear acrylic **(photo 10)**.

Drive the next course of screws through guide holes in the panel and into pilot holes in the PVC ribs.

Cut closure strips to fit at each end and then drive the screws to secure the ends of the panels. Screws should be driven only at troughs in the corrugated panels and should go through panel, closure strip, and rib wall at once.

Attach the acrylic end panels to the canopy frame. Carefully drill guide holes in the acrylic sheeting before driving screws. Use a hand screwdriver to ensure that you do not overdrive the screws and crack the acrylic.

Attach the canopy frame to the base frame with exterior-rated butt hinges.

Attaching a propping stick with multiple height settings lets you vent the cold frame if it gets too hot inside or you want the plants to benefit from a nice rainfall.

INSTALL THE CANOPY

Mount the completed canopy to the cold frame base using a pair of exterior hinges (3½" galvanized butt hinges are shown here). The canopy frame should fit flush over the base on all sides **(photo 11).** Be sure to use exterior-rated screws.

Screw in two hook-and-eye latches in front so you can secure the canopy to help keep critters out and also to hold the canopy closed tightly if the wind should pick up.

ATTACH PROP STICKS

Attach a prop stick to each end of the cold frame, securing each prop with a stainless steel bolt and nut. Insert three washers (or more if necessary) between the prop stick and the 2 × 6 base so the prop stick clears the acrylic end panel. Drill additional ⁵⁄₁₆" holes in the stick and the frame for the eyebolts, so that you can prop the canopy open at different heights **(photo 12).**

Now, prepare the ground and place the cold frame in the desired location. Anchor the base to the ground using 16" treated wood stakes or heavy-duty metal angles driven into the ground and secured to the frame.

It's called a cold frame, not a hot frame ▸

Cold frames often can work too well, capturing and retaining so much heat that it becomes too hot for the plants, even during cool weather. Adding an outdoor thermometer with a remote sensor (wired or wireless) lets you monitor the temperature inside the cold frame without having to lift the canopy. Make sure the thermometer is rated for subfreezing temperatures, since it will be exposed to the elements. Secure the sensor inside the frame as directed by the manufacturer.

Mount the readout unit to the outside of the cold frame base. As an alternative, you can use a wireless system to send a readout to a thermometer inside the house.

As a general guideline, the interior temperature of a cold frame should be no higher than 75°F for summer plants and 65°F or lower for spring and fall plants. But check the recommendations for your specific plantings.

Pagoda Lantern

Enhance your landscape with this decorative pagoda lantern. It will act as an interesting focal point within your garden by day and its glow makes it even more inviting at night. It's made from commonly available dimensional lumber—four pieces of 1 × 6 and one piece of 2 × 2. You can stain the wood to complement the surrounding landscape or you might choose to stain it or paint it to look like the Asian structures that inspired its design.

The stacked tiers of the pagoda are frames that are attached to four corner legs. Connecting four crosspieces with half-lap joints makes each frame. The top frame features similar construction to the sides and is capped with a square piece and a wood ball to create the peak. Any 2"-diameter wood ball (or even a copper ball) will work as the cap ball, but it should ideally be made from exterior-rated wood. You can also use a manufactured post cap for the cap plate and ball.

Candles illuminate this lantern. The candles are placed on a tile base and can be placed within a glass vase or hurricane lantern shade to prevent burning the wood structure.

Materials ▸

1 1½ × 1½" × 8 ft. white oak board	1 6-to 10"-dia. glass hurricane shade
4 ¾ × 5½" × 8 ft. white oak boards	2" exterior-rated screws
1 2"-dia. ball white oak or other	1½" galvanized finish nails
1 12 × 12" ceramic tile	

Big enough to make a statement but compact enough to fit just about anywhere, this oak lantern can house large outdoor candles or even a low-voltage landscape light.

Pagoda Lantern

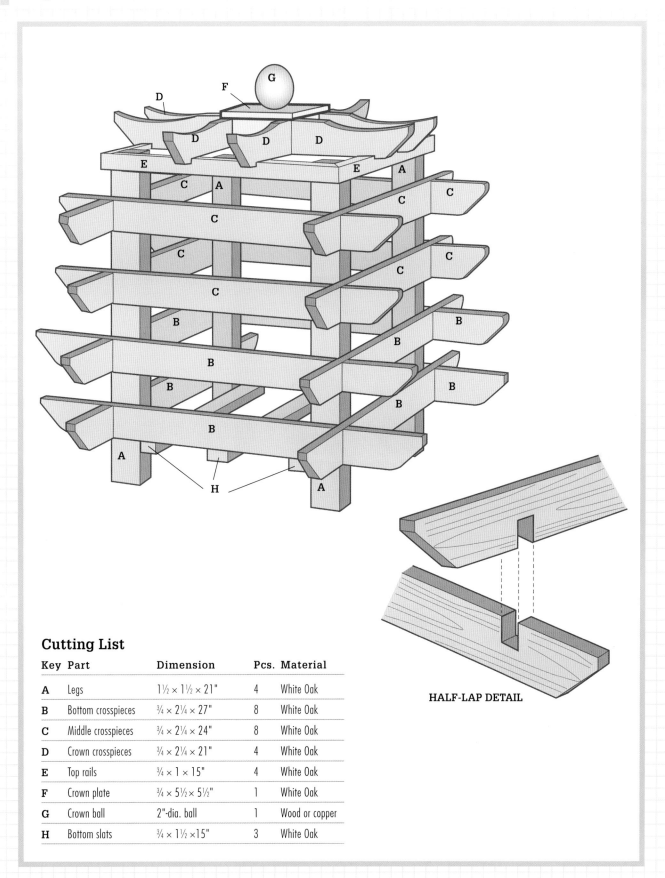

HALF-LAP DETAIL

Cutting List

Key	Part	Dimension	Pcs.	Material
A	Legs	$1\frac{1}{2} \times 1\frac{1}{2} \times 21"$	4	White Oak
B	Bottom crosspieces	$\frac{3}{4} \times 2\frac{1}{4} \times 27"$	8	White Oak
C	Middle crosspieces	$\frac{3}{4} \times 2\frac{1}{4} \times 24"$	8	White Oak
D	Crown crosspieces	$\frac{3}{4} \times 2\frac{1}{4} \times 21"$	4	White Oak
E	Top rails	$\frac{3}{4} \times 1 \times 15"$	4	White Oak
F	Crown plate	$\frac{3}{4} \times 5\frac{1}{2} \times 5\frac{1}{2}"$	1	White Oak
G	Crown ball	2"-dia. ball	1	Wood or copper
H	Bottom slats	$\frac{3}{4} \times 1\frac{1}{2} \times 15"$	3	White Oak

Pagoda Lantern

MAKE THE CROSSPIECES & TOP RAIL

If you do some careful planning and marking, the crosspieces can be cut from three 8-foot-long 1 × 6 boards. First, cut the boards to length. Cut one 1 × 6 into four 24" pieces. Then cut two 27" boards and two 21" boards from each of the other two 1 × 6s. Cut the 1 × 6 pieces in half lengthwise, leaving you with the twenty 2¼" wide crosspieces (**photo 1**).

Use a miter saw to trim the bottom corners (1¾ × 1¾") off each end of the crosspieces (**photo 2**). You can also use a table saw and miter gauge to make these cuts. The crosspieces fit together with half-lap joints in much the manner of toy building logs.

The half-lap notches are 1⅛" deep and equal to the thickness of the crosspieces (¾ to ⅞"). To lay out the notches, mark the center of the middle and bottom crosspieces and then make a mark 7½" on each side of the centerline to designate the inside edge of the notches. Mark the center of the top crosspieces and then make a mark 1¾" on each side of the centerline to designate the inside edge of the notches. Cut the notches in several crosspieces at the same time to save time and ensure consistent notch widths.

You must flip half of the crosspieces for each size upside-down so that you end up with an equal number of pieces with notch cuts on the top and on the

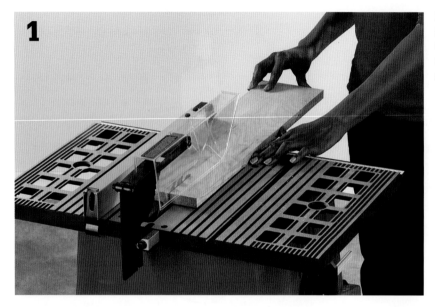

Rip-cut the stock. On a table saw (if you have access to one), rip-cut each piece of 1 × 6 stock for the crosspieces into two equal strips that are approximately 2¼" wide.

Trim the crosspiece corners. Set the miter saw to make a 45° cut and make each cut 1¾" from each end.

bottom edge. You can use a table saw, router, or circular saw to cut the half-lap notches. Use a miter gauge to guide the pieces on a table saw, making several passes to cut the full width. Use a straight-edge to guide a circular saw or router (**photo 3**).

Mark the arc profile along the top edge of the four top crosspieces. Cut along the arc line with a jigsaw or band saw.

Cut 15"-long top rail pieces to length from 1× 2 stock. Then, rip the four pieces down to 1" wide. Cut 45° miters in each end of the top rails. Mark the center of each top rail piece and then make a mark 1¾" on each side of the centerline to designate the inside edge of the notches that will hold the top crosspieces. Use the same method

you used to cut the notches in the crosspieces to cut two ¼"-deep notches in the top edge of each top rail piece (**photo 4**). Sand the faces smooth and ease the outside edges of all of the crosspieces.

BUILD THE BASE

Assemble the crosspiece frames. Apply exterior-rated glue to the notches and clamp the crosspiece frames together. Drill countersunk pilot holes through the bottom of each joint and drive a 2" screw into each joint (**photo 5**).

Cut the legs to length and then attach them to the crosspiece frames. Cut four 3"-wide spacer blocks to position the bottom frame on the legs. Apply glue to the inside faces of the crosspiece-frame corners and

Cut half-lap notches. Clamp the crosspieces together with the notch cutout marks aligned. Use several passes with a router and straight bit to remove the waste material from the notches, lowering the bit ¼" for each pass.

Scrap

Notch the top rails. Clamp the top rails together and cut two ¼"-deep notches that are the same width as the rail stock. Use a router setup with a straight bit and straightedge guide. *TIP: Position a piece of scrap the same thickness as the workpieces on each side so the router bit will enter the workpieces cleanly with no tear-out.*

clamp them to the legs. Drill one countersunk pilot hole at each corner and secure with a 2" screw.

Cut four 2"-wide spacer blocks to position each of the next three frames over the previous frame. Secure each frame to the legs with glues and 2" screws (**photo 6**). Glue and clamp the top rails to the legs and attach them with 2" screws. Attach the bottom slats to the bottom crosspiece frame with 2" screws.

BUILD THE CROWN

Apply glue to the crown crosspiece notches and clamp them together. Secure them by driving 2" screws through the bottom of the joint. Cut the crown plate to size and drill a ¼"-diameter pilot hole through the center of the crown plate and a ³⁄₁₆"-diameter × 1¼"

pilot hole in the center of the base of the ball. Position the crown ball over the center of the cap plate and attach it with a 2" screw (**photo 7**). Attach the cap plate to the top crosspiece frame with 1½" galvanized finish nails (**photo 8**). Drill a ¹⁄₁₆" pilot hole for each nail.

LIGHT YOUR LANTERN

You can apply an exterior stain to add color to the wood and help protect it from decay or you can let it age naturally. Place a 12" square tile on the bottom slats inside the base. Use one to three candles to illuminate the lantern. Place large candles inside a glass vase or hurricane shade to protect the wood parts from burning and protect the candle flame from the wind.

Pin the crosspieces together. Drill a ³⁄₁₆"-dia. x 2"-deep pilot hole in the bottom of each crosspiece joint and secure the joints with 2" screws.

Join the crosspiece frames. Use 2" spacer blocks to position each frame over the previous frame. Attach the frames to the legs with glue and 2" screws.

7

Make the crown. Attach the crown plate to the crown ball with a 2" screw.

8

Make the crowning touch. Attach the cap plate to the top crosspiece frame with galvanized finish nails. Drill a pilot hole for each nail to prevent splitting the wood.

Firewood Shelter

This handsome firewood shelter combines rustic ranch styling with ample sheltered storage that keeps firewood off the ground and obscured from sight. Clad on the sides and roof with beveled cedar lap siding, the shelter has the look and feel of a permanent structure. But because it's freestanding, you can move it around as needed. It requires no time-consuming foundation work. As long as it's loaded up with firewood it is very stable, even in high winds. But if it has high exposure to the elements and is frequently empty, secure it with a pair of wood stakes.

This firewood shelter is large enough to hold an entire face cord of firewood. (A face cord, also called a rick, is 4 feet high, 8 feet wide, and one log-length deep— typically 16".) Since the storage area is sheltered and raised to avoid ground contact and allow airflow, wood dries quickly and is ready to use when you need it. Raising the firewood above the ground also makes the woodpile a much less attractive nesting area for rodents.

Materials ▶

10 2 × 4" × 8 ft. cedar boards	8 ⅜ × 4" lag screws
5 2 × 6" × 8 ft. cedar boards	1½" spiral siding nails
10 ⅝ × 8" × 8 ft. cedar lap siding	Deck screws (2½", 3")
24 ⅜ × 3½" lag screws	Finishing materials

Stacks of firewood will stay drier and be less of an eyesore if you build this rustic firewood shelter.

Firewood Shelter

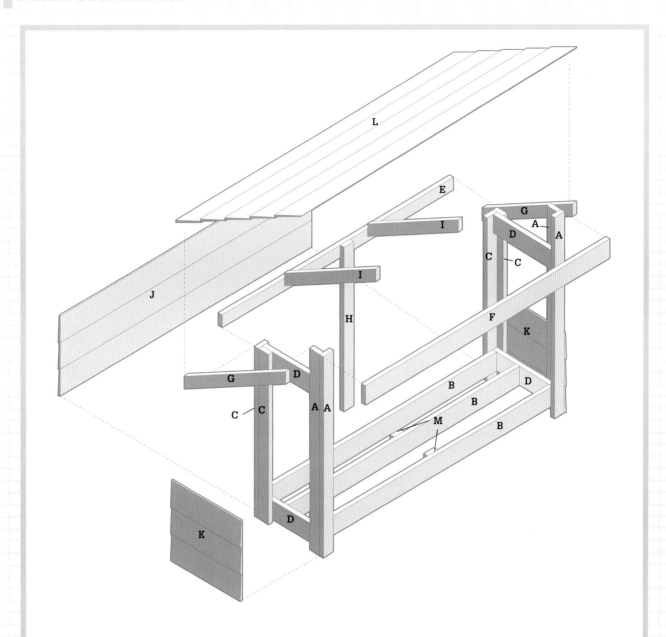

Cutting List

Key	Part	Dimension	Pcs.	Material
A	Front posts	1½ × 3½ × 59"	4	Cedar
B	Bottom rails	1½ × 5½ × 82½"	3	Cedar
C	Rear posts	1½ × 3½ × 50"	4	Cedar
D	End rails	1½ × 5½ × 21"	4	Cedar
E	Back rail	1½ × 3½ × 88½"	1	Cedar
F	Front rail	1½ × 5½ × 88½"	1	Cedar
G	Roof supports	1½ × 3½ × 33¾"	2	Cedar

Key	Part	Dimension	Pcs.	Material
H	Middle post	1½ × 3½ × 50"	1	Cedar
I	Middle supports	1½ × 3½ × 28"	2	Cedar
J	Back siding	⅝ × 8 × 88½"	3	Cedar siding
K	End siding	⅝ × 8 × 24"	6	Cedar siding
L	Roof strips	⅝ × 8 × 96"	5	Cedar siding
M	Prop	1½ × 3½ × 7½"	2	Cedar

Firewood Shelter

BUILD THE FRAME

Cut the front posts and rear posts to length. Butt the edges of the front posts together in pairs to form the corner posts. Drill ⅛"-diameter pilot holes at 8" intervals. Join the post pairs with 2½" deck screws, driven into countersunk pilot holes. Follow the same procedure to join the rear posts in pairs.

Cut the bottom rails and end rails. Assemble two bottom rails and two end rails into a rectangular frame, with the end rails covering the ends of the bottom rails. Set the third bottom rail between the end rails, centered between the other bottom rails. Mark the ends of the bottom rails on the outside faces of the end rails. Drill two ⅜"-diameter pilot holes for lag screws through the end rails at each bottom rail position—do not drill into the bottom rails. Drill a ¾"-diameter counterbore for each pilot hole, deep enough to recess the screw heads. Drill a smaller, ¼"-diameter pilot hole through each pilot hole in the end rails, into the ends of the bottom rails (**photo 1**). Drive a ⅜ × 3½" lag screw fitted with a washer at each pilot hole, using a socket wrench.

Draw reference lines across the inside faces of the corner posts, 2" up from the bottom. With the corner posts upright and about 82" apart, set 2"-high spacers next to each corner post to support the frame. Position the bottom rail frame between the corner posts, and attach the frame to the corner posts by driving two 2½" deck screws through the corner posts and into the outer faces of the bottom rails. Drill counterbored pilot holes in the sides of the corner posts. Drive a pair of ⅜ × 4" lag screws, fitted with washers, through the sides of the corner posts and into the bottom rails. The lag screws must go through the post and the end rail, and into the end of the bottom rail. Avoid hitting the lag screws that have already been driven through the end rails.

Complete the frame by installing end rails at the tops of the corner posts. Drill countersunk pilot holes in the end rails. Drive 2½" deck screws through the end rails and into the posts. Make sure the tops of the end rails are flush with the tops of the rear posts (**photo 2**).

MAKE THE ROOF FRAME

Cut the back rail, front rail, roof supports, middle post, and middle supports to length. The roof supports and middle supports are mitered at the ends. To make the miter cutting lines, mark a point 1½" in from each end,

Drill pilot holes through ¾"-dia. counterbores when preparing to drive the lag screws into the ends of the bottom rails.

Attach the end rails between the front and rear corner posts.

Miter-cut the middle supports and roof supports with a circular saw or with a power miter saw.

Attach the front rail by driving screws through the outer roof supports, making sure the top of the rail is flush with the tops of the supports.

Attach the middle roof supports by driving screws through the front and back rails.

Attach the roof strips with siding nails, starting at the back edge and working your way forward.

along the edge of the board. Draw diagonal lines from each point to the opposing corner. Cut along the lines with a circular saw (**photo 3**) or power miter saw.

Drill countersunk pilot holes in the back rail. Use 3" deck screws to fasten the back rail to the backs of the rear corner posts, flush with their tops and sides. Use the same procedure to fasten a roof support to the outsides of the corner posts. Make sure the top of each support is flush with the high point of each post end. The supports should overhang the posts equally in the front and rear.

Drill countersunk pilot holes in the roof supports and drive deck screws to attach the front rail between the roof supports (**photo 4**). The top of the rail should be flush with the tops of the roof supports. Attach the middle supports between the front rail and back rail, 30" in from each rail end. Drive 3" deck screws through the front and back rails into the ends of the middle supports (**photo 5**). Use a pipe clamp to hold the supports in place as you attach them.

Drill countersunk pilot holes in the middle post. Position the middle post so it fits against the outside of the rear bottom rail and the inside of the top back rail. Make sure the middle post is perpendicular and

extends past the bottom rail by 2". Attach it with 2½" deck screws. Cut a pair of props to length. Attach them to the front two bottom rails, aligned with the middle post. Make sure the tops of the props are flush with the tops of the bottom rails.

ATTACH SIDING & ROOF

Cut pieces of 8"-wide beveled cedar lap siding to length to make the siding strips and the roof strips. Starting 2" up from the bottoms of the rear posts, fasten the back siding strips with two 1½" siding nails driven through each strip and into the posts, near the top and bottom edge of the strip. Work your way up, overlapping each piece of siding by ½", making sure the thicker edges of the siding face down. Attach the end siding to the corner posts, with the seams aligned with the seams in the back siding.

Attach the roof strips to the roof supports, starting at the back edge. Drive two nails into each roof support. Make sure the wide edge of the siding faces down. Attach the rest of the roof strips, overlapping the strip below by about ½" (**photo 6**), until you reach the front edges of the roof supports. You can leave the cedar wood untreated or apply an exterior wood stain to keep it from turning gray as it weathers.

Sheltered Swing

If enjoying an outdoor swing creates a picture in your head of a pleasant, lazy sunny afternoon, you're only seeing half of the picture. The relaxing ritual of passing a long weekend afternoon on a garden swing doesn't need to be limited to bright and sunny days. With this covered unit, you can enjoy the swing in all seasons. You may even find that you look forward to swingin' in the rain.

Sure, you could pick up a canopied glider from the local home center, but be prepared to work on it regularly. Store-bought gliders require regular maintenance and, more importantly, they often look and feel rather cheap. They are no competition for a nicely designed, solidly constructed unit like the one described here. Not only will this swing last a good long time and provide many, many hours of enjoyment, it also provides a handsome addition to your landscape. It can, in fact, even be a centerpiece in your yard or garden.

Set aside a full weekend for building this project. Although the techniques we've used are meant to simplify things for the home craftsman, the project is still fairly involved. Take your time and pay attention to precise measurements and keeping things plumb; a rickety or off-kilter end product will suck the fun out of the experience of a leisurely swing. It will also be a big boon to have a helper on the project—some of

the pieces are fairly large, heavy, and unwieldy. And besides, it will be nice to have company on the swing once it's built! (Do not exceed two people on swing). The only modification you may need to make to the plan is to match the distance between the eyebolts in the stand to the dimension between your porch swing's hanging chains or ropes.

Materials ▸

15	2 × 6" × 8 ft. cedar boards
2	2 × 8" × 10 ft. cedar boards
5	2 × 6" × 8 ft. cedar boards
3	2 × 4" × 10 ft. cedar boards
30	½ × 4" × 8 ft. cedar lap siding
14	2 × 4" × 6 ft. cedar boards
1	2 × 4" × 12 ft. cedar board
1	2 × 6" × 6 ft. cedar board
2	½ × 8" stainless steel eye bolts with washers and locknuts
4	Post-and-beam connectors
10	Rafter ties
30 ft. rope or chain
4	½ × 4" eye bolts or chromed bow eyes (for swing)

Using rope to hang the swing is trickier than using chain but the rope has a more natural quality that supports the overall design of the structure.

Sheltered Swing

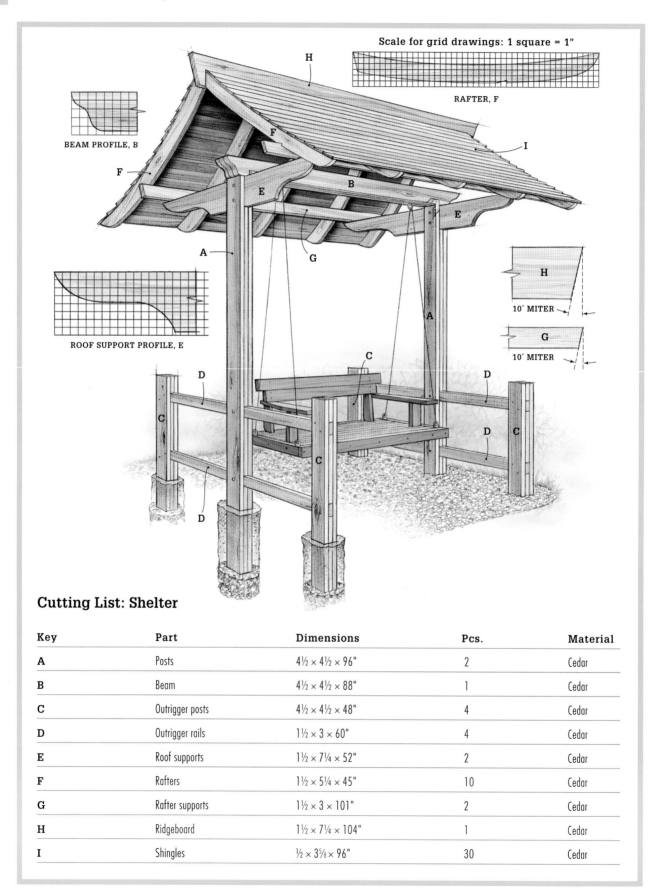

Scale for grid drawings: 1 square = 1"

RAFTER, F

BEAM PROFILE, B

ROOF SUPPORT PROFILE, E

10° MITER

10° MITER

Cutting List: Shelter

Key	Part	Dimensions	Pcs.	Material
A	Posts	4½ × 4½ × 96"	2	Cedar
B	Beam	4½ × 4½ × 88"	1	Cedar
C	Outrigger posts	4½ × 4½ × 48"	4	Cedar
D	Outrigger rails	1½ × 3 × 60"	4	Cedar
E	Roof supports	1½ × 7¼ × 52"	2	Cedar
F	Rafters	1½ × 5¼ × 45"	10	Cedar
G	Rafter supports	1½ × 3 × 101"	2	Cedar
H	Ridgeboard	1½ × 7¼ × 104"	1	Cedar
I	Shingles	½ × 3⅝ × 96"	30	Cedar

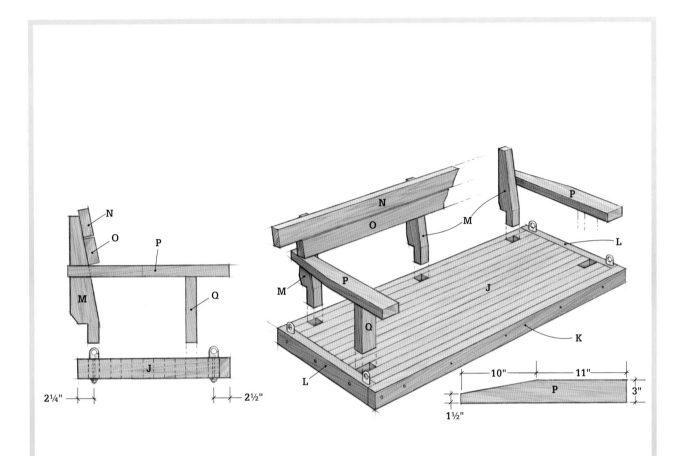

2¼" 2½"

10" 11"
1½" 3"

Cutting List: Swing

Key	Part	Dimensions	Pcs.	Material
J	Seat slats	1½ × 2¾ × 51"	13	Cedar
K	Seat frame front	1½ × 2¾ × 54"	1	Cedar
L	Seat frame sides	1½ × 2¾ × 19½"	2	Cedar
M	Back supports	1½ × 5¼ × 17¾"	3	Cedar
N	Back rail (long)	1½ × 3½ × 54"	1	Cedar
O	Back rail (short)	1½ × 3½ × 50"	1	Cedar
P	Armrests	1½ × 3 × 21"	2	Cedar
Q	Armrest supports	1½ × 2¾ × 12¾"	2	Cedar

Sheltered Swing

SHELTERED SWING DESIGN

When designing a sheltered swing, you want to make the swing roomy enough for two, but not so big that it needs a shelter the size of a two-car garage. Begin planning with the swing. For two adults, you'll want a seating area that's at least 48" wide and 18 to 21" deep. If your swing will have armrests (something we highly recommend), make the seat at least 54" wide. Allow at least 6" of clearance between the swing ends and the shelter posts so the swing won't crash into the posts if it veers to one side.

To protect against head banging, build the shelter so that the lowest horizontal elements (the roof supports in this plan) are at least as high as a standard doorway (80"). If you incorporate a pitched roof into the design, the height of the roof ridge will be 8 or 9 feet. To provide full protection of the swinging area, the roof should span at least 72" from front to back (this design has an 80" span).

MAKE THE SEAT PLATFORM

The success of the design hinges on the beefiness of the 2 × 4 platform. The effect is mostly visual, but the heaviness of the platform also contributes to a rocking motion that's more like a pendulum than a schoolyard swing. Start by cutting thirteen 52"-long 2 × 4s for the seat slats. Cut the front and the side frame pieces slightly long. Using a table saw or jointer, trim ¼" from each edge to reduce the width and remove the bullnose profiles.

If you have access to a planer, face-glue the seat slats in sections that fit into the tool. Be sure to plan for the faux mortises when laying out lumber for gluing (see the drawing on page 171). To join the seat slats, apply exterior-rated glue to the mating faces (**photo 1**), reinforcing each joint by driving a deck screw (centered top to bottom, predrilled and countersunk) every 12". Because of the screws, you don't need clamps.

After the glue dries, run both faces of each seat section through the planer to reduce the pieces to the final thickness (2¾") (**photo 2**). Also plane the 2 × 4 stock for the platform frame and the armrests. After planing, glue and clamp the two seat platform sections together, adding wood cauls above and below the glue-up to align the parts. Trim the platform to 51" wide. Attach the frame sides and the frame front using glue and counterbored deck screws (**photo 3**).

Prepare the seat slats for gluing by trimming off the bullnose edges of the 2 × 4 stock and spreading an even layer of exterior-rated wood glue onto one face in each face-glued joint.

Glue the seat platform in two sections that are narrow enough to fit in a planer; then plane the sections (and the stock for the armrests) to the final thickness.

Attach the front and side seat frames with glue and counterbored deck screws. Cut plugs to fit the counterbores when the swing is completed.

Cut the back supports from 2 × 6 stock using a jigsaw, and fit them into the faux mortises created in the back seat slat. Once they fit snugly, glue them and reinforce each joint with a deck screw.

Once you've built the swing, glue wood plugs into the counterbores and trim them flush. Then sand and apply finish if desired. (The swing shown was finished with medium-dark, semi-opaque wood stain.)

Laminate two sets of 8-ft. 2 × 6s to make the main posts. Use plenty of glue and clamps with clamp pads. The mortises should be about ⅛" longer than the width of the parts they'll house.

BACKREST & ARMRESTS

When paired with a flat seat, a backrest should slant backward 5 to 10°.

You can create backrest supports that form a square connection with the platform but also have an integral slope. We made the back supports from tight-grain 2 × 6 stock, which allowed us to cut an angled part thick enough for good support. Use the grid drawing on page 170 as a guide, and cut three backrest supports **(photo 4).**

Test the fit, then glue the 1½ × 1½" tenons at the bottom of each support into the mortises at the back of the seat platform. Drive a deck screw through a predrilled and counterbored pilot hole in the back slat to reinforce each support.

Install the armrest supports; then cut and attach the armrests with glue and two countersunk screws driven into the tops of the armrest supports and the outside faces of the outer backrest support. The armrests should be parallel to the seat platform and flush with the back edges of the backrest supports.

Finally, cut and install the backrest boards. Rest the back lower edge of the bottom board on the armrests. Fill all counterbores with wood plugs, trim them flush **(photo 5),** and then sand the swing.

MAKE THE SHELTER PARTS

This swing shelter is best built in the workshop and assembled on site. The major structural parts of the shelter are made from three layers of 2 × 6 stock. Laminated posts and beams are straighter and stronger than dimensional 6 × 6 cedar.

You'll use the same basic joinery strategy as with the swing, leaving out sections of the middle 2 × 6 to create through-mortises for the rails that join the posts to the outrigger posts. The outriggers provide stability and visual balance; without them, the structure would be top-heavy and unstable.

The main posts are 8 feet long; the bottom 18" is intended to be set in concrete below grade. The outrigger posts are designed to be 4 feet long with 12" below grade so that you can cut two posts from an 8-foot board.

If you go by the nominal dimensions, sandwiching three 2 × 6s should yield a 6 × 6 post. But because the actual dimensions of a 2 × 6 are 1½ × 5¼", you'll end up with a 4½ × 5¼" post. That's not necessarily a problem, but we trimmed ¾" off the width of each member so the posts and beam were square. Not only do they look better this way, but squaring them gave us the flexibility to orient the edges and faces as we preferred. Lay out and glue the post assemblies, using plenty of clamps and clamping pads to protect the wood **(photo 6).** After the glue dries, remove the clamps and run a belt sander across the glued edges. Cut the end profiles individually on the beam members. After gluing you'll probably need to smooth the profiles with a rasp or sander.

Make a rafter template from plywood, using the drawings on page 170 as a guide. Sand the edges smooth. Trace the template onto each piece of stock (**photo 7**) and cut out the rafters one at a time with a jigsaw. Smooth the cut edges (**photo 8**).

Also trace an end profile (see drawing, page 170) onto the ends of the 2 × 8 roof supports. Cut one support with a jigsaw, smooth the cut, and then trace it onto the other workpiece for cutting. Make 10° miter cuts at the ends of the rafter supports and ridgeboard.

ASSEMBLE THE SHELTER

You can use many strategies to assemble a large (but not too large) outdoor structure that's set in concrete. You can lay out and dig postholes, set the posts, and then build the structure directly on the posts, adjusting as needed. Or do as we did and pre-assemble the main structural elements so you can use the structure to establish the posthole layout.

Insert the upper and lower outrigger rails into the mortises in one main post, and insert the free ends into the mating mortises in the outrigger posts (**photo 9**). Pin these joints temporarily with screws but do not glue them. Make both post assemblies.

Lay each assembly on sawhorses and insert a roof support into the notch at the top of each main post. Use a framing square to make sure the post and support are perpendicular and then drill a pair of guide holes for ½ × 4½", hot-dipped galvanized or stainless steel carriage bolts in the center of the joint. Drill ½"-deep × 1"-diameter counterbores for a washer and nut to accompany each fastener. Also drill a counterbored guide hole through the center of each railing/main post joint and install carriage bolts at all locations (**photo 10**). Secure the railing joints at the outrigger posts by driving a pair of countersunk 3½" deck screws in both sides.

Temporarily erect both post assemblies on site. (Because the main posts are 6" longer than the outrigger posts on the bottom, dig 6 × 6" holes spaced 75" on center for both main posts.)

Make a plywood template of the rafter shape using the drawing as a guide. Trace the shape onto 45" long 2 × 6 workpieces to outline the 10 rafters.

Cut out the rafters using a jigsaw, then smooth the edges. The microplane rotary shaper drill press attachment used here minimizes sawdust and cuts cedar quickly.

Join the main posts to pairs of outrigger posts by inserting the rails through the mortises. Center the main post on the rails. Pin joints temporarily with deck screws. (Do not glue them.)

Center a roof support in the top notch in each main post and fasten with a pair of carriage bolts. Washers and nuts should be installed in counterbored holes.

Temporarily set up the post-and-beam structure near the installation site, tacking the joints. Square the joint on one side and install post-and-beam connectors; then square and fasten the other side.

Brace the posts temporarily with a 2 × 4 and carry the structure to the installation site. Choose the perfect spot and then mark the post locations on the ground.

Set the post-and-beam structure into the holes and adjust its position so it is level and plumb. Fill the holes with concrete, crowning the tops to prevent puddling. Let the concrete cure.

With the assistance of helpers, position the beam on the main posts so it overhangs each post by 4½" at the top edge. Check that the edges are flush, then tack the beam to each post. Make sure the overhang is correct and the beam is perpendicular to the post on one of the assemblies. Secure this joint with a metal post connector. Attach a connector to each side of the post; then adjust and secure the other post/beam connection **(photo 11).** Clamp a 2 × 4 brace between the posts, near the bottom.

With a helper, carry the structure to the installation site and position it. Mark the locations of all six posts **(photo 12),** and move the structure out of the way. Dig 6"-diameter × 16"-deep postholes for

the outriggers and 6"-diameter × 22"-deep holes for the main posts. Carve a bell shape into the bottom of each hole and add 4" of gravel for drainage. Set the structure into the postholes.

Place a level on the beam. If one end is lower, drive a wood stake next to the outrigger rail on the low end, raise that end to level, and screw or clamp the rail to the stake. Also check each top outrigger rail with a level. If one end is lower, raise it by hand and backfill with gravel. Fill the postholes with concrete **(photo 13).**

Work the concrete into each hole with a stick or shovel to eliminate voids. Crown the concrete slightly above grade to prevent water from puddling. Let the concrete set overnight.

INSTALL THE ROOF

Lay the ridgeboard on sawhorses, and attach the rafters with deck screws driven through pilot holes **(photo 14)**. The end rafters should be 5" from the ends of the ridgeboard (top edge). Space the three intermediate rafters evenly—the ends should align where they meet at the ridgeboard. Carefully turn the rafter assembly upside down and attach the rafter supports so they fit into the bird's-mouths on the rafters **(photo 15)**.

Next, install the roof covering. We used 8-foot strips of ½ × 4" beveled lap siding. Let the strips overhang the ends and eaves by ½". Starting at an eave, drive a 1³⁄₈" narrow-crown staple near the top of each strip and into each rafter. Overlap strips by ½" as you work up the roof, concealing the staples **(photo 16)**.

You may need to trim the last strip to width when you reach the ridge.

With a helper, lift the roof onto the roof supports **(photo 17)**, center it, and then drive deck screws through pilot holes in the rafter supports and into the roof supports.

Install rafter hangers at the roof supports and each rafter. (You'll need to trim each hanger slightly with metal snips first.)

Attach the rafters to the ridgeboard with deck screws driven into pilot holes. The bottoms of the rafters should be flush with the bottom of the ridgeboard.

Fit the rafter supports into the bird's-mouth cutouts, and attach the supports to the rafters with deck screws. (A wood pallet makes a perfect holder for the inverted ridgeboard.)

FINISHING UP

The swing itself is finished with dark, semi-opaque deck stain. A coat of lighter-tone deck stain is brushed onto the shelter structure to bring out the richness of the cedar. The differences in tone are subtle, but appealing.

Use stainless steel eye bolts (½ × 3") or marine-style chromed bow eyes to hang the swing seat, along with 30 feet of ⅜" braided marine rope. Attach the eyebolts or bow eyes to the side frames of the seat bench. Position them so they're aligned with the backrest supports and about 2½" from the front of the seat platform.

Install ½ × 8" eyebolts in the beam, spacing them the same distance apart as the rope guides (52" OC). Secure each with a lock washer and nut.

Trying to hang the swing with ropes is more difficult than hanging it with chains. But rope has a softer, more natural feel that harmonizes with the rest of the project. Whether you use rope or chain, cant the swing backward slightly for ease of swinging and greater comfort.

As a final accent (and to simplify mowing), lay down landscape fabric and a layer of washed pond gravel beneath the swing. The gravel prevents anyone from getting their feet muddy when they're swinging.

Attach the shingles (in this case, narrow cedar lap siding strips) to the rafters with 1⅜" narrow-crown staples. Start at the bottom and overlap to conceal the staples.

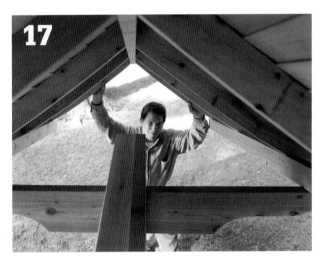

With a helper, raise the roof structure onto the post-and-beam structure, position it, and then secure it with deck screws. Reinforce the connection with rafter ties at the rafter/ridgeboard joints.

Four-post Patio Pergola

Creating shade can be a challenge, especially around hard surfaces like this concrete patio. Awnings and sun sails and patio umbrellas can provide temporary solutions, but wind and the elements can diminish your enjoyment or even lead to minor disasters. If your outdoor living area is overly exposed to sun or wind, a pergola might be just the solution you need.

The four-post patio pergola shown here will withstand just about anything nature can throw at it, plus it adds warmth and architectural interest to a fairly plain setting.

The pergola is typically understood as a freestanding, four-post structure supporting an arbor-type canopy and often used to train vining plants. The elements are simple: posts bases (metal or concrete), four wood posts, joists and corbels that support a series of wood rafters running perpendicular the joists; and often it is capped with thinner purlins running across the rafters to provide shade, trellising and visual interest.

In traditional construction, the structural members of the pergola are fastened together with heavy lag screws, usually countersunk to minimize their visibility. However, as design standards have come to embrace a more industrial aesthetic in recent years, many homeowners may appreciate the unique visual appeal of using exposed hardware. The hardware system we chose to use for this pergola is from a relatively new line called "Outdoor Accents®," manufactured and sold by joist-hanger giant Simpson Strong-Tie (See Resources, page 205). The powder-coat black bases, caps, hangers and fasteners have a very dramatic presence in the final design. But even though they look like they are fastened with typical heavy-duty lag screws, the beefy hex heads you see are actually washers for the primary fasteners: exterior wood screws that do not require pilot holes and can be driven easily by any drill/driver or impact driver, eliminating at least a couple of steps.

You can build your pergola from any exterior-rated lumber. Cedar is a traditional and excellent choice, although its availability is limited in some areas and market prices can be relatively volatile. Treated pine with a relatively contiguous cedar coloration was used

Materials ▸

18	2 × 2 × 8 ft. for purlins	28	rafter ties
6	4 × 4 × 8 ft. for posts and corbels	77	3" exterior wood screws
4	2 × 8 × 12 for joists		5½" wood screws with washers
7	2 × 10 × 12 for rafters		3½" wood screws with washers
4	post base hardware		
4	post anchors		

*As shown:
Base= 7 ft. 7½" wide × 9 ft. 7½" deep
Height: 8 ft. 9½"

in this project, in part because it does not require the application of any stain or wood protection, although you certainly can apply it if you wish. Containers of climbing plants such as clematis or ivy or Virginia Creeper can be positioned at the bases of the posts, or you may choose to plant another vining plants—the homeowner where this structure was built intends to plant it with Cascade Hops.

BEFORE

This decorative hardware from Simpson Strong-Tie's Outdoor Accents line is intended to be seen. It includes post bases with standoff plates, rafter ties, exterior lumber screws and washers that create the appearance of heavy-duty hex heads.

Four-post Patio Pergola

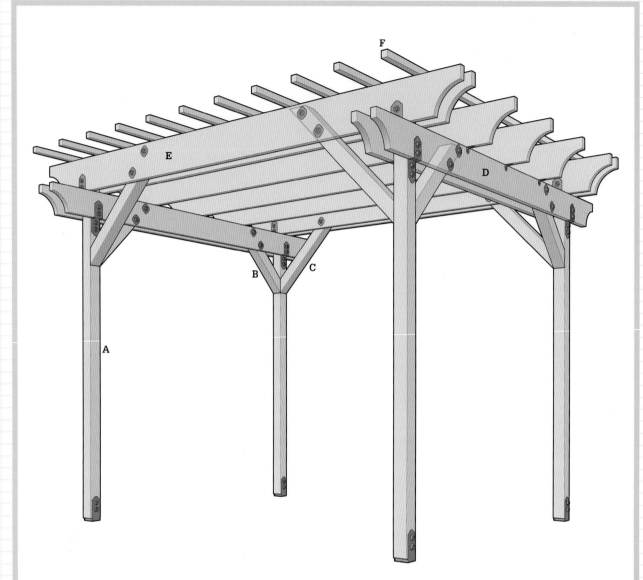

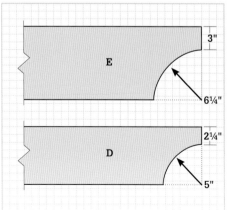

Cutting List

Key	Part	Dimension	Pcs.	Material
A	Posts	3½ × 3½ × 104"	4	Ext. Lumber
B	Corbel-front/back	3½ × 3½ × 30"	4	Ext. Lumber
C	Corbel-side	3½ × 3½ × 43⁷⁄₁₆"	4	Ext. Lumber
D	Joist	1½ × 7¼ × 120"	4	Ext. Lumber
E	Rafter	1½ × 9¼ × 120"	7	Ext. Lumber
F	Purlin	1½ × 1½ × 120"	11	Ext. Lumber

PREPARATIONS

Whether the project is a fence, a deck, an arbors or any other large outdoor structure, you have two basic construction strategies to choose from. First, and more traditionally, you can take painstaking measurements and create a precise layout and then stick-build the project piece by piece assembling as you go. Or you can choose a more mechanical approach where the project itself informs the exact location. This is done by building your project in sections and then using the actual assembled sections a guidance for positioning. The latter approach is what you will see here. Because a pergola is basically two pairs of posts joined on top by rafters and joists, we built the two end post pairs with joists first and used the actual parts to define where the post saddles would go. This is an especially good idea when you are drilling holes in a concrete patio for post anchors and thus have only a very limited about of flexibility to make adjustments. Once the pairs of posts are anchored it is relatively easy to connect them with rafters, and you are virtually finished.

Using this construction strategy does not mean you should not have a good working plan. In fact, in many cases you may need such a plant to obtain a building permit. The plan we used was based on one published by Simpson Strong-Tie, manufacturer of the custom hardware we used. You can download a free copy of this and other outdoor building plans from the ri website (See Resources, page 205).

If you are building your pergola with post set in sand or concrete, you'lll need to dig down at least 24 inches to set the posts. In such cases be sure to contact your local utility company to check and make sure there are no gas, water or electrics lines in the building area. You can call 811 to arrange for a free on-site visit and inspection.

BUILD THE END-POST PAIRS

Select two 4 × 4 posts and one 2 × 10 joist and cut them to length. Also cut the curved end profiles on the joist (**photo 1**). Break the cut edges with a sander (**photo 2**). Lay the posts parallel on a flat surface then position the joist across the tops of the posts. Check to make sure everything is square and the overhangs are correct and even, and then tack the joist to the posts with a couple of deck screws driven at each joint. Then, move the assembly to the building area with the post tops roughly where you want the post bottoms to be anchored in the post bases. Set post base hardware next to the post tops (the tops will give you more accurate post spacing because of the proximity to the crosspiece). Mark the post base locations onto the concrete (**photo 3**) and then remove the assembly. Now that the posts no longer need to be flush on the surface for accurate marking, you can tack the second joist to the posts to stiffen the assembly (**photo 4**).

Use a cutoff piece of the correct width board for each part (the rafters are wider than the joists) and plot the end profile according to the diagram on page 180. Cut the profiles on the cutoff pieces with a jig saw to make templates.

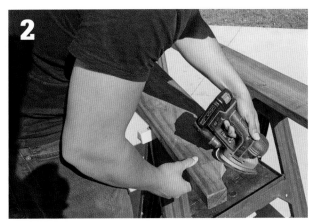

Smooth the cut end profile with a sander and break the edges of the cuts into a slight bevel to help prevent splintering.

INSTALL THE UNDERCARRIAGE

Position the post base hardware according to your marked lines on the surface and trace a drilling point for the anchors. You have multiple options for this: one traditional way is to drill a hole in the concrete for the threaded anchor and then set the anchor into exterior-rate two part epoxy that is injected into the guide hole with a syringe. Another option is to use an expandable masonry anchor: these threaded anchors are flanged so when they are driven into the guide hole they expand and make a compression joint much like wall anchors do. Because it is faster and cleaner we chose this method. Drill the guide holes with a drill (preferably a corded hammer drill and a masonry bit) according to the diameter and depth recommended (**photo 5**). Because the concrete slab drilled into her is 4" thick we used 3-½", ⅝"-dia. anchors you don't want to drill all the way through the slab. The guide hole was drilled to 3" deep so the top of the anchor would extend ½" above the surface. Position the

Lay a post/joist assembly in position on the surface and set post base hardware flush against the post ends. Trace the post base location onto the surface.

Tack the mating joist in position on the opposite sides of the posts from the first joist, using deck screws.

Drill guide holes for the post base anchors using a hammer drill and masonry bit.

After driving the anchor bolt into the guide hole, fasten down the pedestal bases for the first end post pair assembly. Install the post standoff platforms.

post base hardware onto each anchor and then add a washer and nut and tighten the nut with a ratchet or impact driver **(photo 6)**.

With both anchors installed and aligned, set the offset pedestal into each saddle to protect the nut and keep the post ends from having ground contact. Set your joist-and-post assembly into the post bases (a helper is a good idea here) and check for plumb with a level **(photo 7)**. Secure the posts in the post bases with the recommended fasteners **(photo 8)**.

Erect the end post assembly in the post bases, checking with a level to make sure the posts are plumb. Tack the posts temporarily to the bases with deck screws.

Drive the post base fasteners through the base saddles and into the post. Keep them slightly loose so you can still adjust the assembly later.

Install all fasteners for both posts a little loose so you can doublecheck the assembly for plumb and level **(photo 9)** before fully installing the fasteners. Install the post-to-joist hardware to secure the connections **(photo 10)**. Attach the other post-and-joist assembly, measuring and testing for square to make sure it is positioned correctly relative to the first pair.

Double check that the posts are plumb and the joists are level.

Attach the finished hardware for permanently connecting the joists and posts.

INSTALL THE RAFTERS AND PURLINS

With both base/end assemblies secured, cut a rafter to length and Create the end profiles (**photo 1 and 2**). Lay the cut rafter across the joist tops, pressed against the outsides of the posts. Adjust the overhangs at both ends and check for square. Tack the rafter to the posts with deck screws (**photo 11**). Install a rater the same way on the other side and tack it in place. Your

With both post assemblies secured, position and tack and outer rafter at each corner.

Finish driving the final fasteners at all post bases and check again for plumb and square.

structure should now be square and in final position. Finish tightening any fasteners that you left a little loose (**photo 12**) and attach the remaining outer rafter hardware (**photo 13**).

To add visual interest and prevent racking, 4 × 4 corbels are added to each post/rafter joint. The easiest way to get them exactly right is to cut some 4 × 4 stock slightly overlong and clamp it into position.

Attach the finished rafter hardware to the outer rafter at each corner.

Clamp 4 x 4 stock across the corbel locations at each corner and transfer cutting lines where they cross the rafter tops.

Trace the cutoff lines where they join the rafter tops and inside post edge (**photo 14**) then remove the stock and make the angled cuts (**photo 15**). Tack the corbels in place (**photo 16**) and then secure them with the finished hardware (**photo 17**). Cut and install the rest of the rafters, using metal rafter ties at each joint (**photo 18**). Finally, cut the 2 × 2 purlins to length and screw them down to the rafter tops, working from above. Apply a UV-resistant finish if desired.

Remove the corbel stuck and make the angled cuts with a power miter saw.

Make the angled cuts where the corbels meet the posts and then tack into position with deck screws.

When all the corbels are cut, aligned and tacked into place, attach the final hardware.

Install the remaining rafters, using L-brackets to reinforce the joints.

Attach the purlins to the rafter tops with exterior screws driven from above.

SPECIAL SECTION: Garden Bridges

Whether incorporated as a decorative feature, a functional asset, or a combination, a garden bridge is an alluring landscape addition. Depending on the design, a small footbridge can be an easy project; but no matter how much work you put into it, a garden bridge usually has big visual impact. That's because these structures call to us like no other element in a landscape. A bridge beckons to be crossed. Our curiosity naturally wants to know what's on the other side, and the view from the bridge itself is a tempting draw. But that subtle magic aside, you'll want a bridge that appeals to your sense of design so that you get the most bang for your lumberyard buck.

Next to the design, the secret to any garden bridge is placement. It might actually cross a barrier such as a waterway, or it may just be placed to connect a patch of grass with a pathway; regardless, the bridge embodies a sense of mystery and an invitation to explore further. The pages that follow describe several ways to use and place garden bridges—including how to create the appearance of an obstacle that needs bridging.

The style of the bridge you choose should relate to the style of your home, the landscape aesthetic you've chosen, and your own personal tastes. In designing the bridge, size it appropriately for the space you have and to keep it in proportion to other garden structures. But no matter what style or design you choose, this much is true—the garden bridge is one of the most unique and appealing structures you can add to your yard.

Garden bridges can be broken down into three structural systems: (A) The undercarriage—beams, spreaders, and sometimes deck-support ledges; (B) the decking; and (C) the posts and rails.

DESIGNING THE BRIDGE

The terrain and contours of your yard can dictate the characteristics and scale of your bridge. But rough standards exist: Typical garden bridge sizes range from 28 to 60" wide and from 4 to 12 feet long. If you are unrestricted by terrain, consider building a garden bridge that's 36 to 48" wide and 8 to 12 feet long. A structure of this size has adequate mass for a strong presence but is still portable and inexpensive to construct. Peak deck elevation seldom exceeds 18 to 24".

The appearance of a bridge should be based on aesthetic preferences and the overall style of your house and yard. Most bridge designs conform to one of these styles: Oriental, Victorian, contemporary, or rustic.

- *Oriental* is the most traditional bridge style, mainly because the basic form of the decorative garden bridge (called the "Edo" bridge) originated in ancient Japan. Bridges styled in this manner tend to be spare and elegant.
- *Victorian* bridges are fancy, with lavish fretwork and gingerbread. Often painted, they succeed best in country-style settings or where the home itself is from the Victorian era.
- *Contemporary* bridges tend to extol a prominent engineering feature. Metal and other non-wood materials are most likely to be used for contemporary garden bridges. Informal in appearance, they command attention by making a design statement.
- *Rustic* bridges are made from timbers, rough-sawn lumber and even tree trunks or limbs. They are of heavier proportions and do not feature sophisticated joinery or detailing.

Along with the design style, consider the type of bridge that suits your situation: flat, arched, low-arched, or angled-platform (see next page "Garden Bridge Types").

Flat bridges are created to span two points of comparable elevation separated by a narrow area of lower elevation. These bridges are the easiest to design

Rustic garden bridges often are made with found logs and timbers that are native to the building site. Because these materials are not structurally rated, try to reserve them for decking and decorative functions and use pressure-treated lumber for the undercarriage.

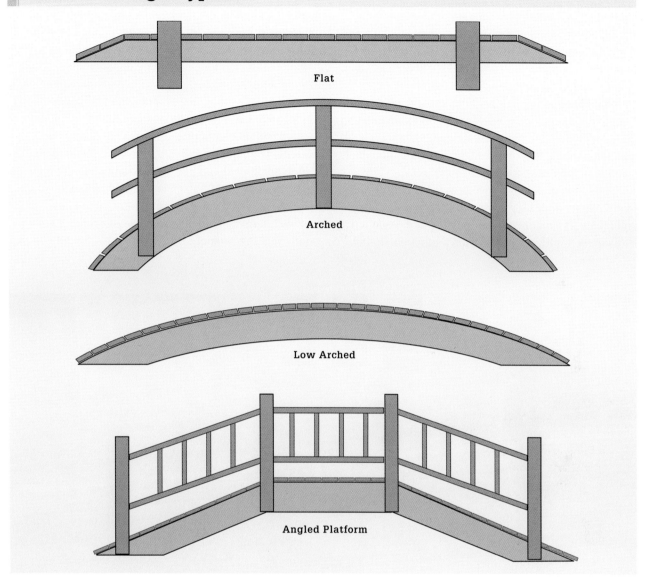

Flat

Arched

Low Arched

Angled Platform

and build — they can be as simple as a pair of timbers topped with deck boards or 2 × 4s. A basic flat bridge will offer rustic charm when its function trumps its form.

Arched bridges have unique structural and aesthetic properties. They can span greater distances than other bridge types because of their ability to transfer load, and they exude an elegance and grace that set them apart from bridges with more geometric configurations. But these advantages come at a price: An arched bridge is considerably more difficult to design and build than flat or angled bridges. Full-size arched garden bridges typically feature handrails that echo the curve of the undercarriage.

Low-arched bridges are simpler, scaled-down versions of full-size arched bridges. They are subtle and can virtually disappear along a winding pathway or in a casual garden. Railings on this type of bridge

are typically low and mostly decorative—you can omit them altogether if you prefer. The shallow incline and short length of a low-arched bridge enable you to cut each undercarriage support out of a single piece of dimensional lumber.

Angled-platform bridges can provide the lift of an arched bridge but with less demanding construction. On this bridge type, ramps beginning at each end meet in a central landing point, simplifying the undercarriage. The flat planes of the ramps and the landing make fastening deck boards and installing posts and rails easier.

Because of the flat landing, an angled-platform bridge is an excellent choice if you plan to spend time standing or sitting on the bridge deck, gazing across your landscape.

CHOOSING A SITE

A garden bridge can be sited practically anywhere you wish. You don't need a stream, a gulch, or even a berm. In fact, few yards contain natural obstacles requiring bridging. Many garden bridges are simply plopped down in the middle of a flat lawn. Sheer decorative appeal is a fine reason to build a bridge. However, if you are a pragmatist who can't abide the thought of a bridge that leads to nowhere or spans no obstacle, you can justify the presence of the bridge by creating a dry rock bed (sometimes called an *arroyo*), a planting bed, a landscape berm, or a drainage swale for it to cross.

Above all, a garden bridge is a decorative landscape feature. Its primary purpose is to beautify and create a visual focal point in your yard or garden. But a garden bridge also performs a function. To be effective and safe to cross, it must be sturdy and have a manageable incline. With a few exceptions, a bridge should be equipped with posts and grippable handrails. The access points to the bridge should be stable and well-drained and provide solid footing. The height of the decking should be no more than a couple of inches above the ground at the ends of the bridge.

A garden bridge is not intended to support vehicles. (A typical garden bridge can be picked up intact and moved fairly easily.) Bridges designed for vehicle traffic or to span a public waterway, culvert, or ditch are considered permanent structures. They must meet specific load, safety, and environmental impact standards. They require professional engineering and special permits. Building this type of bridge is not a do-it-yourself project.

When siting a garden bridge, the best results often come when the site is custom-landscaped for the bridge. This plain front yard was not a good candidate for a bridge until the dry creek "arroyo" was added.

BUILDING BRIDGES

Bridges are composed of three elements: the undercarriage, the decking, and a post-and-rail system. Because they are freestanding structures, garden bridges are not normally attached to piers, pilings, or footings.

The success of a garden bridge depends on the integrity of the undercarriage—the matrix of supports and spreaders that bear the decking and posts. Where possible, design your bridge so each support can be cut from a single piece of dimensional lumber.

To increase the maximum lift generated by a single board, graft the arched cutout from the bottom edge of the board onto the top edge.

The bigger and higher your bridge is, the more complex the geometry of the supports. If you want more than 1 foot of rise, make the undercarriage from multiple segments (see sidebar, below) or bent laminations. The large bridge in the photo on page 188 has three undercarriage support beams. Each beam is made from 10 segments glued and bolted together in a double layer. The joints between segments are staggered so they do not align.

If your bridge will be wider than 30", include a central support beam along with the outer beams. Single-layer beams are adequate for smaller bridges that have less rise. But if you are creating segmented beams, you should use double layers, with each layer functioning as a gusset for the opposing layer. Pressure-treated pine is the best wood to use for the undercarriage. The beams should be connected with spreaders to set the bridge width and prevent racking.

Building the Undercarriage ▸

Bridges that rise more than a foot generally are supported by beams fashioned from multiple segments. Each beam for the bridge shown on page 188 is made from 10 angled segments joined into a double layer.

The inner layer of each outer beam is trimmed along the top to create a support ledge for the decking, and both layers of the center beam are trimmed. Spreaders are installed between the beams to establish spacing and prevent racking.

DECKING

Use 5/4 deck boards or 2× dimensional lumber for the bridge decking. On flat or angled-platform bridges you can attach 6"-wide decking, but for arched bridges 4"-wide stock is better. The curved tops of the arched bridge beams greatly reduce the amount of bearing surface for the decking, causing wider deck boards to rock.

In most cases, the deck boards should be screwed to—not nailed to the supports. Snap a chalkline first to align the screws. If you want to avoid exposed fasteners (or use wider decking on an arched bridge), hidden fasteners, such as stair angles, may be used.

Options for Attaching Decking ▸

OPTION 1: Rest deck boards directly on the top edges of the beams, providing at least 1" of overhang.

OPTION 2: Add a ledge or create one by trimming the inner layer of double-layer beams.

OPTION 3: Use hidden metal hardware attached to the inside faces of the support beams.

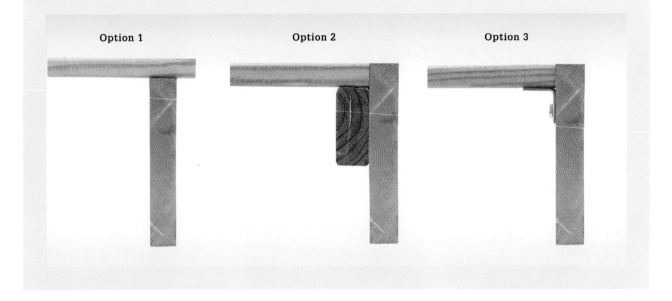

Option 1   Option 2   Option 3

WOOD DECKING

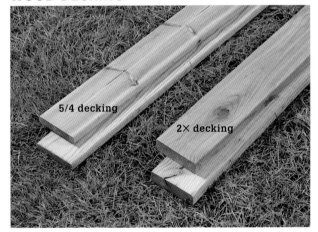

5/4 decking

2× decking

Both 2x and 5/4 lumber are suitable for use as decking. However, 5/4 will generally be of higher quality, and the radiused edges prevent splintering—an important consideration for bare feet or if you have young children.

If you hand-select each of your deck boards, look for pieces with vertical grain pattern (left in photo). They'll be less inclined to cup and warp than flat-grain lumber (right), but the wood tends to be significantly heavier.

POSTS AND HANDRAILS

Posts and handrails are not always required, but they can enhance safety and appearance. If the bridge is more than 12" high or spans a dangerous or delicate obstacle, such as a creek or flowerbed, you should include railings. Ideally, railings should be grippable and about 36" above the decking. If you choose to include balusters in your railing system, make sure they conform to your local building codes.

Posts can be connected with lag screws, carriage bolts, or deck-post connectors (see sidebar, below).

Some low-arched bridges include railings that are only 12 to 24" above the bridge decking. Obviously, these are not intended as handrails. Their function is almost exclusively visual, relating to matters of scale, mass, balance, and ornamentation. If you incorporate low railings into your design, make them stand out visually or they could be a tripping hazard.

Examining various bridge designs reveals little consistency in how to orient the posts that support the handrails. In some cases, the posts are perpendicular to the ground; in others, they're perpendicular to the deck boards. Use whichever method you find more visually appealing, unless your bridge deck rises at a steep incline. If your bridge has a slope greater than 1" per foot, install the posts perpendicular to the ground, not the bridge deck.

Options for Attaching Posts ▶

OPTION 1: Posts are attached to the bridge undercarriage with carriage bolts. Half-laps on the bottom ends stabilize the posts and make them look trimmer and more proportional to the rest of the bridge.

OPTION 2: Posts are attached with lag screws.
OPTION 3: Posts are attached using metal deck-post connectors. This is a utilitarian option and less handsome than the other mounting styles.

Option 1

Option 2

Option 3

TIPS FOR BUILDING BRIDGES

Build as much of the bridge as possible in the workshop, then transport the parts to the installation site for assembly. Before you assemble the bridge, excavate and backfill the site as needed to make the contact points for the bridge ends as level as possible. It's always a good idea to add a thick layer of compactable gravel at these points for drainage. Flat stones at each end of the site create stable landings for entering and exiting the structure. Pay attention to these transition areas, especially if the bridge is incorporated into a raised walkway or boardwalk. Transitions should be as seamless and level as possible.

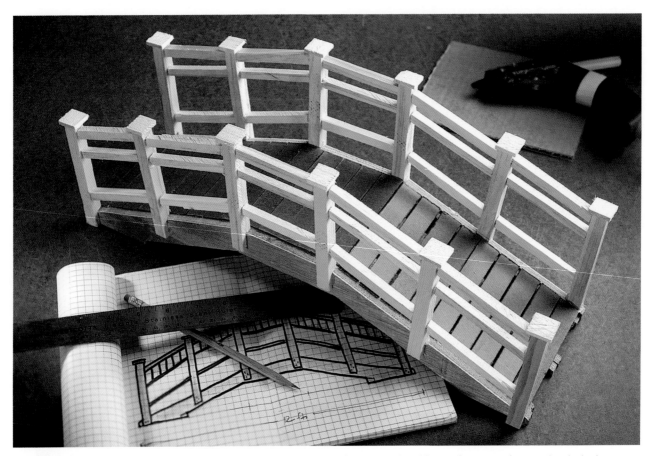

Building a scale model is a good idea when designing any construction or woodworking project. But when you're designing a bridge, a model is a virtual necessity to help you make decisions about proportion and scale.

Prepare the site. The ends of the bridge should rest on flat, well-drained ground. Compactable gravel can provide both attributes.

Tips for Building Bridges ▶

- Use hot-dipped galvanized or stainless steel fasteners wherever possible to inhibit rust and corrosion.
- Dry-assemble the bridge and take physical measurements for post angles **(photo A)**.
- Build and assemble the undercarriage components in your shop if possible. Also cut the deck boards to uniform length, and predrill for fasteners **(photo B)**.

- Wait until the bridge is assembled on site to cut handrail sections to length.
- If you use pressure-treated lumber, wait a minimum of three to six months before applying finishing products.
- Attach posts to the outer beam structures with half-lap joints. Gang-cut the half-lap shoulders for consistency **(photo C)**.

THE X-BRIDGE

In terms of technique, bridge building is similar to deck building. But that doesn't mean your garden bridge must look like a deck. One clever variation on garden bridge building is the "X-Bridge", where traditional railing balusters with railing supports are replaced with a rail system inspired by steel-truss bridge design. The railing is kept low because the proportions worked better visually and the low elevation of the bridge doesn't require a functioning handrail. This "X" design also employs an arched bridge deck instead of a flat deck. The result has a pleasing contemporary appearance. Constructing the supports and handrails is not difficult. Simply overlap six pieces of tapered, pressure-treated 1 × 8 pine to make the X-shaped railing supports. Cut the handrails and beams from 2× stock.

THE SIX-FOOT FOOTBRIDGE

You can build a low-arched or flat bridge like this in an hour or two for a minimal expense.

Whenever possible, cut the support beams from a single piece of stock. You can increase the lift by grafting the arched cutouts onto the top of the beam.

Along with the screwed-down 2 × 4 decking, simple 2 × 4 spreaders at each end and another near the middle provide lateral support.

Simple Garden Bridge

An elegant garden bridge invites you into a landscape by suggesting you stop and spend some time there. Cross a peaceful pond, traverse an arroyo of striking natural stone, or move from one garden space to the next and explore. While a bridge is practical and functions as a way to get from point A to point B, it does so much more. It adds dimension, a sense of romanticism, and the feeling of escaping to somewhere special.

The bridge you see here can be supported with handrails and trellis panels. But left simple as pictured, we think the sleek, modern design blends well in the landscape, providing a focal point without overwhelming a space.

Materials ▶

4 4 × 4" × 8 ft. cedar boards	8 1 × 2" × 8 ft. cedar boards
2 2 × 10" × 8 ft. cedar boards	2 ½ × 2" × 8' cedar lattice
10 2 × 4" × 8 ft. cedar boards	Lag screws (⅜ × 4")
2 1 × 8" × 8 ft. cedar boards	Deck screws (2", 3")
2 1 × 3" × 8 ft. cedar boards	Finishing materials

Unlike many landscape and garden bridges that are large, ornate, and designed to be the center of attention, this low cedar bridge has a certain refined elegance that is a direct result of its simple design.

Cutting List

Key	Part	Dim.	Pcs.	Material
A	Stringers	1½ × 9¼ × 96"	2	Cedar
B	Stretchers	1½ × 3½ × 27"	4	Cedar
C	Treads	1½ × 3½ × 30"	26	Cedar

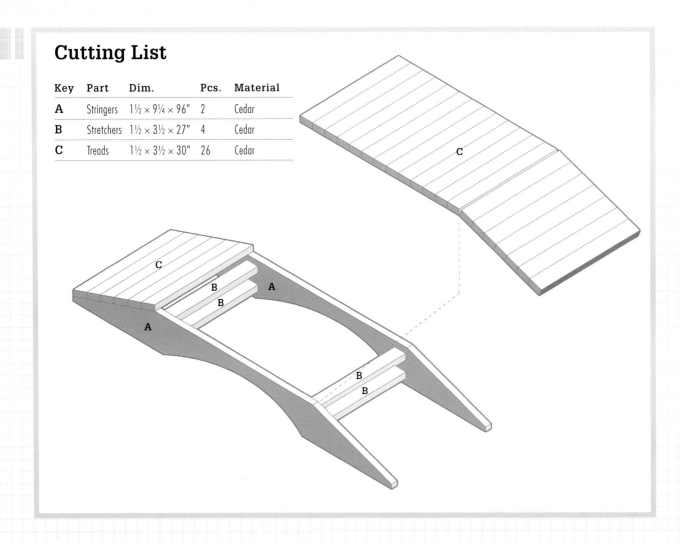

Preparing Bridge Pieces

Study the cutting list carefully and take care when measuring for cuts. The building blocks of this bridge are: stringers, a base, and treads. Read these preliminary instructions carefully, then study the steps before you begin.

Stringers: This first step involves cutting the main structural pieces of the bridge. The stringers have arcs cut into their bottom edges, and the ends of stringers are cut at a slant to create a gradual tread incline. Before you cut stringers, carefully draw guidelines on the wood pieces:

- A centerline across the width of each stringer
- Two lines across the width of each stringer 24" to the left and right of the centerline
- Lines at the ends of each stringer, 1" up from one long edge

- Diagonal lines from these points to the top of each line to the left and right of the center

Base: Four straight boards called "stretchers" form the base that support the bridge. Before cutting these pieces, mark stretcher locations on the insides of stringers, 1½" from the top and bottom of the stringers. The outside edges of the stretchers should be 24" from the centers of the stringers so the inside edges are flush with the bottoms of the arcs. When working with the stretchers, the footboard may get quite heavy, so you will want to move the project to its final resting place and finish constructing the project there.

Treads: Cut the treads to size according to the cutting list. Once laid on the stringers, treads will be separated with ¼" gaps. Before you install the treads, test-fit them to be sure they are the proper size.

Simple Garden Bridge

Use a circular saw to cut the ends of stringers along the diagonal lines, according to the markings described on page 201.

Tack a nail on the centerline, 5¼" up from the same long edge. Also tack nails along the bottom edge, 20½" to the left and right of the centerline.

Make a marking guide from a thin, flexible strip of scrap wood or plastic, hook it over the center nail, and slide the ends under the outside nails to form a smooth curve. Trace along the guide with a pencil to make the arc cutting line.

Use a jigsaw to make arched cut-outs in the bottoms of the 2 × 10 stringers after removing the nails and marking guide.

Assemble the base by preparing stringers and positioning the stretchers between them. Stand the stringers upright (curve at the bottom) and support the bottom stretchers with 1½"-thick spacer blocks for correct spacing. Fasten the stretchers between the stringers with countersunk 3" deck screws, driven through the stringers and into the ends of the stretchers.

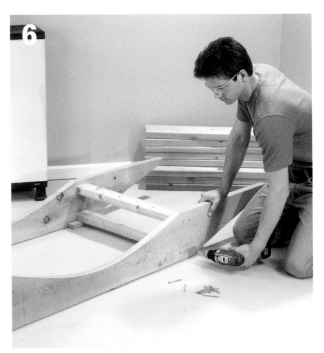

Turn the stringer assembly upside down and attach the top stretchers, securing them through the outside face of each stringer into the stretcher.

Attach the treads after test-fitting them. Leave a ¼" gap between each tread. Secure them with 3"-long countersunk deck screws driven into the edge of the stringers.

Sand all surfaces to smooth out any rough spots, and apply an exterior wood stain to protect the wood, if desired. You can leave the cedar untreated and it will turn gray, possibly blending even with other landscape features.

Reference Charts

Metric Conversions

To Convert:	To:	Multiply by:
Inches	Millimeters	25.4
Inches	Centimeters	2.54
Feet	Meters	0.305
Yards	Meters	0.914
Square inches	Square centimeters	6.45
Square feet	Square meters	0.093
Square yards	Square meters	0.836
Ounces	Milliliters	30.0
Pints (U.S.)	Liters	0.473 (Imp. 0.568)
Quarts (U.S.)	Liters	0.946 (Imp. 1.136)
Gallons (U.S.)	Liters	3.785 (Imp. 4.546)
Ounces	Grams	28.4
Pounds	Kilograms	0.454

To Convert:	To:	Multiply by:
Millimeters	Inches	0.039
Centimeters	Inches	0.394
Meters	Feet	3.28
Meters	Yards	1.09
Square centimeters	Square inches	0.155
Square meters	Square feet	10.8
Square meters	Square yards	1.2
Milliliters	Ounces	.033
Liters	Pints (U.S.)	2.114 (Imp. 1.76)
Liters	Quarts (U.S.)	1.057 (Imp. 0.88)
Liters	Gallons (U.S.)	0.264 (Imp. 0.22)
Grams	Ounces	0.035
Kilograms	Pounds	2.2

Converting Temperatures

Convert degrees Fahrenheit (F) to degrees Celsius (C) by following this simple formula: Subtract 32 from the Fahrenheit temperature reading. Then, multiply that number by $5/9$. For example, 77°F - 32 = 45. 45 × $5/9$ = 25°C.

To convert degrees Celsius to degrees Fahrenheit, multiply the Celsius temperature reading by $9/5$. Then, add 32. For example, 25°C × $9/5$ = 45. 45 + 32 = 77°F.

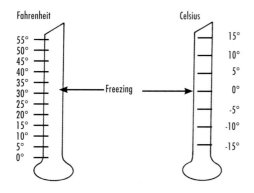

Metric Plywood Panels

Metric plywood panels are commonly available in two sizes: 1,200 mm × 2,400 mm and 1,220 mm × 2,400 mm, which is roughly equivalent to a 4 × 8-ft. sheet. Standard and Select sheathing panels come in standard thicknesses, while Sanded grade panels are available in special thicknesses.

Standard Sheathing Grade		Sanded Grade	
7.5 mm	(5/16 in.)	6 mm	(4/17 in.)
9.5 mm	(3/8 in.)	8 mm	(5/16 in.)
12.5 mm	(1/2 in.)	11 mm	(7/16 in.)
15.5 mm	(5/8 in.)	14 mm	(9/16 in.)
18.5 mm	(3/4 in.)	17 mm	(2/3 in.)
20.5 mm	(13/16 in.)	19 mm	(3/4 in.)
22.5 mm	(7/8 in.)	21 mm	(13/16 in.)
25.5 mm	(1 in.)	24 mm	(15/16 in.)

Lumber Dimensions

Nominal - U.S.	Actual - U.S. (in inches)	Metric
1 × 2	3/4 × 1 1/2	19 × 38 mm
1 × 3	3/4 × 2 1/2	19 × 64 mm
1 × 4	3/4 × 3 1/2	19 × 89 mm
1 × 5	3/4 × 4 1/2	19 × 114 mm
1 × 6	3/4 × 5 1/2	19 × 140 mm
1 × 7	3/4 × 6 1/4	19 × 159 mm
1 × 8	3/4 × 7 1/4	19 × 184 mm
1 × 10	3/4 × 9 1/4	19 × 235 mm
1 × 12	3/4 × 11 1/4	19 × 286 mm
1 1/4 × 4	1 × 3 1/2	25 × 89 mm
1 1/4 × 6	1 × 5 1/2	25 × 140 mm
1 1/4 × 8	1 × 7 1/4	25 × 184 mm
1 1/4 × 10	1 × 9 1/4	25 × 235 mm
1 1/4 × 12	1 × 11 1/4	25 × 286 mm
1 1/2 × 4	1 1/4 × 3 1/2	32 × 89 mm
1 1/2 × 6	1 1/4 × 5 1/2	32 × 140 mm
1 1/2 × 8	1 1/4 × 7 1/4	32 × 184 mm
1 1/2 × 10	1 1/4 × 9 1/4	32 × 235 mm
1 1/2 × 12	1 1/4 × 11 1/4	32 × 286 mm
2 × 4	1 1/2 × 3 1/2	38 × 89 mm
2 × 6	1 1/2 × 5 1/2	38 × 140 mm
2 × 8	1 1/2 × 7 1/4	38 × 184 mm
2 × 10	1 1/2 × 9 1/4	38 × 235 mm
2 × 12	1 1/2 × 11 1/4	38 × 286 mm
3 × 6	2 1/2 × 5 1/2	64 × 140 mm
4 × 4	3 1/2 × 3 1/2	89 × 89 mm
4 × 6	3 1/2 × 5 1/2	89 × 140 mm

Liquid Measurement Equivalents

1 Pint	= 16 Fluid Ounces	= 2 Cups
1 Quart	= 32 Fluid Ounces	= 2 Pints
1 Gallon	= 128 Fluid Ounces	= 4 Quarts

Credits

Handyman Club of America
pp. 28-65, 71-121, 134-143, 148-163, 168-177, 188, 193, 195, 196, 197 (top left), 198-199

Shutterstock
pp. 70, 190

Christopher Mills
pp. 180

Resources

Aluminum Angle
859-745-2650
www.metalsdepot.com

Axle Push Cap
888-713-2880
www.sportsmith.net

Black & Decker (power tools and accessories)
800-544-6986
www.blackanddecker.com

Rockler Woodworking (decorative finish washers & router bits)
800-279-4441
www.rockler.com

Dek-Block Piers (precast concrete piers)
800-664-2705
www.deckplans.com

Fiskars (posthole digger)
800-500-4849
www.fiskars.com

Handyman Club of America
http://handy.scout.com

Killian Hardware (gate hardware)
215-247-0945
www.killianhardware.com

McFeely's (stainless steel lag screws and fasteners)
800-443-7937
www.mcfeelys.com

Penofin (oil stain and finishes)
800-736-6346
www.penofin.com

Simpson Strong-Tie
800-999-5099
www.strongtie.com

West Marine (chromed bow eyes)
800-262-8464
www.westmarine.com

Index

A
Adirondack chairs
    Classic Adirondack Chair, 16–21
    design and, 16
    paint colors for, 16
    Sling-Back Adirondack, 32–37
adjustable back, 63–65
adjustable squares, 106
angled platform bridges, 191
arbors
    Freestanding Arbor, 128–133
arc cuts, 202
arched bridges, 191

B
barbecuing, 114
bench grinder, 116
benches
    High-low Potting Bench, 134–137
    Knockdown Garden Bench, 26–31
    Recyclables Bench, 52–57
    Slatted Garden Bench, 22–25
    Trestle Table and Benches, 72–79
bevel cuts, 140
bridges. See garden bridges
butt hinges, 95

C
candles, 158, 162
canvas seats, 32, 36–37
caulk, 108, 112-113
cedar, 22
cedar lap siding, 164, 167
Cedar Patio Table, 80–83
chairs
    Classic Adirondack Chair, 16–21
    Luxury Sun Lounger, 58–65
    Side-by-Side Patio Chair, 10–15
    Sling-Back Adirondack, 32–37
chamfered edges, 84, 89–90
children
    Children's Picnic Table, 100–103
    Timberframe Sandbox, 118–121
circular tabletops, 88–89
Classic Adirondack Chair, 16–21
clear wood sealer, 16, 21, 22, 25, 69, 99, 127, 132
Cold Frame, Jumbo, 152–157
composite boards
    advantages of, 72, 134, 136
    cutting, 79
    screws for, 78, 137
    working with, 74
Compost Bin, 124–127
composting, 124

construction adhesive, 108, 112–113, 151
copper pipes, 147
countertop edging, 113
cup hooks, 137
cypress, 60

D
decking
    composite, 74
    options for attaching, 194
deck-support ledges, 190
design
    Adirondack chairs and, 16
    around propane tank storage, 114
    for sheltered swing, 172
dining. See tables
drainage
    for garden bridges, 196
    for planters, 143
    for postholes, 175
    for stationary benches, 29

E
end-post pairs, 181
entertaining
    Patio Prep Cart, 108–113
    Pitmaster's Locker, 114–117
    See also tables
entryways, 52
eyebolts, 50–51

F
fence panels, 126
Firewood Shelter, 164–167
flat bridges, 190-191
Folding Table, 92–95
Four-post Patio Pergola, 178–187
Freestanding Arbor, 128–133

G
garden bridges
    building, 193–197
    choosing site for, 192
    decking for, 194
    designing, 190–191
    dimensions of, 190
    handrails for, 195
    placement of, 189, 192
    posts for, 195
    scale models of, 196
    Simple Garden Bridge, 200–203
    Six-foot Footbridge, 199
    styles of, 190
    tips for building, 196–197

types of, 191, 198–199
    undercarriage for, 193
    vehicle bridges vs., 192
    X-bridge, 198
gardening
    Compost Bin, 124–127
    High-low Potting Bench, 134–137
    Jumbo Cold Frame, 152–157
    Raised Bed with Removable
        Trellis, 144–147
    Trellis Planter, 138–143
    Versailles Planter, 148–151
gliders, 169
gravel
    garden bridge drainage and, 196
    for planter drainage, 143
    for postholes, 175
    as sandbox bed, 118, 120
    stationary benches and, 29

H
hacksaws, 116
half-lap joints, 86, 88, 158, 197
hardware
    brass, 58, 61
    chest handles, 57
    cup hooks, 137
    eyebolts, 50–51
    for folding tables, 94–95
    hinges, 57, 112
    latches/strikeplates, 111
    for pergola, 178–179
    stainless steel, 32
    strap hinges, 94, 95
    wheels/casters, 65, 111–112
High-low Potting Bench, 134–137
HVLP sprayers, 44

J
jointers, 60
Jumbo Cold Frame, 152–157

K
kerf edges, chiseling, 30
kids. See children
Knockdown Garden Bench, 26–31

L
landscape fabric, 177
lattice, 66
lighting, 158
linseed oil, 80, 83, 102
liquid measurement equivalents, 204
low arched bridges, 191

lumber
cedar, 22
cypress, 60
milling, 60
preparing stock, 60
redwood, 43, 58, 60, 104
rip-cutting, 12, 34, 41–43, 54, 58, 62, 75, 94, 140, 151, 160
treated, 100
for undercarriage, 190
See also composite boards
lumber dimensions, 204
Luxury Sun Lounger, 58–65

M
metal cutoff saw, 116
metal frames, 114–116
metric conversions, 204
metric plywood panels, 204
mortise-and-tenon joints, 72, 173
mortises, faux, 172, 173

P
Pagoda Lantern, 158–163
paint
for Adirondack chairs, 16
for garden bridges, 190
for pagoda lantern, 158
for planters, 151
for porch swing, 40
on recyclables bench, 52, 55, 56
for tables, 92, 95, 96, 99, 100, 102, 107
Patio Chair, Side-by-Side, 10–15
Patio Prep Cart, 108–113
pavers, 118, 121, 152
Pergola, Four-post Patio, 178–187
picnic tables
Children's Picnic Table, 100–103
Traditional Picnic Table, 104–107
Pitmaster's Locker, 114–117
planers, 60, 172
planters
gravel for drainage, 143
lining, 142–143
Raised Bed with Removable Trellis, 144–147
Trellis Planter, 138–143
Versailles Planter, 148–151
plastic sheathing
as planter liner, 142
as sandbox liner, 118, 120
plumb cuts, 12
plywood
metric panels, 204

for outdoor use, 116–117
Porch Swing, 38–45
Porch Swing Stand, 46–51
post assemblies, 174–175
postholes, 175
posts, options for attaching, 195
Potting Bench, High-low, 134–137
power planers, 60
precast concrete piers, 29
profiled rails, 54
propane tanks, 114
pullout trays, 58, 64–65
purlins, 185–187
PVC plumbing pipe, 144, 147

R
rabbets, 150
rafters, 185–187
Raised Bed with Removable Trellis, 144–147
Recyclables Bench, 52–57
redwood, 43, 58, 60, 104
reverse tapered legs, 84–91
roofing panels, polycarbonate, 152, 156–157

S
Sandbox, Timberframe, 118–121
saw protractors, 102
scale models of garden bridges, 196
seating
adding to arbor, 133
Classic Adirondack Chair, 16–21
comfort and, 9
Knockdown Garden Bench, 26–31
Luxury Sun Lounger, 58–65
Porch Swing, 38–45
Porch Swing Stand, 46–51
Recyclables Bench, 52–57
Sheltered Swing, 168–177
Side-by-side Patio Chair, 10–15
Slatted Garden Bench, 22–25
Sling-Back Adirondack, 32–37
Trellis Seat, 66–69
Sheltered Swing, 168–177
shoulder cuts, 141
Side-by-Side Patio Chair, 10–15
Simple Garden Bridge, 200–203
site preparation
for cold frame, 152
for garden bridges, 196
for sandbox, 118
for sheltered swing, 174–175
Six-foot Footbridge, 199
slats, spacing, 25

Slatted Garden Bench, 22–25
Sling-Back Adirondack, 32–37
speed squares, 48
spreaders, 190
stainless steel screws, 32, 34–35
stock, preparing, 60
storage
Firewood Shelter, 164–167
Recyclables Bench, 52–57
Timberframe Sandbox, 118–121
strap hinges, 94, 95
swings
comfort and, 38
hanging, 45, 50–51
Porch Swing, 38–45
Porch Swing Stand, 46–51
Sheltered Swing, 168–177

T
tables
Cedar Patio Table, 80–83
Children's Picnic Table, 100–103
Folding Table, 92–95
Occasional Table, 96–99
planter as, 151
Teahouse Table Set, 84–91
Traditional Picnic Table, 104–107
Trestle Table and Benches, 72–79
tapered legs, reverse, 84–91
Teahouse Table Set, 84–91
temperature conversions, 204
thermometers for cold frames, 157
tile
cart top installation, 108, 113
as pagoda lantern base, 158, 162
Timberframe Sandbox, 118–121
Traditional Picnic Table, 104–107
Trellis Planter, 138–143
Trellis Seat, 66–69
trellises
Freestanding Arbor, 128–133
Raised Bed with Removable Trellis, 144–147
Trellis Planter, 138–143
Trellis Seat, 66–69
Trestle Table and Benches, 72–79

U
umbrellas
Cedar Patio Table, 80, 83
holes for, 15, 83
securing, 10
Side-by-Side Patio Chair, 10–15
undercarriage, 182–184, 190, 191, 193, 197

V
vehicle bridges, garden bridges vs., 192
Versailles Planter, 148–151

W
wheels, 65, 111–112
wood. *See* lumber
wood finish/sealer, 16, 21, 22, 25, 44,
  69, 99, 127, 132
wood plugs, 16, 44

X
X-bridge, 198

Y
yard accessories
  Firewood Shelter, 164–167
  Four-post Patio Pergola, 178–187
  Freestanding Arbor, 128–133
  Pagoda Lantern, 158–163
  Sheltered Swing, 168–177
  See also garden bridges